IMAGES of America

TOWN OF OWEGO

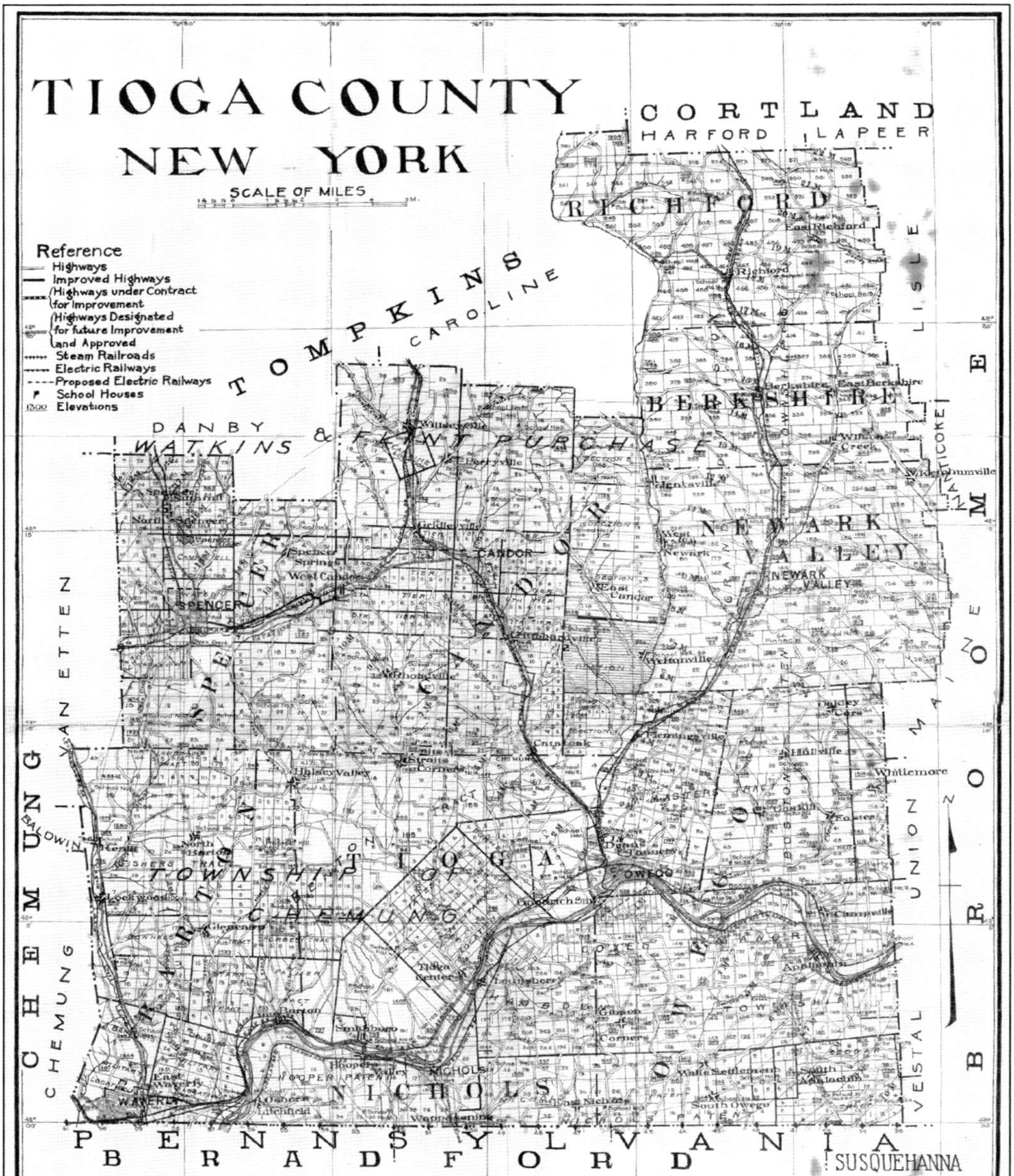

This undated map appears to be from around 1900. Shown are the nine towns and six villages, with the Susquehanna River passing from east to west, from Broome County through to Pennsylvania.

On the cover: From the time the county was formed in 1791 to the present, lumber has been an important business. The men worked hard all year and really earned their pay. The mill has been long gone, but new and more modern ones have taken its place. This photograph was taken at Palmer's Mill in Apalachin, around 1900. Pictured are, from left to right, George Hill, Harrison Hill, Charles Hill, and Bill Gibson. (Tioga County Historian's Office.)

IMAGES
of America

TOWN OF OWEGO

Emma M. Sedore

ARCADIA
PUBLISHING

ISBN 978-0-7385-6264-3

Published by Arcadia Publishing
Charleston, South Carolina

Printed in the United States of America

Library of Congress Catalog Card Number: 2008932697

For all general information contact Arcadia Publishing at:
Telephone 843-853-2070
Fax 843-853-0044
E-mail sales@arcadiapublishing.com
For customer service and orders:
Toll-Free 1-888-313-2665

Visit us on the Internet at www.arcadiapublishing.com

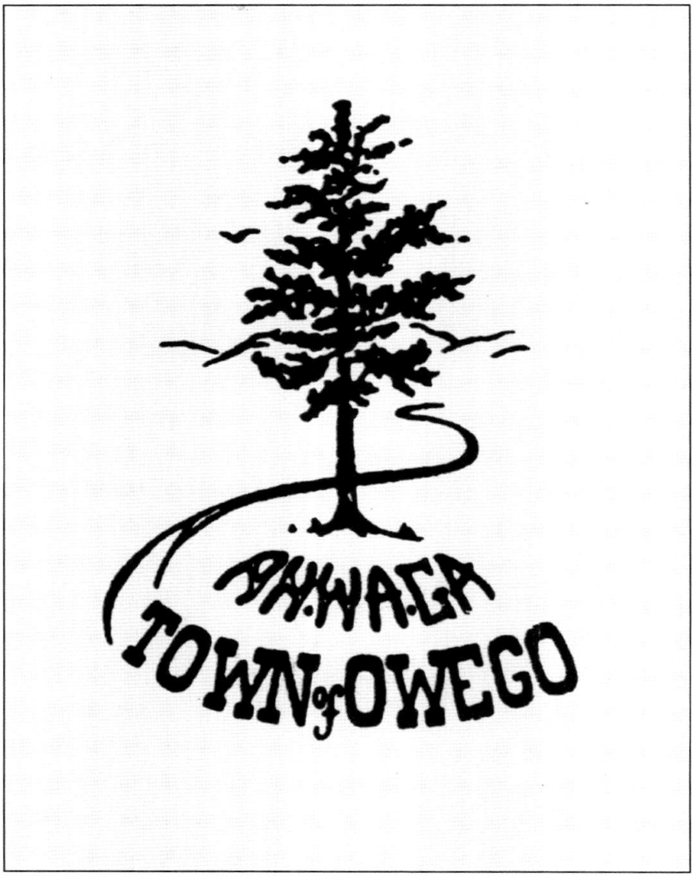

The artist used a Native American theme, with the tree representing their love for nature. The roots spell out *ahwaga*, also Native American in origin, meaning "Where the valley widens," and the name Owego is derived from it. Eda Brent of Apalachin designed the Town of Owego logo in 1978 when she entered a competition through the Tioga County Council on the Arts and won first place. The Owego Town Board adopted it, and it has been in use ever since.

Contents

ACKNOWLEDGMENTS

One of the best things about doing this book was networking with people who care enough about history and were willing to share their photographs and personal memories about the town of Owego. At first, I wondered where I would be able to come up with at least 200 images; but when I advertised in the newspapers and personally contacted people, they answered my call.

I am especially grateful to the people who welcomed me into their homes and spent so much time recalling and reminiscing about their families and enlightening me about local history that I am sure I would never find in any book. Some of the people include Virginia Milligan (who was the first to call), Howard Seymour, Jeannette Baldwin, Frieda Baker, Bill Caloroso, Nancy P. Ellis, David Geller, Mary Ann Sacharov, Carolyn Gordner, Joyce Ingersoll, Bruce DeVlieger, George Penney, Laura Spencer, and Mary Ellen Kishpaugh, to name most of them. A very special thank-you goes to Margaret Hadsell, who made it possible for me to meet my deadline. I am also grateful to the Tioga County Historical Society, which let me search to my heart's content.

Introduction

According to Lewis Henry Morgan, the earliest inhabitants of the town of Owego were Native Americans, specifically the Cayuga and Onondaga tribes of the Iroquois Nation. After the Revolutionary War, the majority of them left and early settlers moved in. Most of them came from the New England states, New York, New Jersey, and Pennsylvania. The Town of Owego was formed on March 14, 1800, and called the town of Tioga, located on the east side of the Owego Creek. The town on the west side of the creek was first called Owego, but because the village of Owego was on the east side, people assumed the town of Tioga was Owego. To eliminate the confusion, the names were officially exchanged in 1813. The town of Owego is the largest in Tioga County and is composed of numerous hamlets. They are Apalachin (the largest), Campville, Gaskill Corners, Flemingville, Gibson Corners, South Apalachin, South Owego, and Waits.

The Susquehanna River weaves its way through the center of it, past Hiawatha Island, where a myth persisted for years that it was the place where the Iroquois Confederacy was formed. The island has a history of its own, especially the period between 1874 and 1888, when huge steamboats that were built on the banks of the river in the village of Owego would carry happy excursionists to and from the island to picnic, dance, and even stay overnight at the Hiawatha House hotel. The hotel register at the Tioga County Historical Society Museum shows that between the years 1876 and 1884, visitors came there from 26 different states and nine foreign countries. John D. Rockefeller, who was born in Tioga County, lived right across from the island from 1849 to 1854. In his biography, written by Allen Nevins, Rockefeller recalls ice-skating and swimming there as a boy. He came back to visit his old homestead numerous times until the late 1920s, and since 2004, there has been a historic marker to denote his home, which is still occupied today.

The year 1849 was a big one for Owego. That was when the New York and Erie Railroad came through on the north side of the river. At that time, Ransom Steele and William Pearsall, of Apalachin, owned lumber mills on the south side of the river. They shipped the lumber to various ports in Pennsylvania on large rafts in the spring when the ice on the river broke. When they heard that the railroad was coming through, they made an agreement with the railroad officials to build a bridge across the river to the north side, where the officials agreed to build a train depot at the end of it. However, after the bridge was built, the railroad reneged on its agreement and put the depot a few miles west at Campville. Building the bridge turned out to be fruitless anyway, because by 1854, it washed away in a flood, and another bridge would not be built until 2002.

During the Civil War, the town and village counted more than 500 men who had enlisted in the army and navy. Two Apalachin men became brigadier generals, Benjamin F. Tracy and Isaac S. Catlin. General Tracy went on to become secretary of the navy from 1884 to 1889.

Beginning in 1837, the Chenango Canal was built from Utica to Binghamton as an extension of the Erie Canal. By 1862, work was started to build an extension from the Chenango Canal, west, through Tioga County to connect with the North Branch Canal, near the state line at Athens, Pennsylvania, for a distance of about 38 miles on the south side of the Susquehanna River. The canal commissioners felt it would increase business, even though the Erie Railroad was already operating on the north side of the river. It was built in sections, "as money became available." Because of the Civil War, prices of material and labor increased, which caused construction costs to be greater than expected. As the years passed, enthusiasm waned, and people wanted the project halted. When the canal was completed between Binghamton and Smithboro in 1872, they got their wish and the project was abandoned. Some remains of the Chenango Canal Extension can still be seen today, and a historic marker was installed near a section of it at Apalachin in 1993.

The 20th century in the town saw historic changes through the world wars, Prohibition, women's rights, the Great Depression, transportation, and especially technology. The most important event happened in the 1950s, when International Business Machines (IBM) built a million-dollar military products plant in the town and hired thousands of engineers and manufacturing and office personnel. It seemed as if almost overnight, the town and village and areas for miles around were put to a test to see how quickly housing developments, roads, schools, banks, hotels, a sewage treatment facility, and everything else could be built or improved. Government officials were forced to revise and implement rules and regulations to meet the needs of all the changes taking place. In 1988, the town built a new building on Route 434, and since 1996, the Town of Owego elected its first female supervisor. IBM left Owego in 1994, then the Loral Corporation, a high-technology company, moved in until 1996, when Lockheed Martin Systems Integration took over and has since won the contract to build the presidential helicopter.

Probably the most infamous event that ever happened in the town of Owego was on November 14, 1957, when a group of about 60 Mafia kingpins gathered at the home of Joseph Barbara Sr., allegedly to attend a barbecue. The police and FBI raided the gathering, and many were brought to trial at the Tioga County Courthouse in Owego. Among those arrested were Vito Genovese, Russell Bufalino, Anthony Guarnieri, Joseph Profaci, and others. It drew worldwide attention to the quiet hamlet of Apalachin.

Today it would be hard to find Native Americans canoeing down the river, or seeing huge steamboats docking at Front Street, but wouldn't it be fun if they were? Perhaps some of the images in this book will prod your imagination. It is impossible to have photographs of everything and everyone for the history of the town, but hopefully this book will give you a broad range, inform you about something you did not know, and perhaps even stir up some pleasant memories.

One

Apalachin

Apalachin is located on the south side of the Susquehanna River, approximately eight miles east of the village of Owego. It derives its name from the township of Apalacon, Pennsylvania, where the Apalachin Creek originates. The name is Native American in origin and means "from whence the messenger returned." The earliest settler was Isaac Harris, who came in 1786. As the hamlet developed, much activity occurred at the port in the river where the Apalachin Creek and the road met to launch huge rafts of lumber in early spring. Because of this, by 1829, it was known as the "Corners." It was next known as Apalachin Corners, and when the first post office was established in 1835, the name officially became Apalachin. A few of Apalachin's most prominent citizens were Benjamin F. Tracy, a Civil War general and secretary of the navy, appointed by Pres. Benjamin Harrison in 1889, and his brother-in-law, Gen. Isaac S. Catlin. The 20th century boasted Eugene Manlove Rhodes, popular writer of western novels through the 1930s. When the Delaware, Lackawanna and Western Railroad built its first station there in 1882, businesses thrived. Farmers brought everything from potatoes to horses to load on the train and enabled people to work in surrounding communities. Major changes took place in the 20th century after IBM built its plant in Owego. Housing developments went up, and old structures came down. Today it has settled into a quiet, productive community.

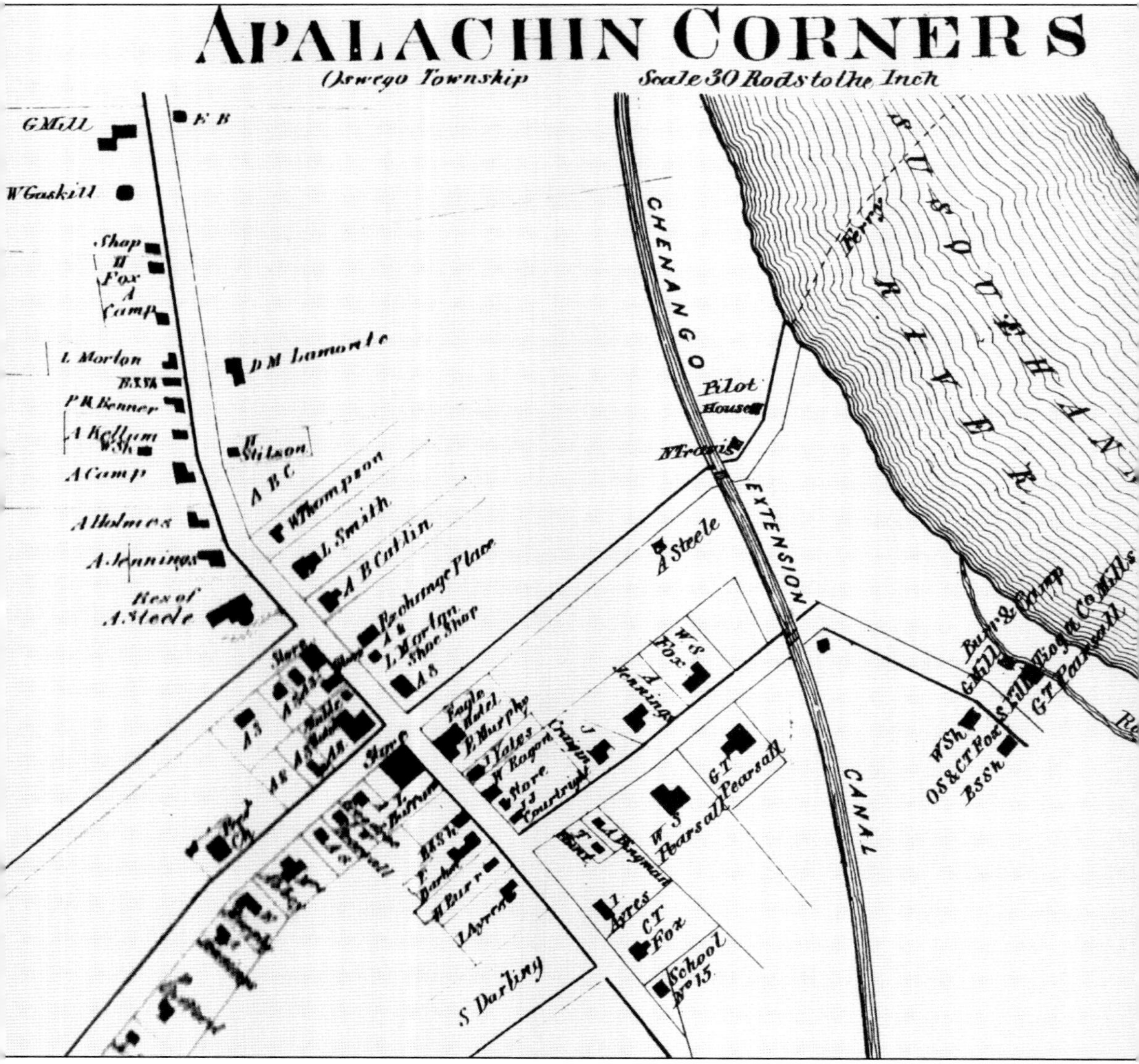

This inset is from an 1869 map and shows a close-up of Apalachin Corners, later called Apalachin. The Chenango Canal Extension is clearly shown as it was being built, although it was never completed. Notice the misspelling of Owego as Oswego.

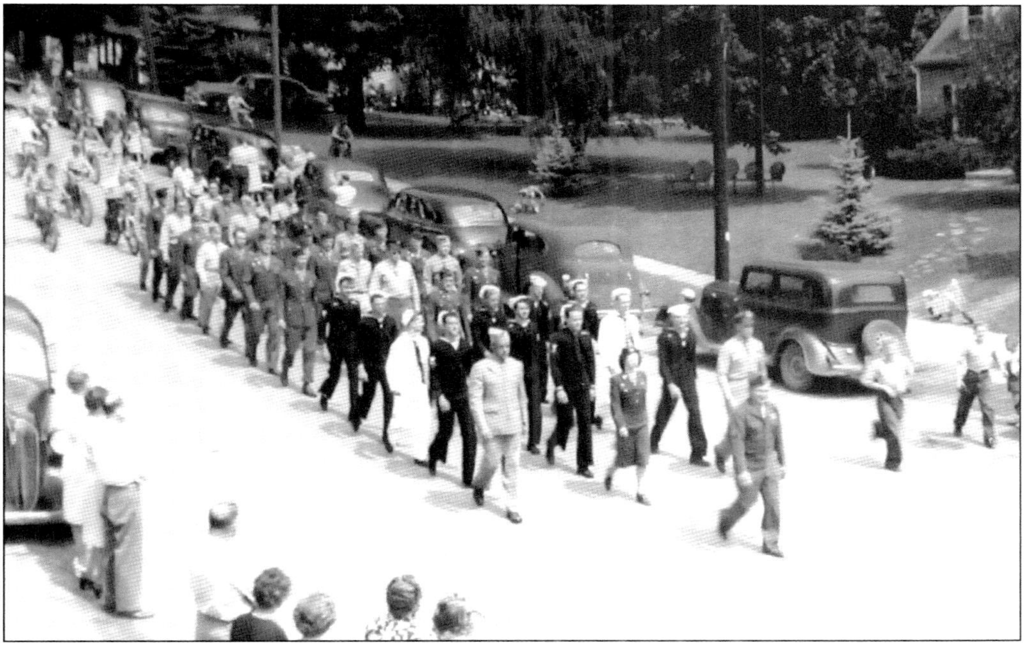

It seemed that whenever there was something to celebrate, Apalachin had a parade to go along with it, and even though the crowds were minimal, the spirit was always there. This one was in 1950 in honor of the World War II soldiers who returned home.

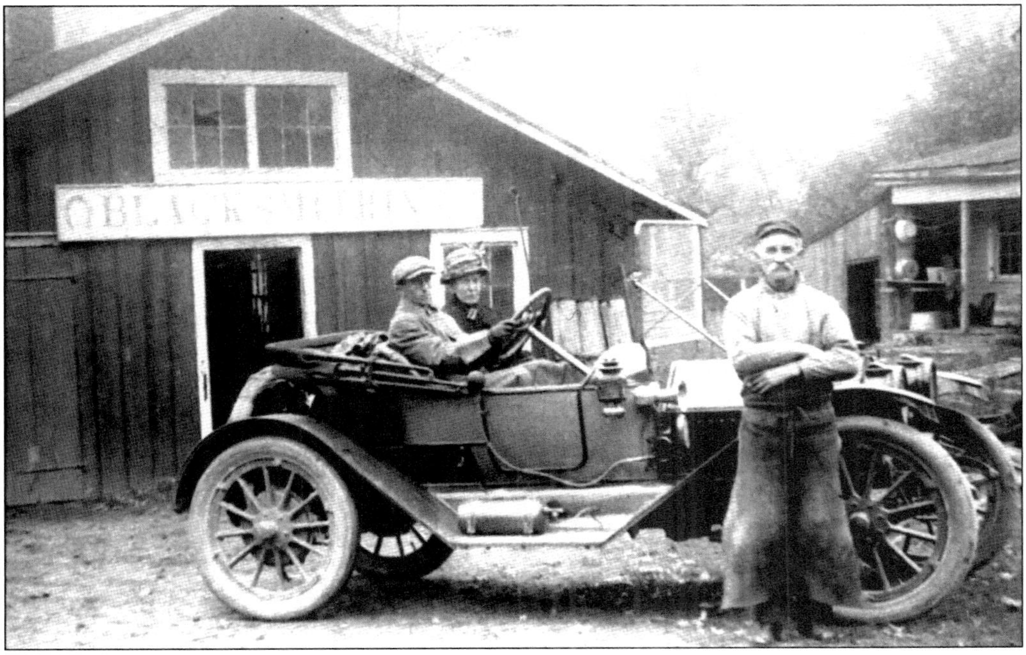

It almost looks as if Apalachin blacksmith John Ryan is thinking, "This contraption will never put me out of business!" However, Louise Benner's brand-new 1914 car is running just fine, as her friend and justice of the peace Robert Ryan can attest to. Benner was a well-known piano teacher for many years.

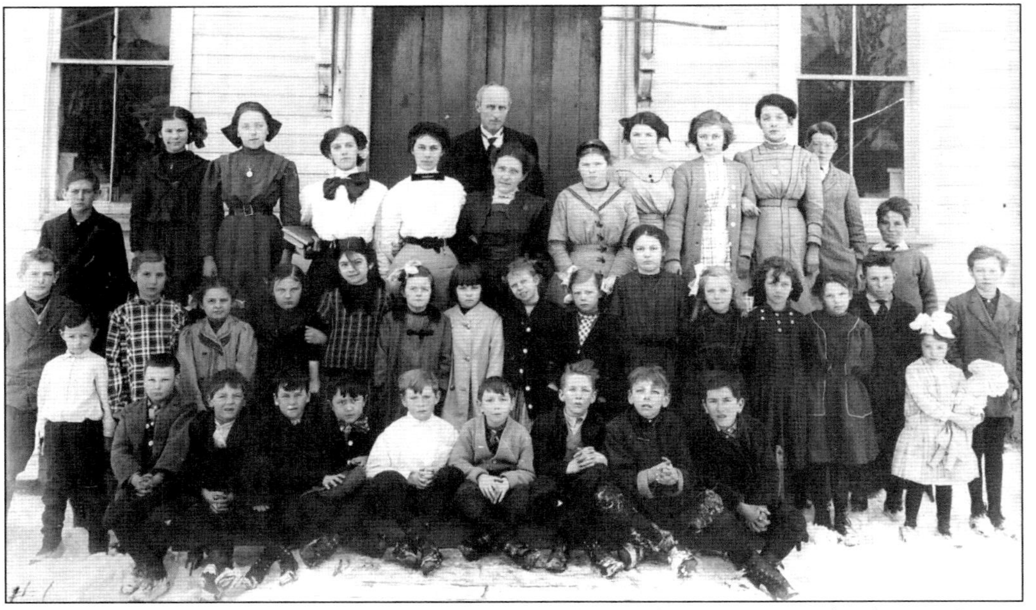

Teacher William E. Lambert stands with his class at the Apalachin Union School around 1910. Although the list of names on the back of the photograph is not complete, nor is it in order, it includes Steve Holmes, Wallace Beach, Wallace Curtis, Dean Sleeper, Dan Hill, Effie Hill, Bert Hill, Catherine Johnson, Ross Knapp, Ben Guilian, Amelia Knapp, Thelma Glann, Laura Hilton, Marion Bates, and Earl Knapp.

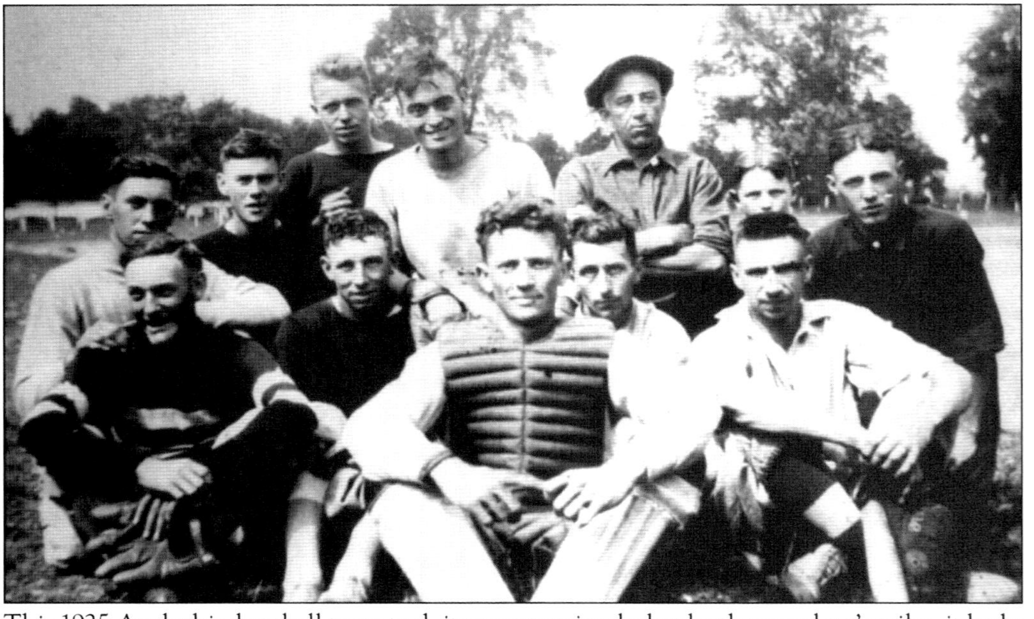

This 1925 Apalachin baseball team took its games seriously, but by the members' smiles, it looks like they managed to have a lot of fun. Shown from left to right are (first row) W. Beach, R. Knapp, ? Bouton, Robert Ryan, and W. Guiles; (second row) Burt Darling, Howard Beach, Ralph Gould, Fred Hickey, Francis Palmer, unidentified, and Steven Holmes.

It is amazing how accommodations have improved since motels like the Hillside Cabins of the 1930s and 1940s offered the latest in comfort, with a full bath and heated rooms, with the heater next to the bed.

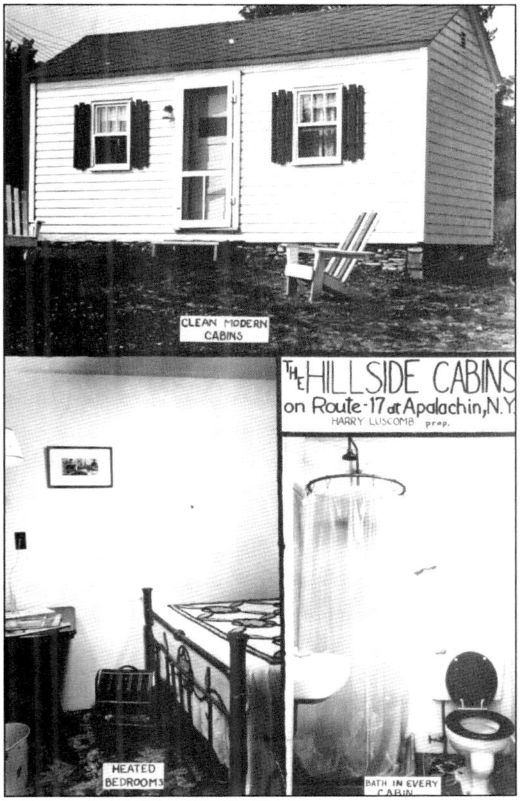

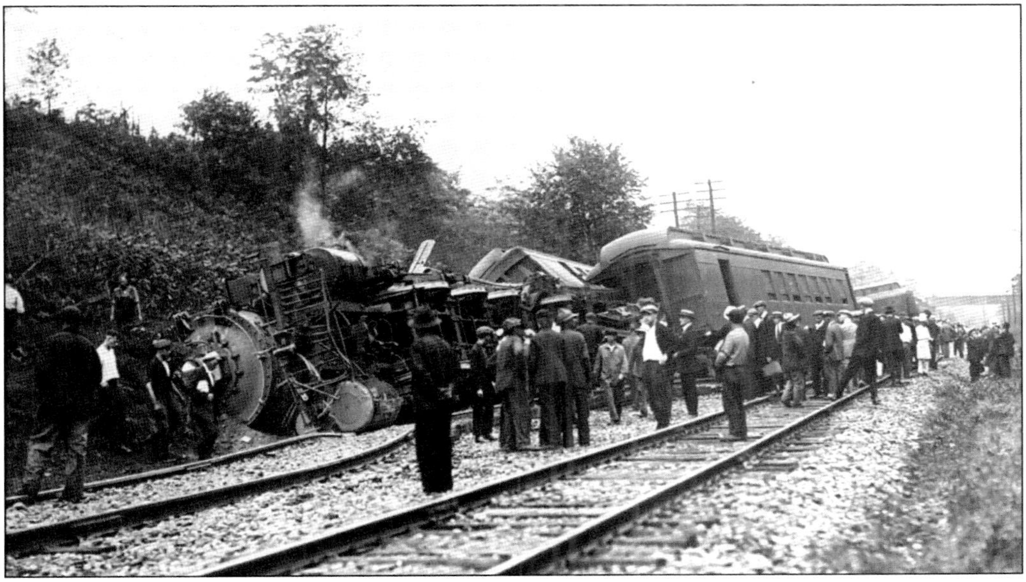

The westbound Lackawanna Limited passenger train No. 3 is shown after it plowed into an embankment just west of Apalachin at 4:20 p.m. on September 3, 1921. The accident was due to a problem with the tracks, which cost one man his life and caused many to be injured. Thousands of people showed up to see the huge wreck.

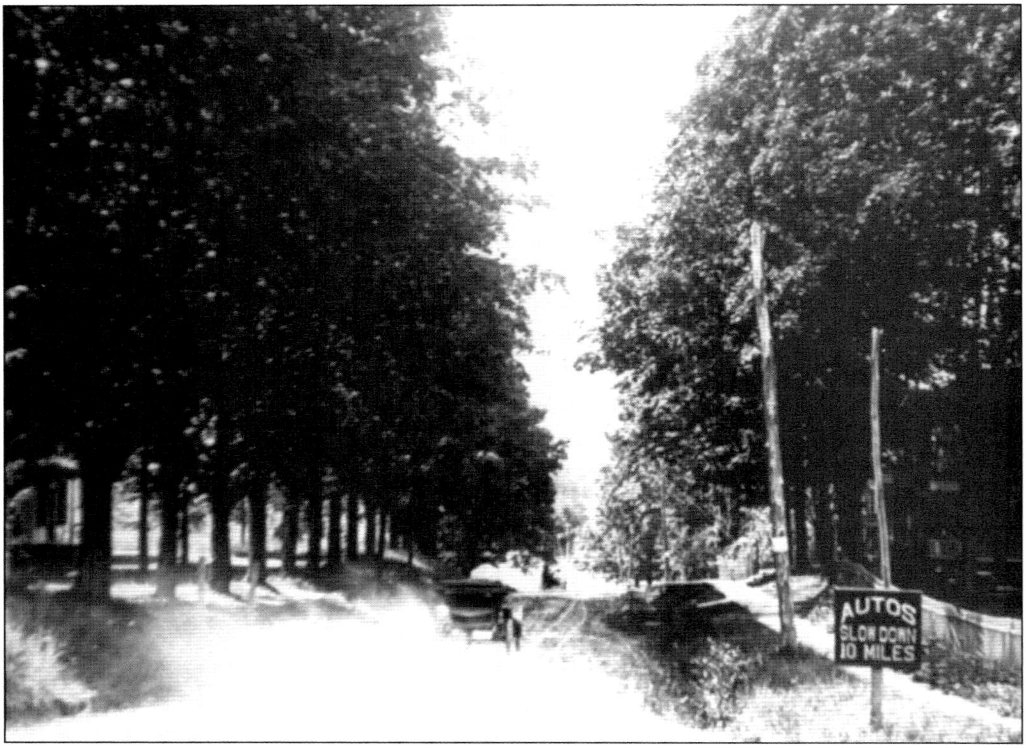

The Marshland Road sign warns drivers to slow down to 10 miles per hour, probably because there were more horses on the road than cars in the early 1900s.

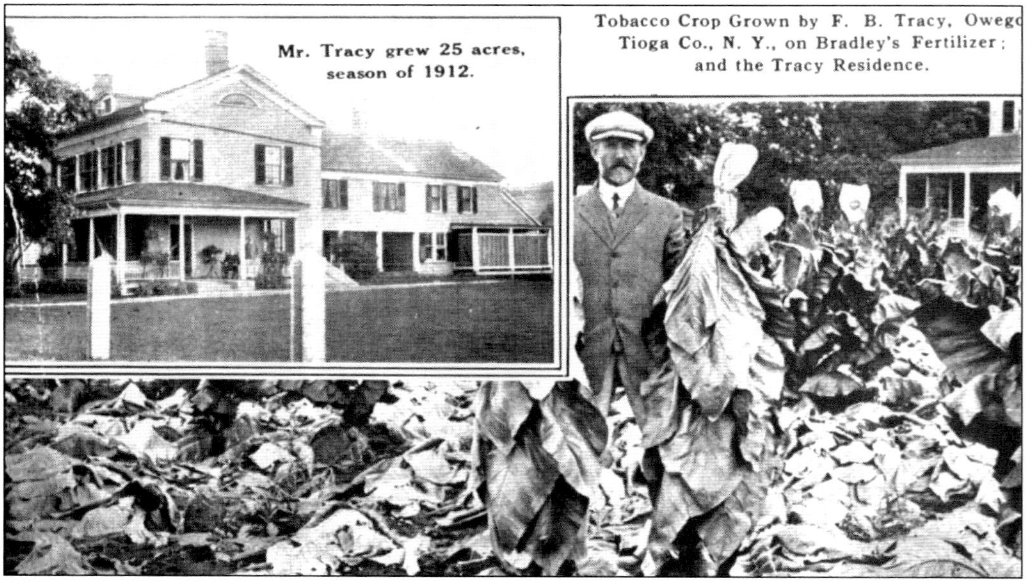

Tobacco was big business on the Tracy farm in Apalachin around the beginning of the 20th century on into the 1920s. This postcard shows the Tracy home on Marshland Road and Frank B. Tracy holding up large sheaves of tobacco that were just harvested. Some years were good for growing, but if the weather turned bad with rain and hail, it would destroy the crops.

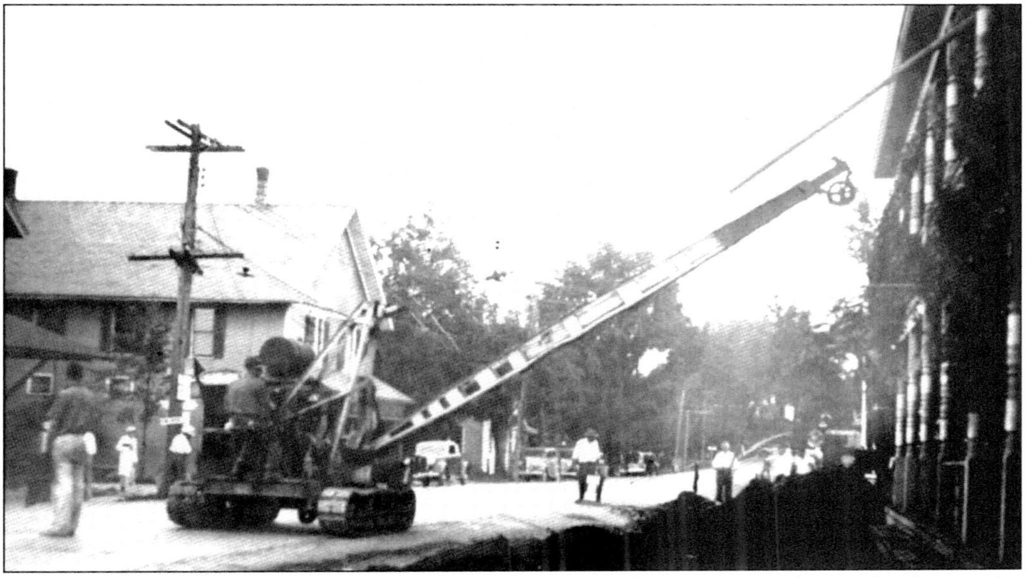

Taken in September 1936, this photograph shows the workmen putting the dirt back into the trench in front of the hotel on Main Street after installing a new water system.

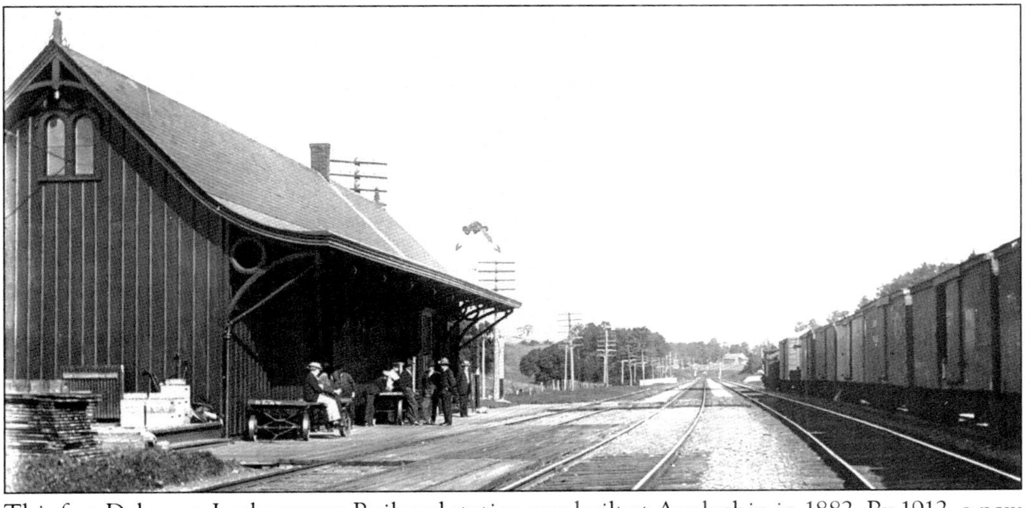

This first Delaware-Lackawanna Railroad station was built at Apalachin in 1882. By 1912, a new one was constructed, and businesses expanded. People traveled more frequently and students used it to get to school in the village of Owego every day. It was abandoned in 1954 by order of the Public Service Commission as a losing proposition for the railroad. Today it houses small businesses.

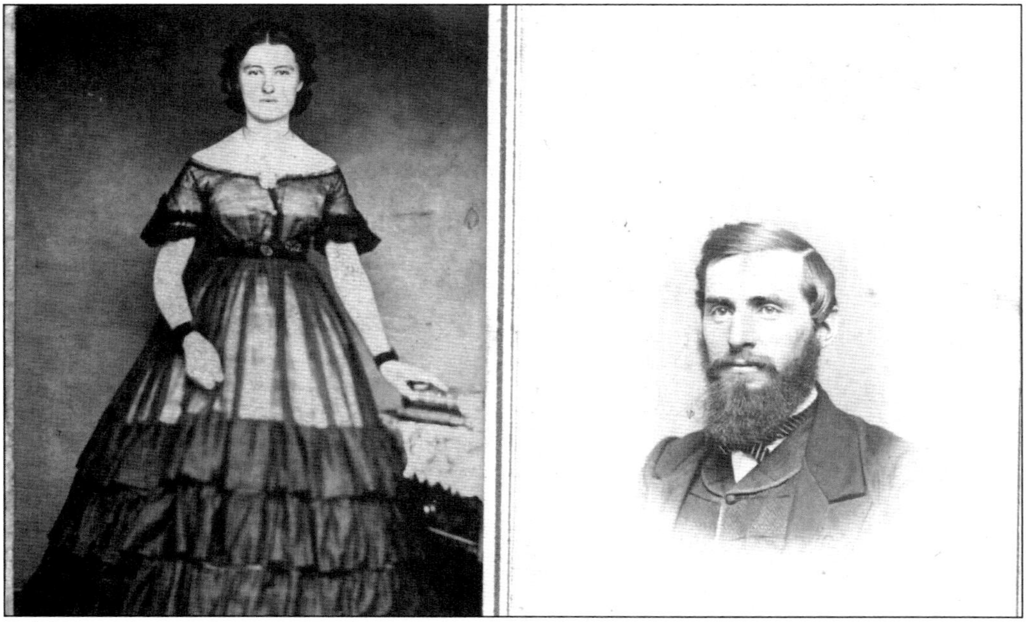

Adeline Valeria Billings Pearsall was only 19 when she posed for this formal photograph, the same year she became the bride of Ransom S. Pearsall on February 22, 1865, both of Apalachin. Ransom is 27 in this photograph, taken the year he and Adeline married. An educated man, he conducted a lumber business in Apalachin and piloted rafts to Pennsylvania and Maryland every spring. He was a justice of the peace from 1884 to 1888, was the postmaster of Apalachin, and held various other community posts.

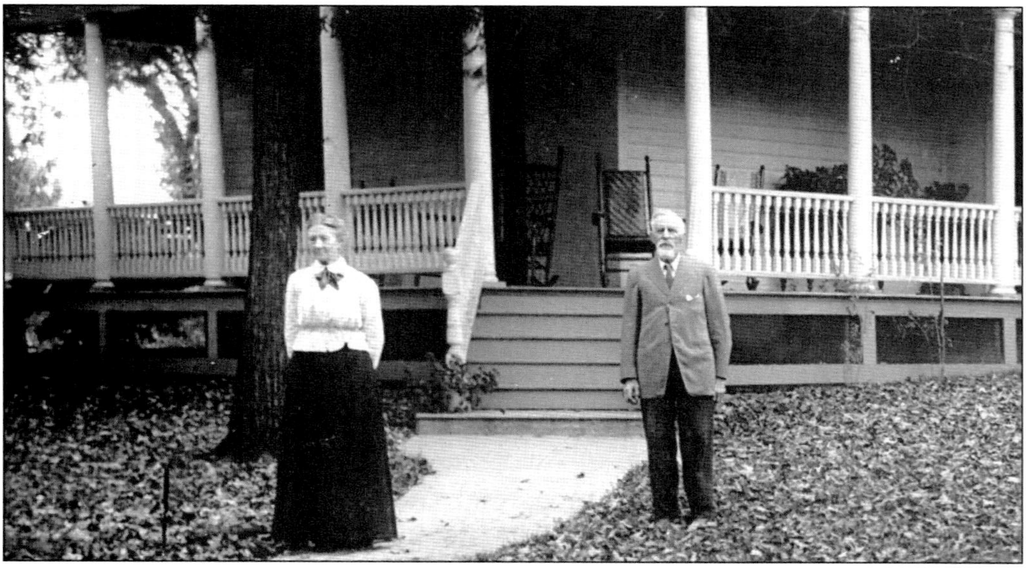

Adeline and Ransom are shown in front of their home on William Street in Apalachin around 1915. This photograph appeared in a 1935 newspaper article to commemorate their 70th anniversary. They had four children, Grace L., William C., Anna L., and Emily G. Emily and Grace worked at the state capitol in Albany and came home every chance they had. In 1915, Emily composed and published a waltz titled "Ripples on the Susquehanna."

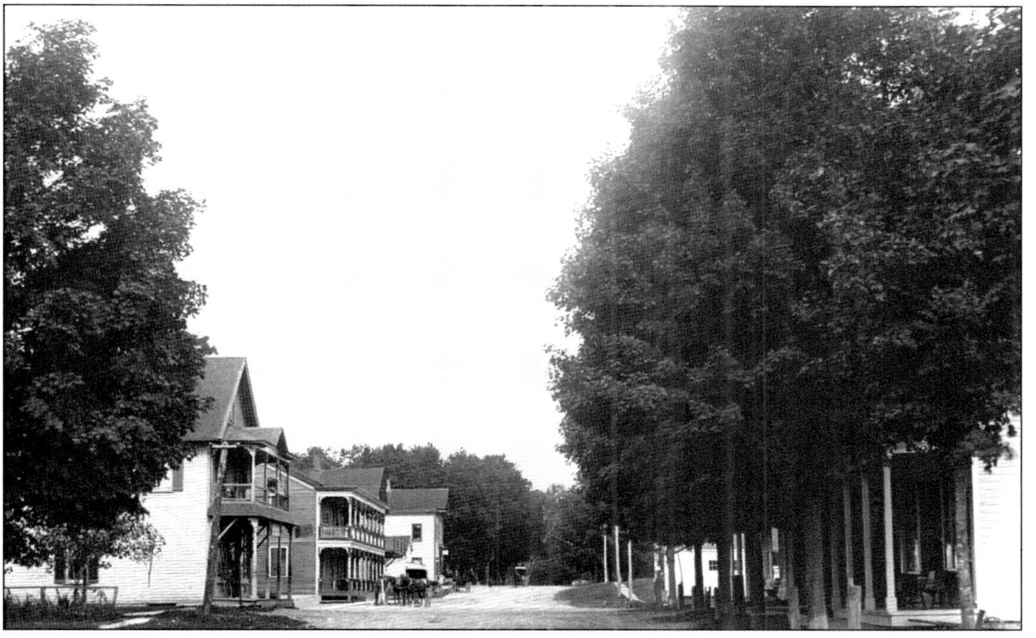

The hub of Apalachin was at the corner of Main Street and Pennsylvania Avenue, formerly known as Church Street, and as a result numerous photographs were taken in this section. The pleasant view shown here is looking west, past the Exchange Hotel. Today the road is paved, and a number of the buildings have either burned or have changed in appearance due to age or remodeling.

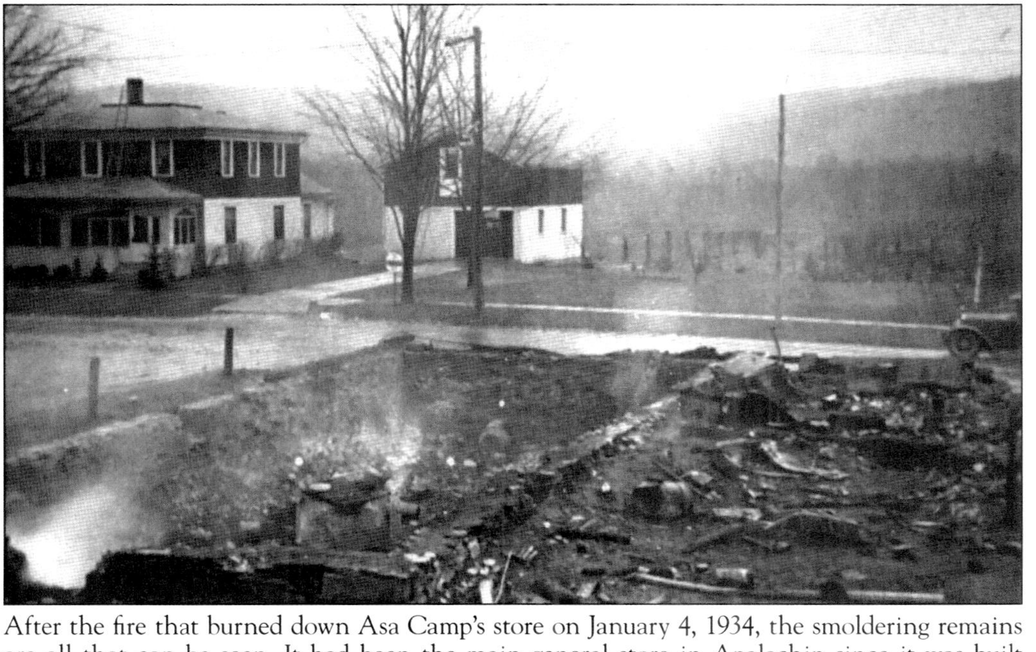

After the fire that burned down Asa Camp's store on January 4, 1934, the smoldering remains are all that can be seen. It had been the main general store in Apalachin since it was built around 1854 and was located on the corner of Main and New Streets. It housed a post office and meeting hall upstairs.

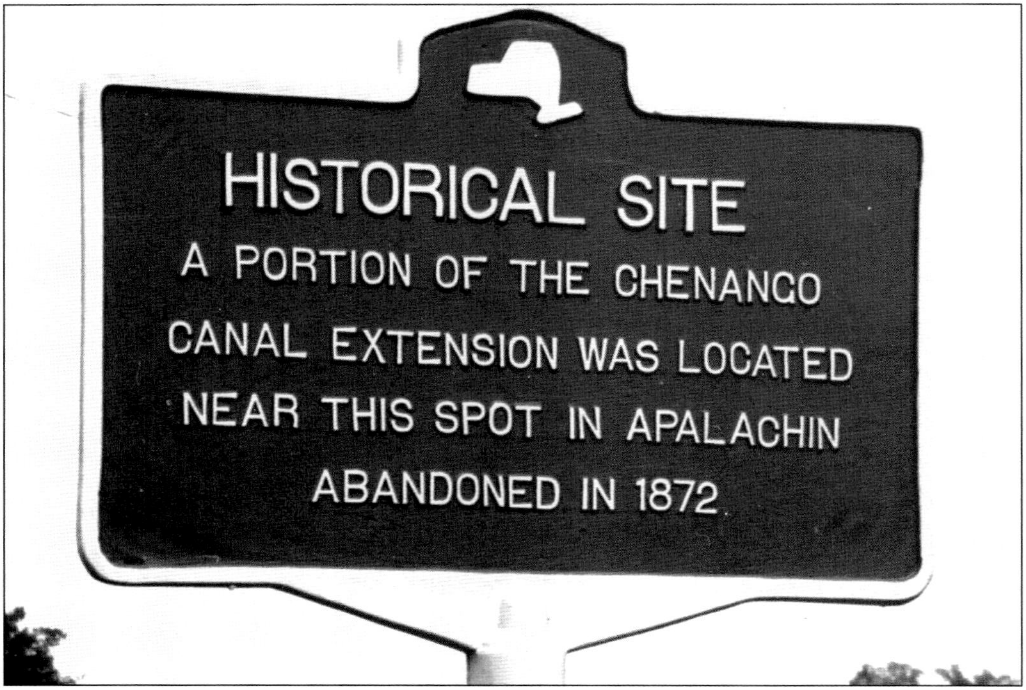

The Chenango Canal ran from Utica to Binghamton for 97 miles, opening in 1837, and was quite successful for a long time. It encouraged legislators in 1862 to begin construction of an extension of the canal through Tioga County on the south side of the Susquehanna River and connect it with the North Branch Canal, near the state line at Athens, Pennsylvania, a distance of about 38 miles. The canal commissioners in Pennsylvania felt it would increase business from their state up to the Erie Canal. It was built in sections, "as money became available." It went slowly due to the Civil War raging and prices skyrocketed, not to mention that the Erie Railroad ran on the north side of the river. By 1872, it was finished to about Nichols, but taxpayers had had enough, and it was never completed. The historic marker was erected by the Town of Owego in 1993 and is located on Route 434 in Apalachin near the remains of the once-proposed canal.

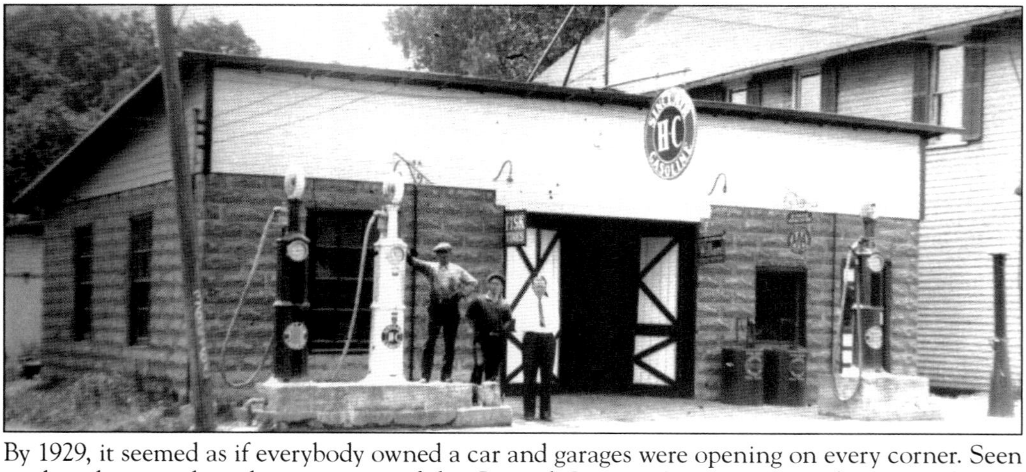

By 1929, it seemed as if everybody owned a car and garages were opening on every corner. Seen in this photograph is the proprietor of the Central Garage, C. Harrison, and two people who may be keeping him company until a customer arrives.

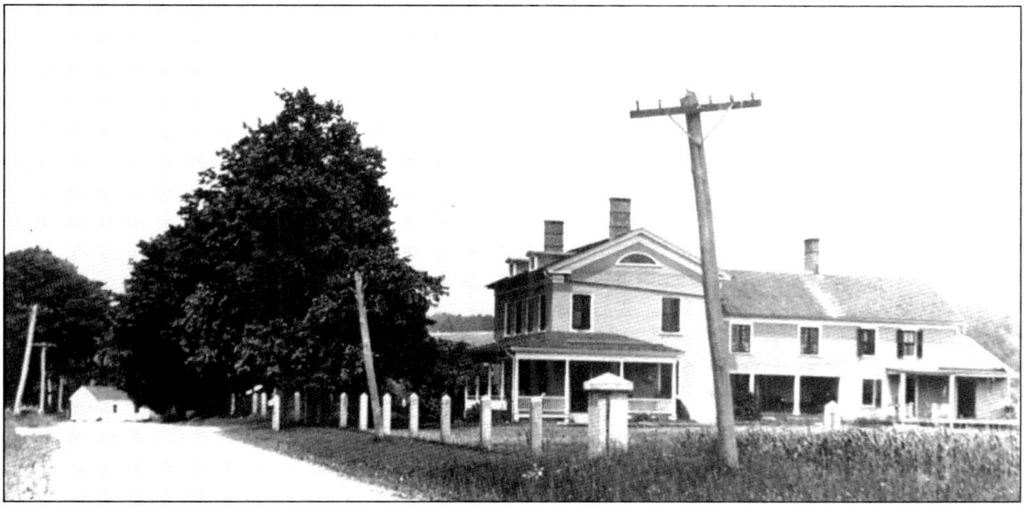

This fine home was built around 1835 on Marshland Road, Apalachin. Its most notable owner was Gen. Benjamin F. Tracy, who fought in the Civil War and was later appointed secretary of the navy in 1889 by Pres. Benjamin Harrison. The 1851 schoolhouse can be seen in the distance.

Alan Tucker Sr. was a bright, well-respected man and the Owego town clerk for 28 years. He had also been a member of the Owego police, but the other hat he wore earned him the nickname of "Owego's outstanding musician and band lover." He was a director of the Owego Village Band and the Kirby Band in Nichols for several years and was the band instructor in the Owego schools; he also conducted his own dance band. Born in 1901, he passed away in 1977.

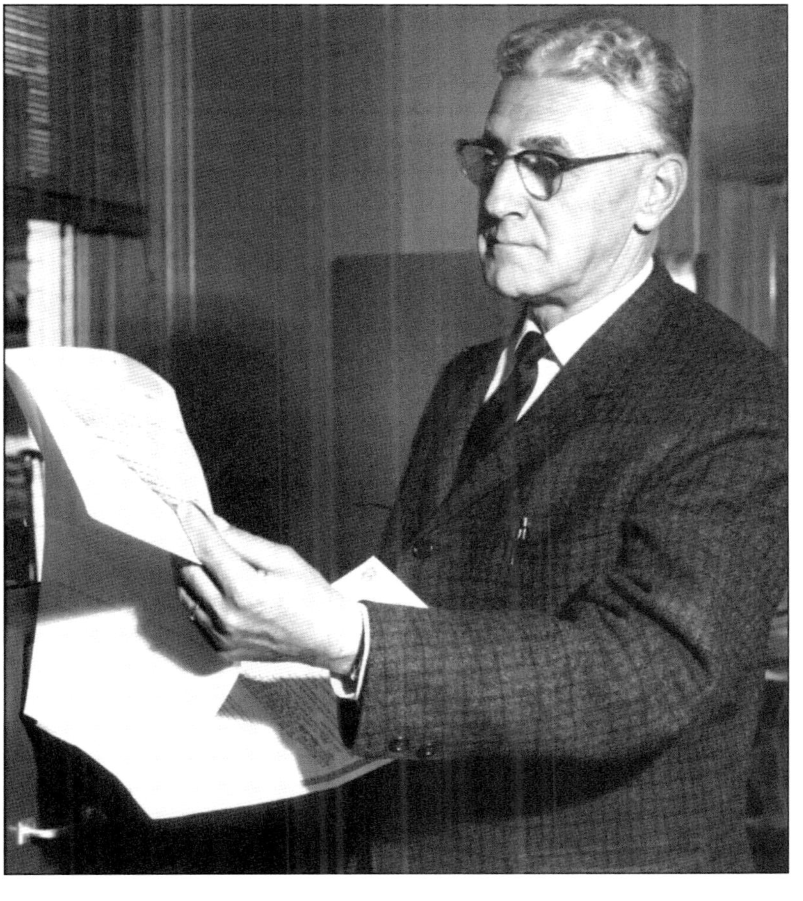

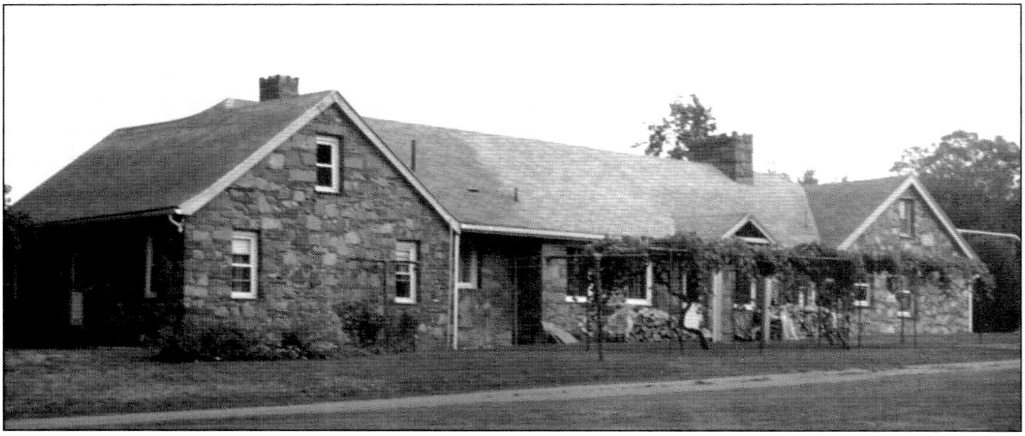

The lovely Barbara estate on McFall Road in Apalachin has a bit of a notorious past. On November 14, 1957, more than 60 members of organized crime gathered to allegedly attend a barbecue and to pay their respects to their ailing host, Joseph Barbara Sr. The police and FBI were alerted when the guests registered at a local motel. They blocked the entry road to the house but were spotted and many of the guests ran into the woods. After they were rounded up, a newspaper declared that the incident "touched off one of the most widespread crime investigations in the country's history." It drew national attention, including that of the United States Senate Select Committee on Improper Activities in Labor or Management, with Robert Kennedy as counsel. Trials were held at the Tioga County Courthouse and most of those arrested took the Fifth Amendment. By the end of the following year, some had been deported, some were jailed for refusing to answer questions from the grand jury, and one was convicted of criminal contempt, but when it was all over, the reason for the meeting remained a mystery. The home is now privately owned.

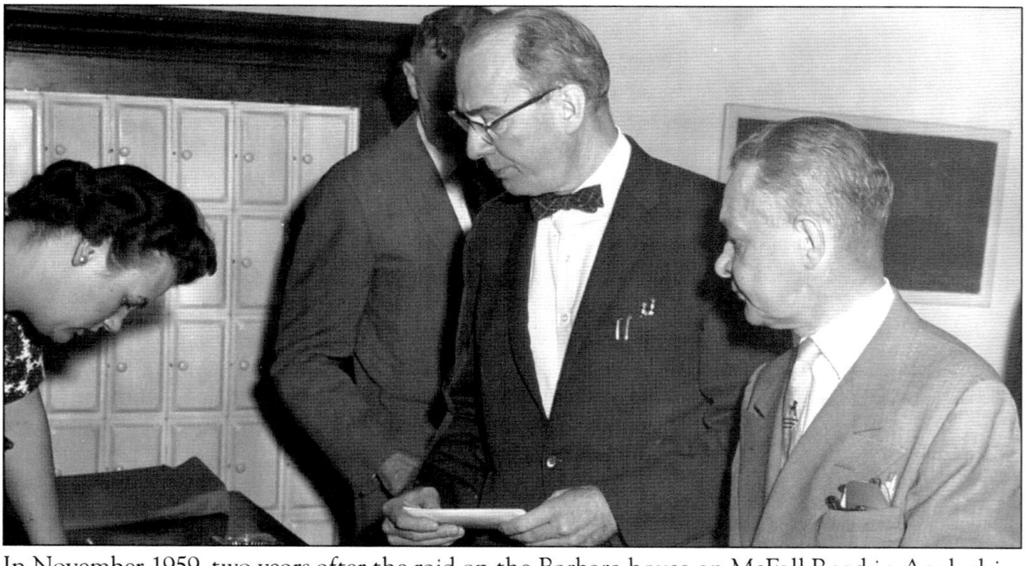

In November 1959, two years after the raid on the Barbara house on McFall Road in Apalachin, the owner wanted to rezone the property to turn it into a tourist attraction and let the public get a close-up view of the inside of the home. Shown here are attorney Harry S. Travis, right, and Owego town attorney Lewis Parmerton conferring with Rita O'Brien, court stenographer, after a town board hearing on the rezoning issue.

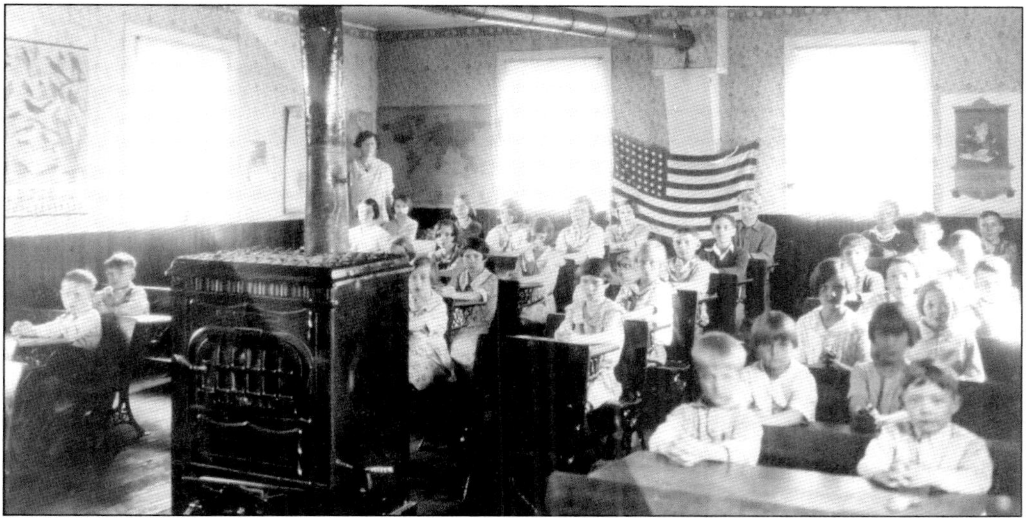

L. M. Hall, the teacher of this one-room school in 1932, probably instructed the children to "sit up straight and fold your hands" for the picture, because that is what they are all doing. The school was in District No. 31 in Apalachin and housed grades one through seven. The Heatorola stove looks like it does a good job of keeping them warm. The names were listed in alphabetical order, but not as they are seated. The girls are Anna Abbey, Irene Bakeman, Mary Buckner, Helen Buckner, Viola Card, Violet Card, Myrtle Darrah, Betty Darrah, Betty Degnan, Martha Denning, Betty Frazer, Rita Frazer, Georgia Frazer, Frances Gaylord, Dorothy Martin, Jean Rider, Alberta Stanley, Margaret Stephens, Lena Storozow, and Helen Storozow. The boys are Donald Abbey, Howard Allen, William Darrah, Norman Darrah, Albert Darrah, Edwin Fancher, Junior Frazer, Harold Lillie, Orin Lillie, John Lopke, Charles Martin, Frank Mroczck, Elmer Rider, and Ezra Stephens.

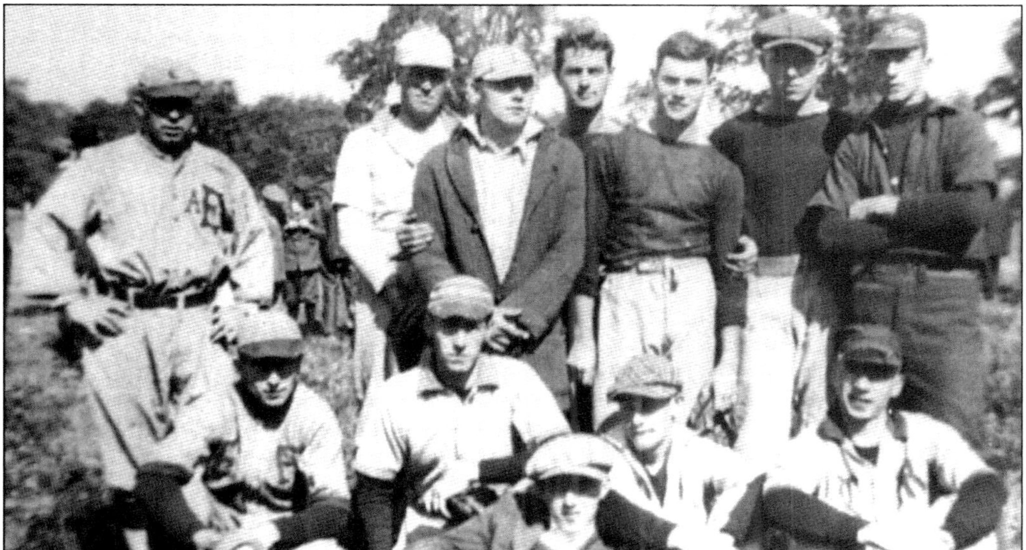

Baseball was very competitive in Apalachin, especially in the 1920s and 1930s. The teams played in local ball fields but also traveled to surrounding towns and cities, and newspapers eagerly wrote up the results.

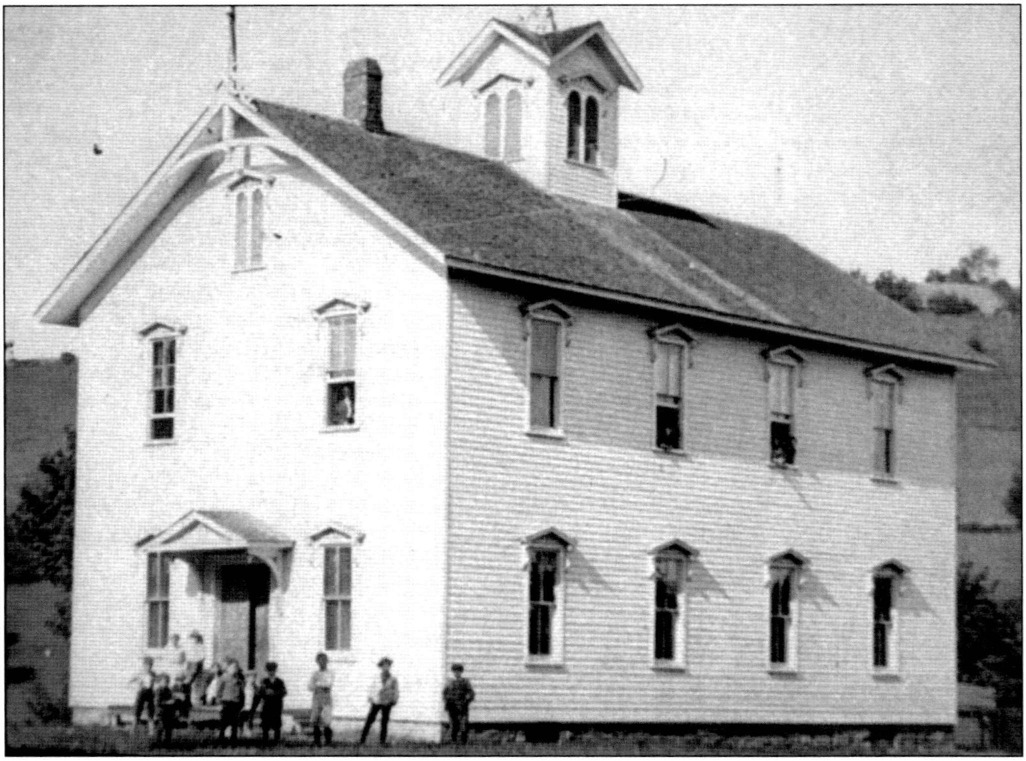

This schoolhouse stood on Pennsylvania Avenue from 1879 to 1957, in District No. 15. After it closed, it was used for a while as the Apalachin Library. It was finally razed, and the Apalachin Fire Department built its new firehouse on the property.

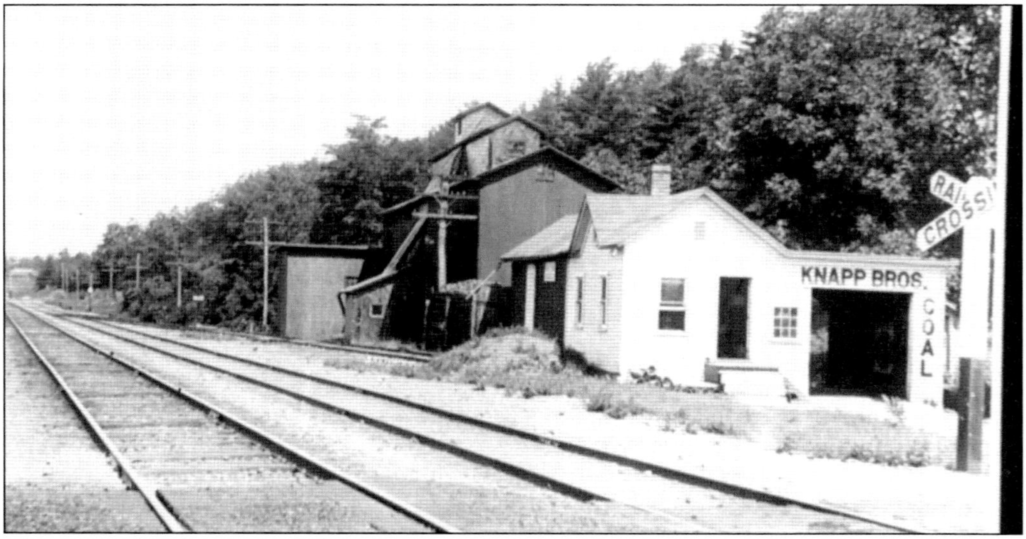

The Knapp brothers owned the coal yard just west of the Delaware, Lackawanna and Western Railroad station for a number of years. This view, looking west, was taken in 1913 when business was at its peak. In 1915, the firm of Knapp Brothers was dissolved, but Charles R. Knapp and his son formed a partnership and continued in the business.

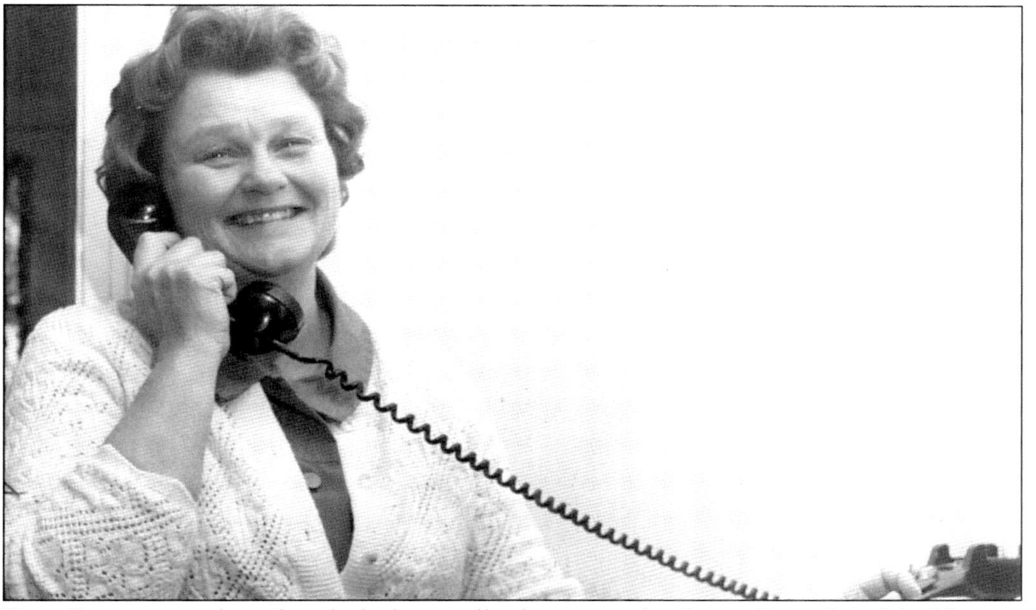

Doris Scott was used to a lot of telephone calls; she was on the Owego Town Board for 28 years, beginning in 1974, when this photograph was taken, until just before her death in 2002. A graduate of Keuka College, she continued her education at Columbia University and the University of Pennsylvania. Because she was so involved with programs and the improvement of Hickories Park, the town board dedicated the park bandstand in her honor.

The sign reads, "Apalachin Public Library," but it was so much more than that. Built in 1874, it opened as Grange No. 177, and over the years, it was used by the Ladies Aid Society, a center for community activities and social affairs, and even as a place of worship as late as 1958. It served as the Apalachin Public Library for a while and finally came to a close and began to deteriorate until it was beyond repair and was finally razed.

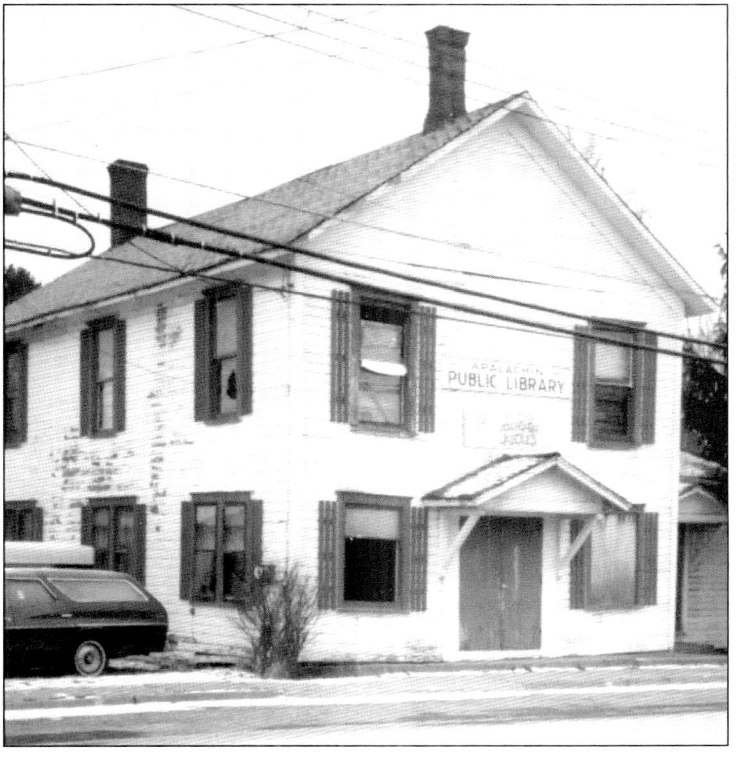

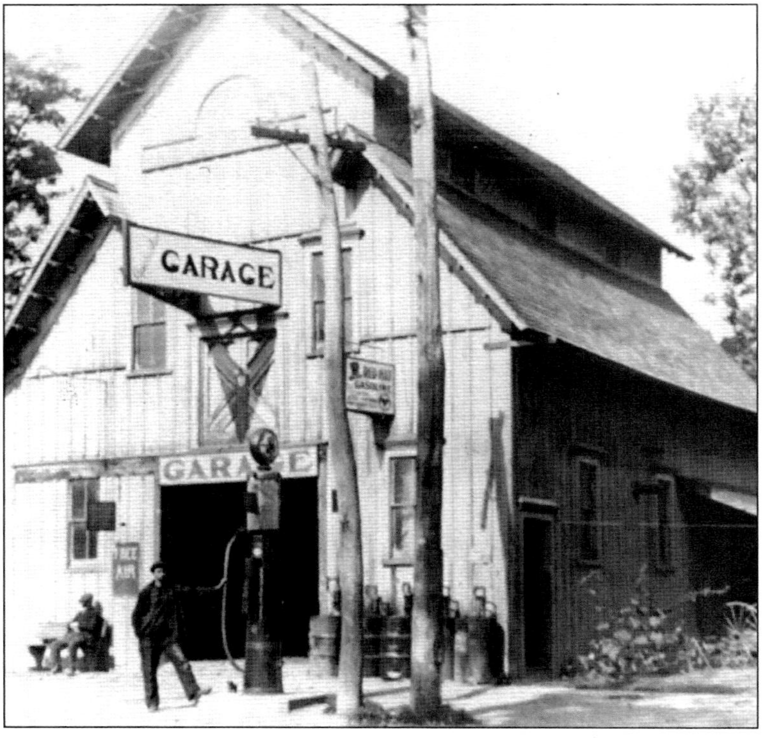

It looks like this Apalachin garage from the 1920s was converted from what used to be a barn; but if a customer needed gas, that was not important. The sign reads, "Red Hat Gasoline," with a top hat as a logo. Standing by the pump is Harry Gray and asleep on the bench behind him is Jim Knapp. The garage burned down in a disastrous fire in 1932.

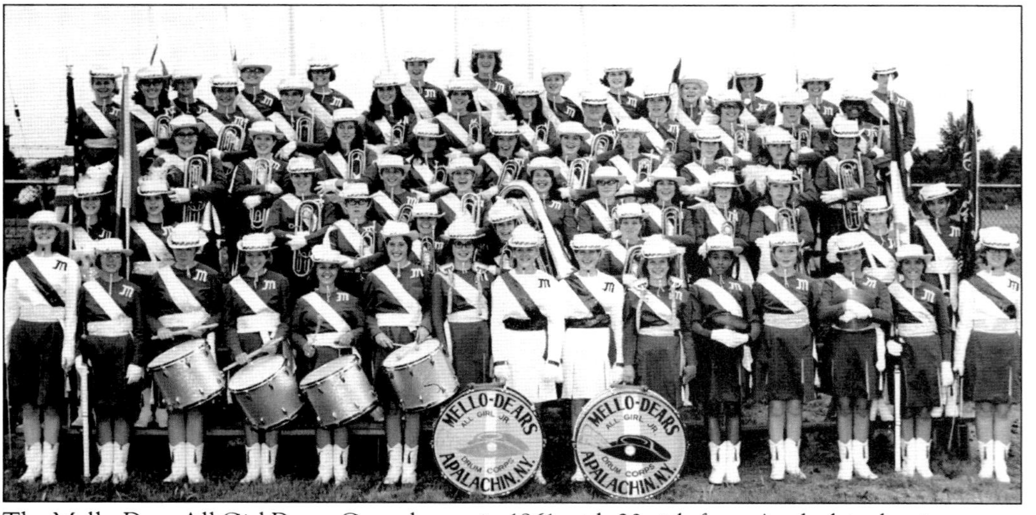

The Mello-Dear All Girl Drum Corps began in 1961 with 20 girls from Apalachin, but it was not long before it expanded to over 100 from New York and Pennsylvania. The girls first marched in parades and wore makeshift uniforms and used borrowed equipment from the American Legion. In 1962, they began entering competitions, and in 1963, they had a new 66-passenger school bus to transport them. By 1967, the Mello-Dears were undefeated for the entire year in 19 consecutive parades. They went on to win many victories, including the one on August 4, 1972, when they won the World Open Class A All-Girl Championship, defeating 10 other all-girl corps from the United States and Canada. The corps director was Fred Ford of Owego, who served as director until it disbanded after it returned from the Orange Bowl.

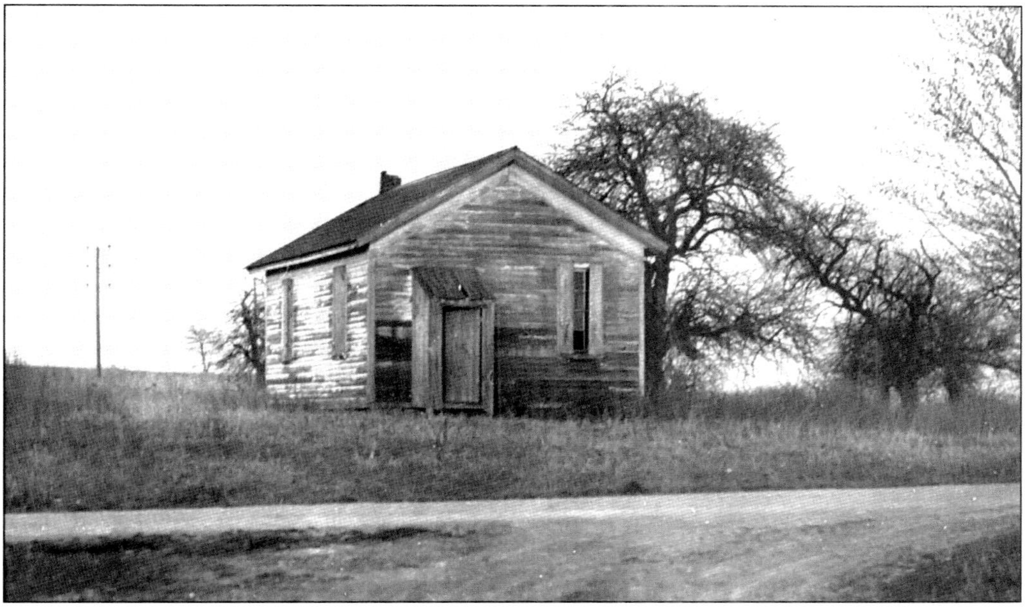

Built in 1830, this is the Mutton Hill School in District No. 19, in Apalachin. The photograph was taken in 1942 and clearly shows its age. As with so many old buildings, it burned several years later.

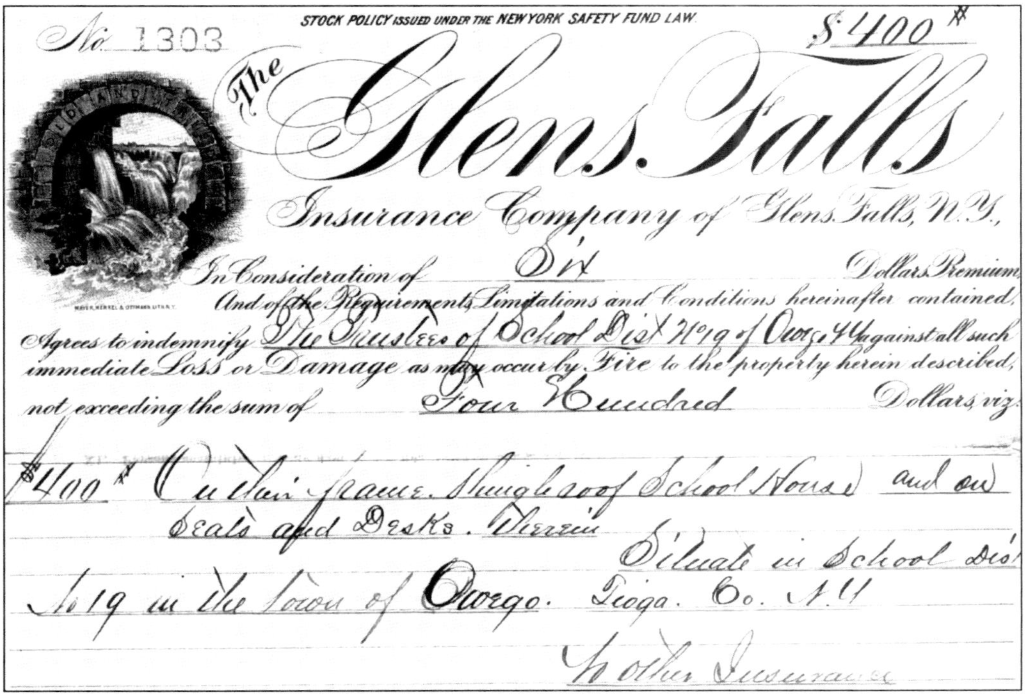

No. 1303

STOCK POLICY ISSUED UNDER THE NEW YORK SAFETY FUND LAW.

$400

The Glens Falls Insurance Company of Glens Falls, N.Y.,

In Consideration of Six Dollars Premium And of the Requirements, Limitations and Conditions hereinafter contained, Agrees to indemnify The Trustees of School Dist No 19 of Owego NY against all such immediate Loss or Damage as may occur by Fire to the property herein described, not exceeding the sum of Four Hundred Dollars, viz:

$400 On their frame Shingle roof School House and on Seats and Desks therein

Situate in School Dist No 19 in the town of Owego. Tioga Co. N.Y.

No other Insurance

Shown is annual insurance policy No. 1303 for $400, at a premium of $6 per year for the schoolhouse in District No. 19. It was known as the Mutton Hill School and located west of Apalachin. The insurance covered loss and damage by fire to the property for one year, expiring in 1881.

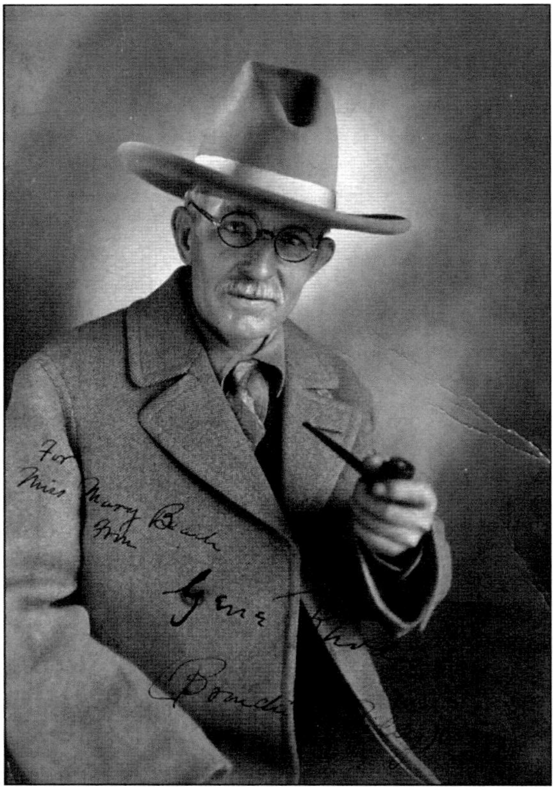

Eugene Manlove Rhodes, a cowboy author of 14 western novels, short stories, and poetry often sent photographs of himself to his son, Alan Rhodes of Apalachin. Alan carried a business card with him at all times that read, "Alan Rhodes, Apalachin, N.Y. The only claim I have to fame is having had my father's name." Eugene came to Apalachin after May Louise Davison Purple read some of his poetry and wrote to him in New Mexico. They corresponded on a regular basis, and a romance was kindled, which led to marriage in 1899. For a short time, they lived at his home in Tularosa, New Mexico, but later moved back to Apalachin, where Eugene continued to live for the next 20 years.

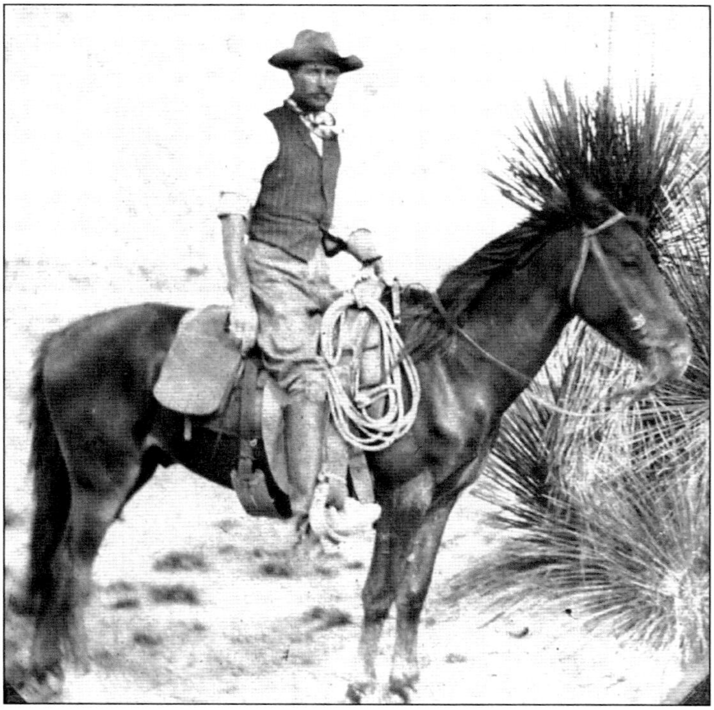

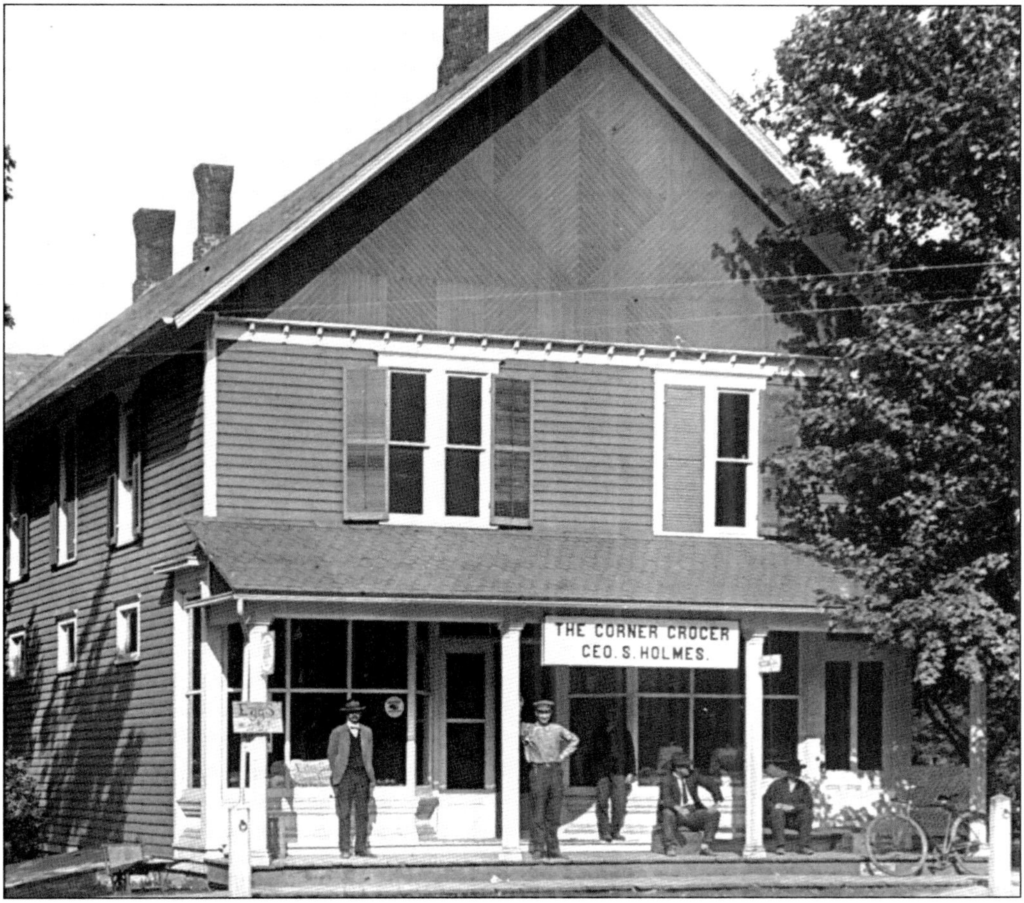

George S. Holmes's corner grocery store was a handsome building on Main Street in Apalachin, as this photograph shows. It was sold later on and became the Grand Union store until it burned down.

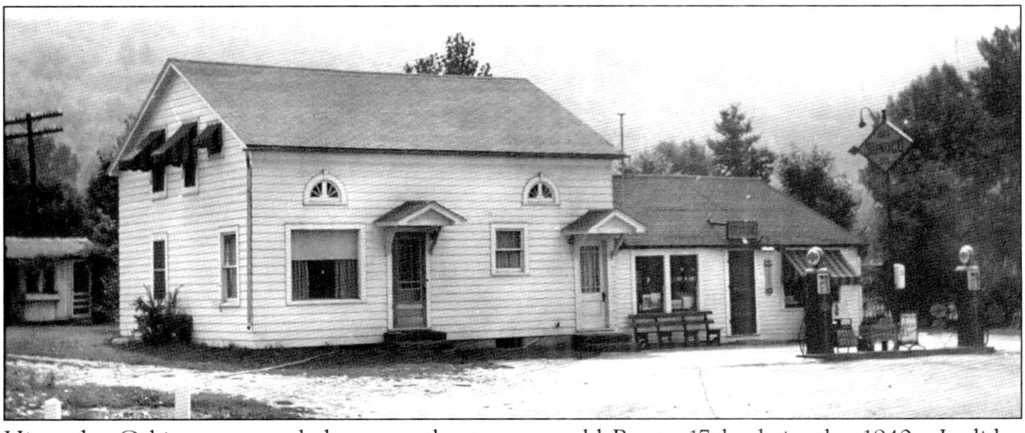

Hiawatha Cabins was nestled among the trees on old Route 17 back in the 1940s. It did a thriving business, but as with most of the motels of that era, it came to a close as roads improved and speed limits went up, spurring tourists to keep on going.

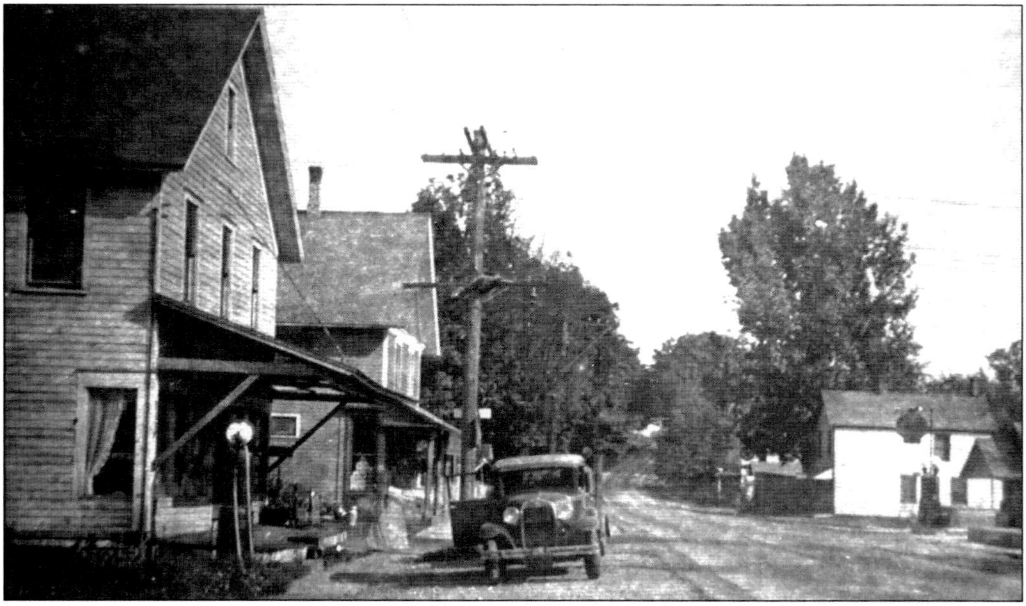

The cameras in 1932 were a far cry from what is available today, but even though the sun was 90 degrees eclipsed on August 31, 1932, this photograph taken near the Exchange Hotel does not look too bad.

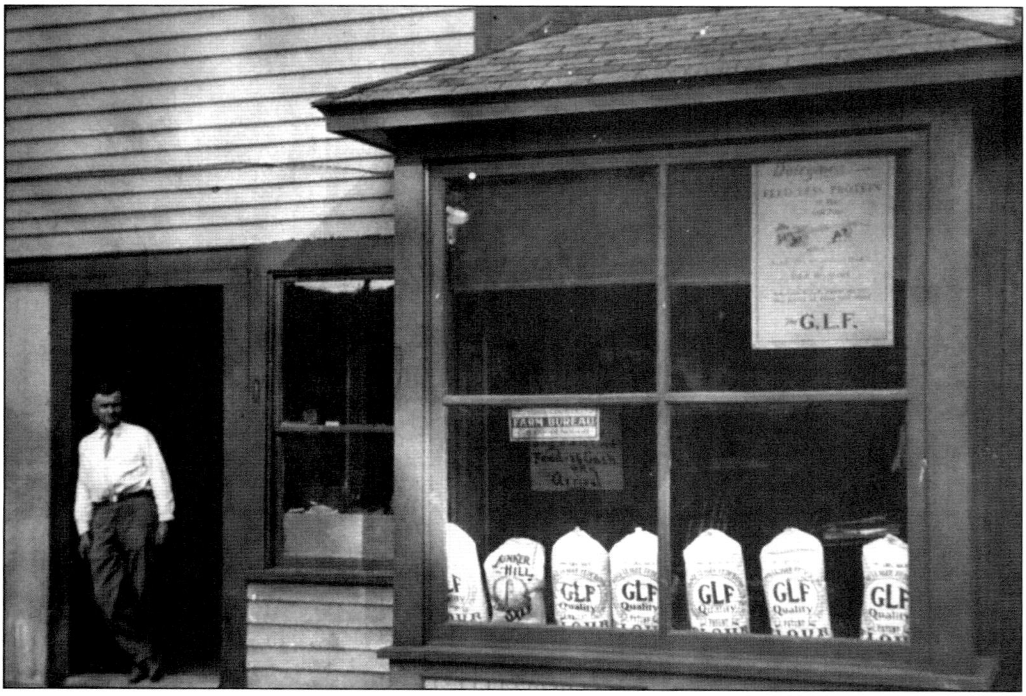

Perhaps C. B. Goodnough is waiting for a delivery truck or simply for some business. As shown by the sacks in his store window, he specialized in feed in 1928. His handwritten notice reminds his customers, "Feed is Cash on Arrival."

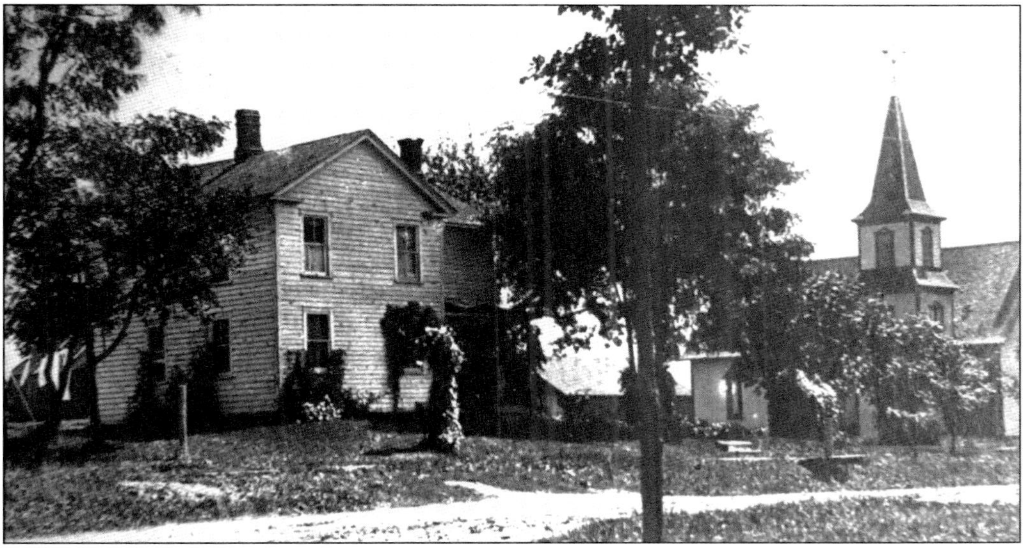

The Methodist Episcopal church was built in 1887 on Church Street, now named Pennsylvania Avenue. The parish house is next to it and looks as if it must have been laundry day from the wash on the line.

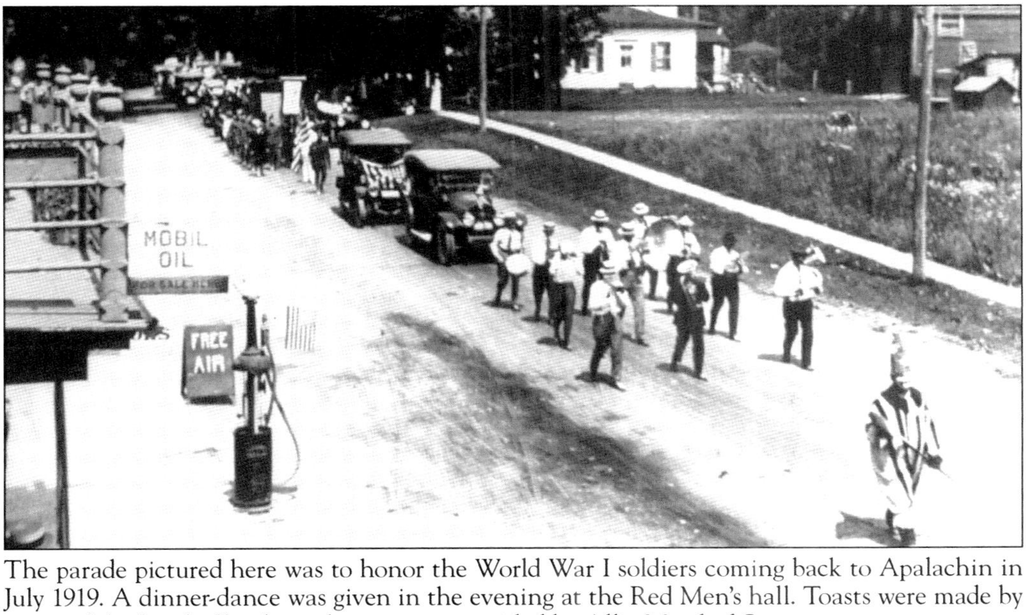

The parade pictured here was to honor the World War I soldiers coming back to Apalachin in July 1919. A dinner-dance was given in the evening at the Red Men's hall. Toasts were made by many of the local officials, and music was provided by Allie Mead of Owego.

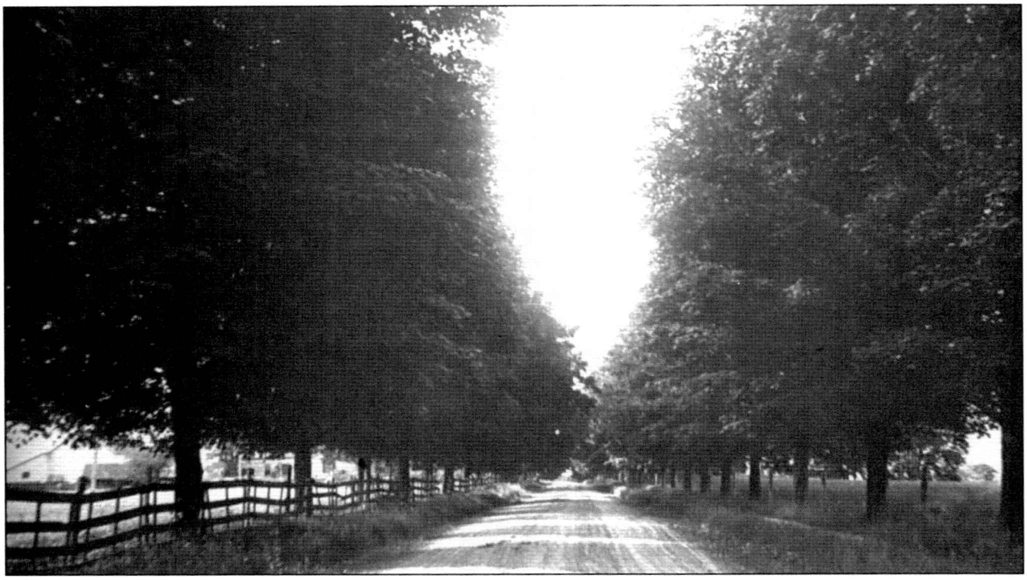

In its earliest history, this road was a narrow trail used by the Native Americans who lived here. It was called River Road up until the mid-19th century and then finally, Marshland Road. It is still a beautiful tree-lined road, looking much like this photograph.

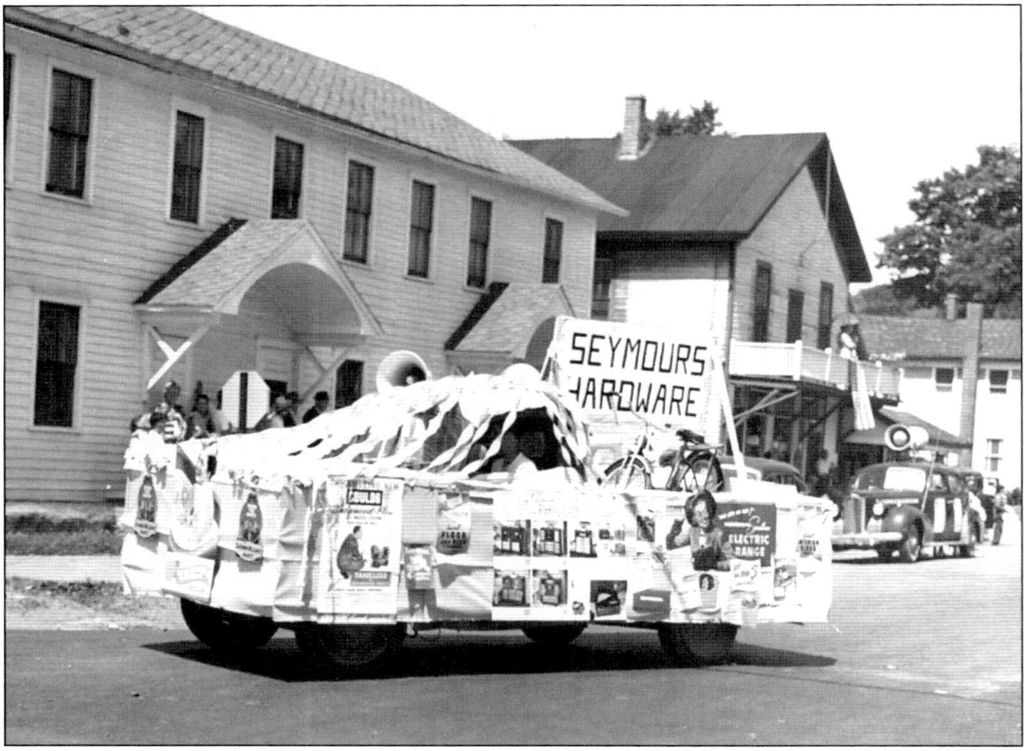

Using advertising for decorations on a float was probably a good idea. Richard Seymour, son of Apalachin hardware store owner Harmon Seymour, took on the job of driving the float in a 1940s parade, and it looks like he did a good job of including everything on it.

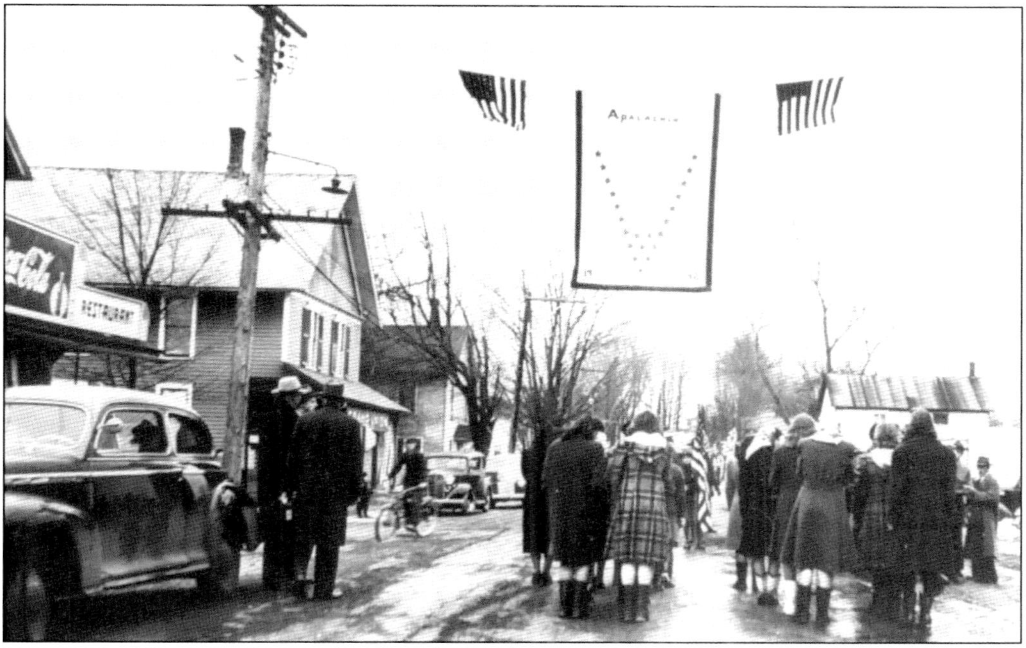

During World War II, the people of Apalachin had a 22-star flag made in the shape of a V, with each star representing a military man from Apalachin. This photograph was taken during a ceremony as the flag was hung across Main Street.

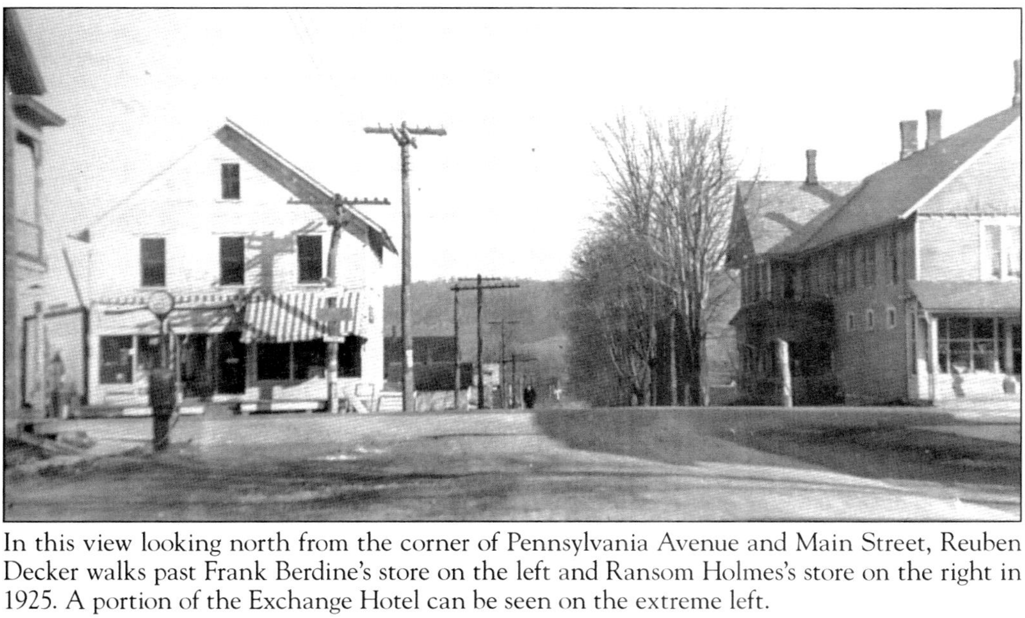

In this view looking north from the corner of Pennsylvania Avenue and Main Street, Reuben Decker walks past Frank Berdine's store on the left and Ransom Holmes's store on the right in 1925. A portion of the Exchange Hotel can be seen on the extreme left.

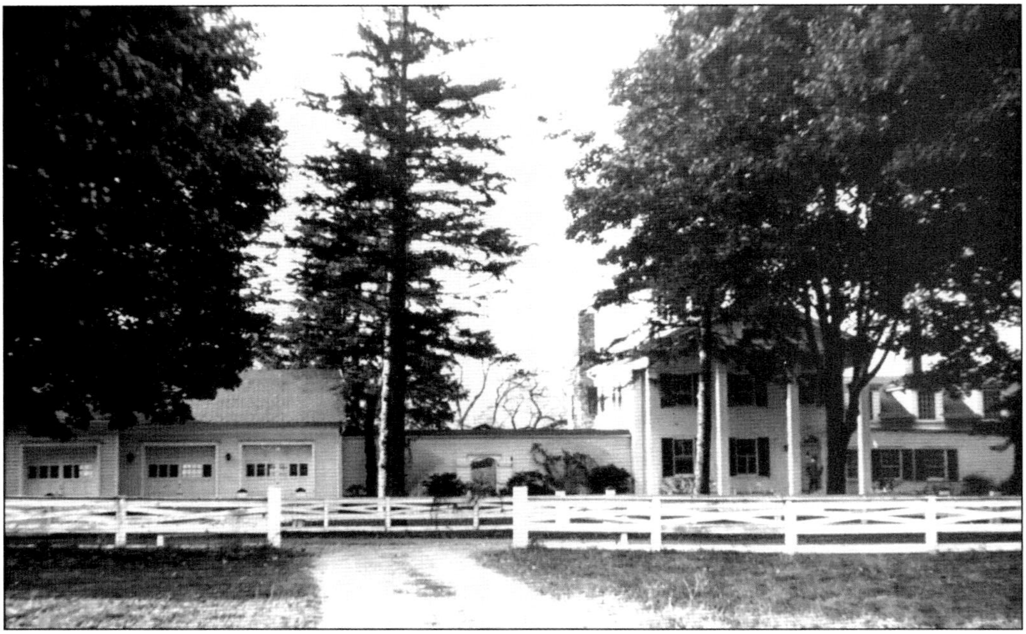

The beautiful Mercereau estate was built about 1826 by David Mercereau from the trees on his property, as well as the fieldstones for the fireplace and chimney. The home was passed on to George Mercereau in 1934. He and his wife Edna named it Edgefield, taking the first two letters of Edna and the first two letters of George and adding *field*.

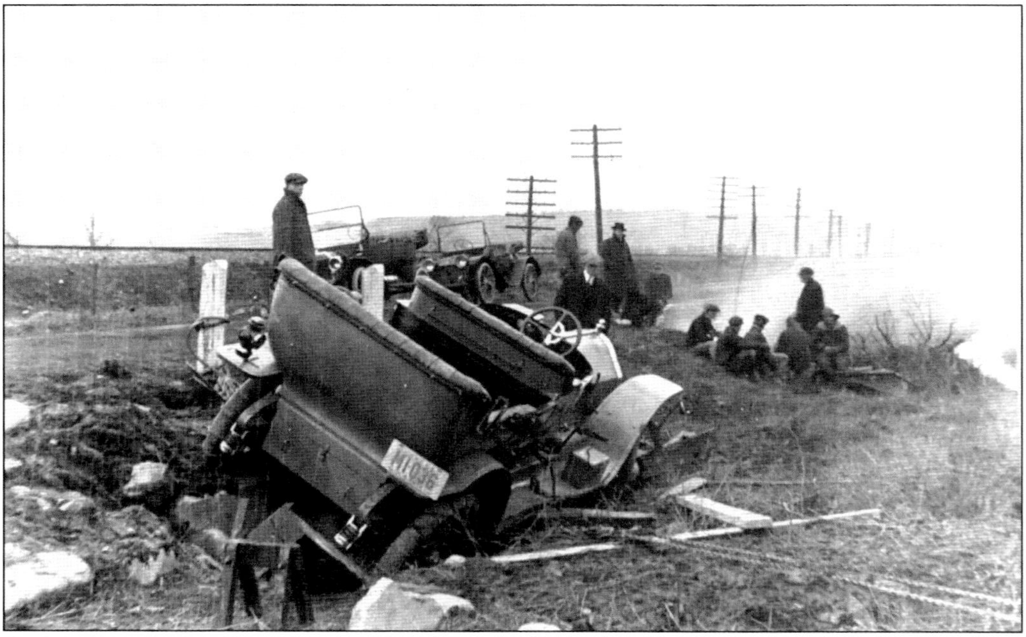

Car accidents were all too common in the early days. The combination of skinny tires and bad roads were accidents waiting to happen. This one occurred by the railroad tracks on April 2, 1916, about three miles west of Apalachin. It looks as if owner Thomas Flyer had some major repairs to make.

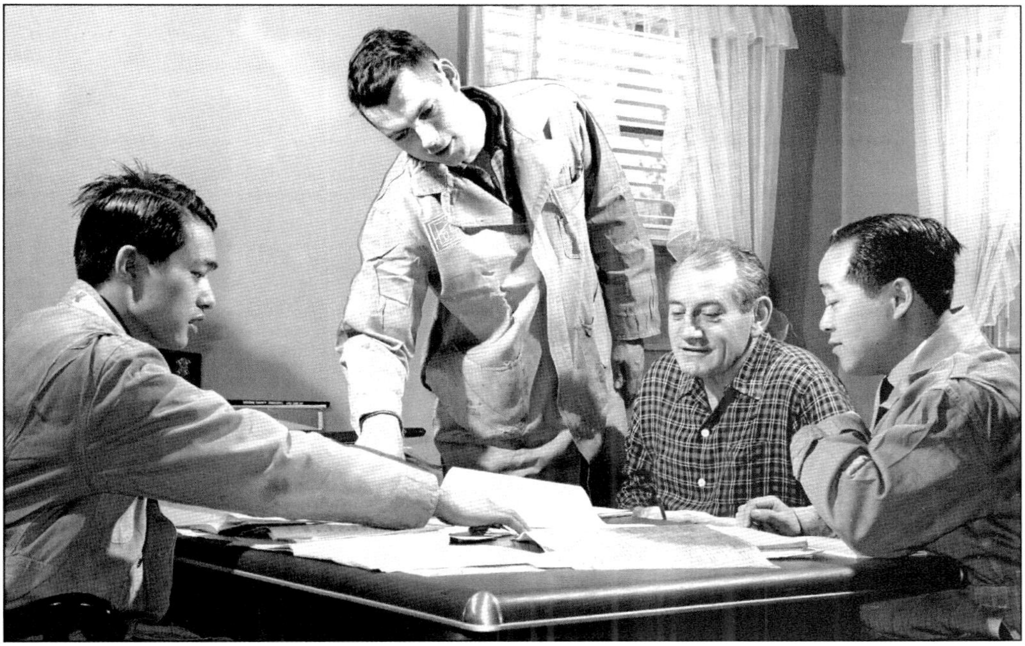

In 1964, officials of Owego Heat Treat of Marshland Road in Apalachin and Yoshino Kogyosno Company of Tokyo review plans for licensing of the Japanese firm to use processes patented by the town of Owego firm for treating metal in industrial processes. Japanese engineers studied various American methods before making a deal with Owego Heat Treat. From left to right are Masanora Nishikawa (technology supervisor of the Tokyo firm), Edward L. Englehard (manager), William E. Englehard (president of Owego Heat Treat), and Hiroyasu Koike (assistant manager of the technology department of the Japanese firm).

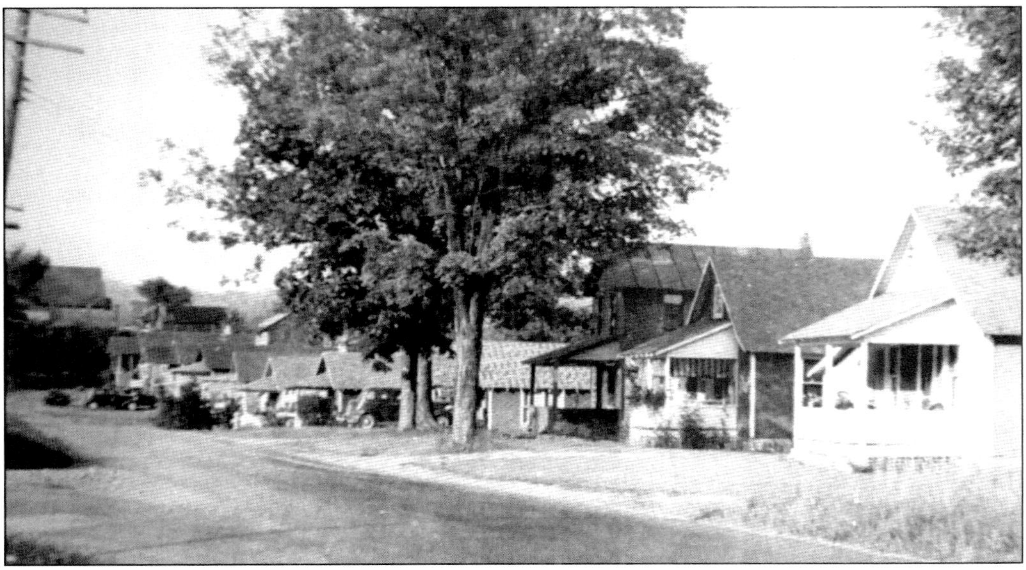

"Poverty Row" was the nickname given to this group of homes on Pennsylvania Avenue in Apalachin, because they were built of recycled lumber. David Gardiner built them in the late 1930s and early 1940s.

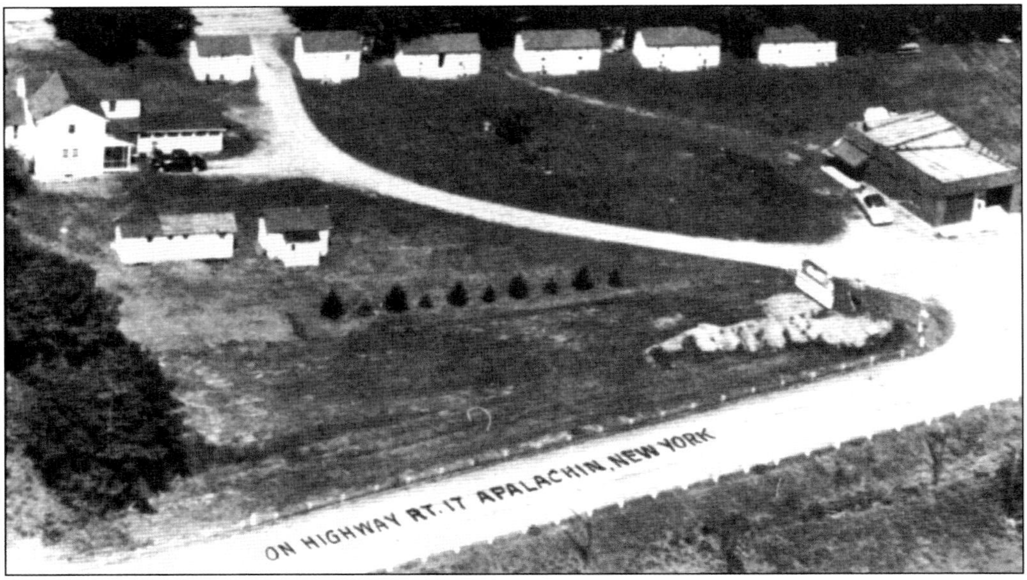

The Rainbo Cabins in Apalachin were built around 1937 and owned by the Wooden family. Betty Hawkins Brown told how she worked there and noted that tourists were scarce in the 1940s. Besides having a large dining area where meals were served on Sundays, baked goods, ice cream, candy, and other homemade foods were sold every day.

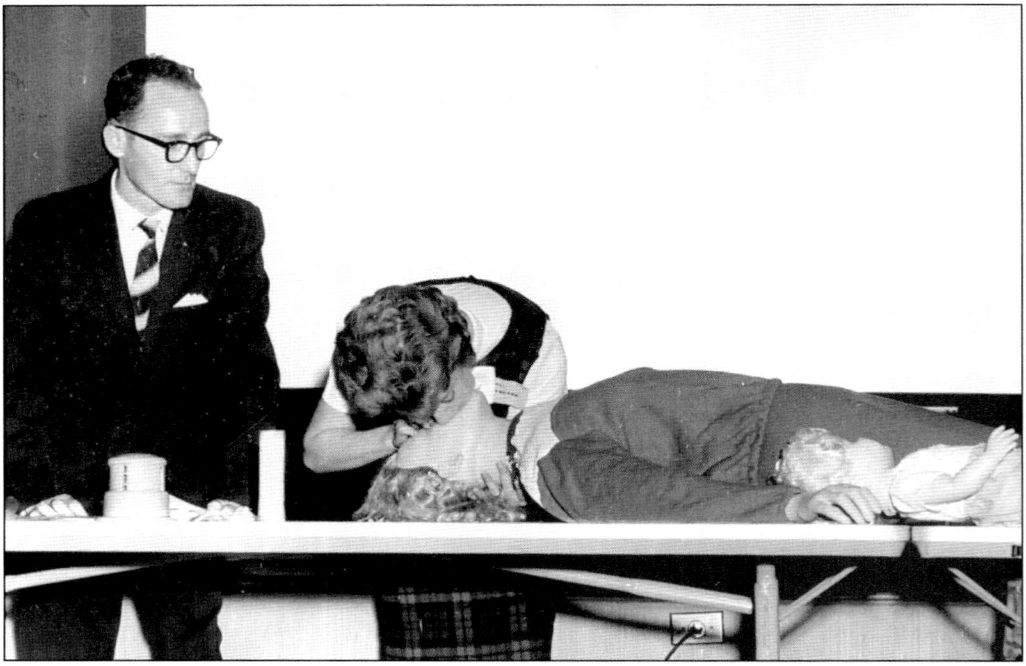

Captain of the Apalachin Emergency Squad, Eugene Mac Daniels watches Mrs. Pat Scovell of Apalachin demonstrate mouth-to-mouth resuscitation on "Resusa-Kate." The mannequin was purchased by the Apalachin Fire Department for $22.50 in 1965, and many community residents took advantage of learning this lifesaving technique.

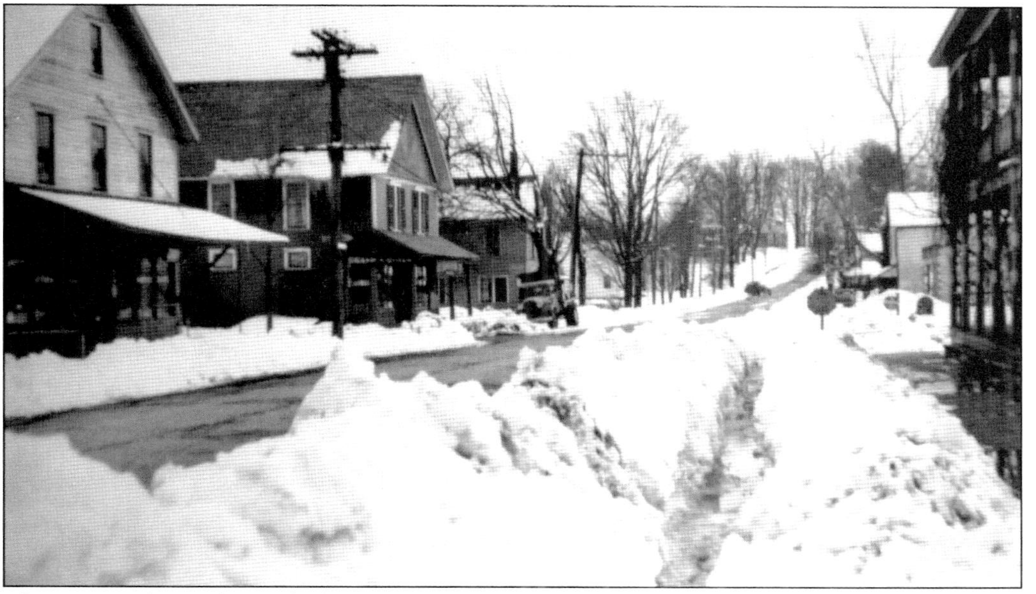

The winter of 1940 dumped a lot of snow on Apalachin, and plows were scarce. This photograph was taken in front of the Exchange Hotel on Main Street.

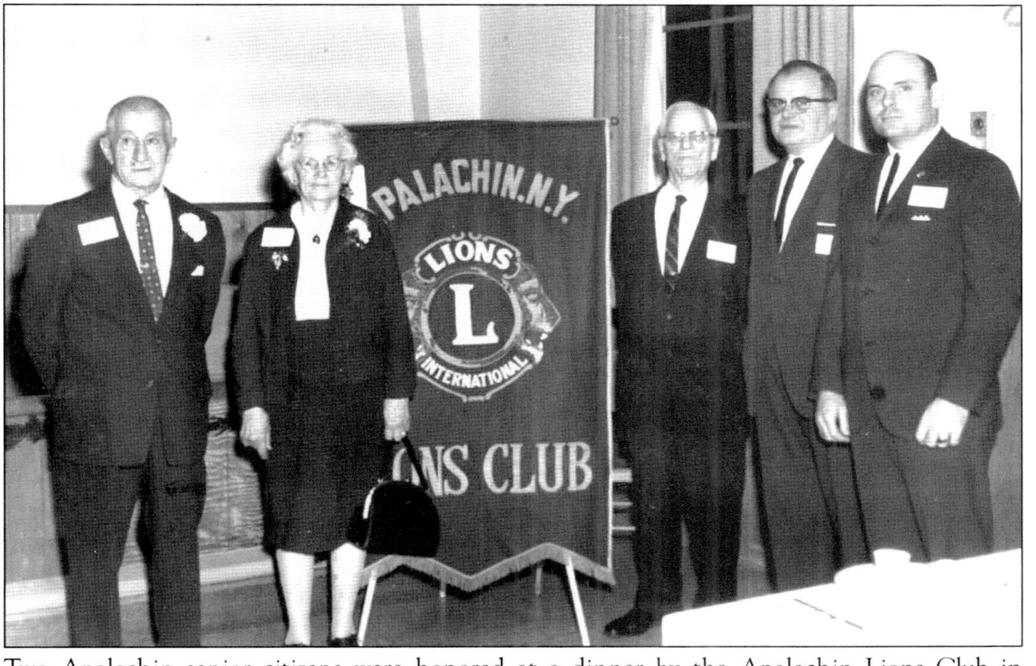

Two Apalachin senior citizens were honored at a dinner by the Apalachin Lions Club in December 1966. Shown are, from left to right, Robert Ryan and Mary Rider, guests of honor; Peter T. Campon, of Binghamton; Robert Donnelly, program chairman; and Jack Smith, Lions Club president.

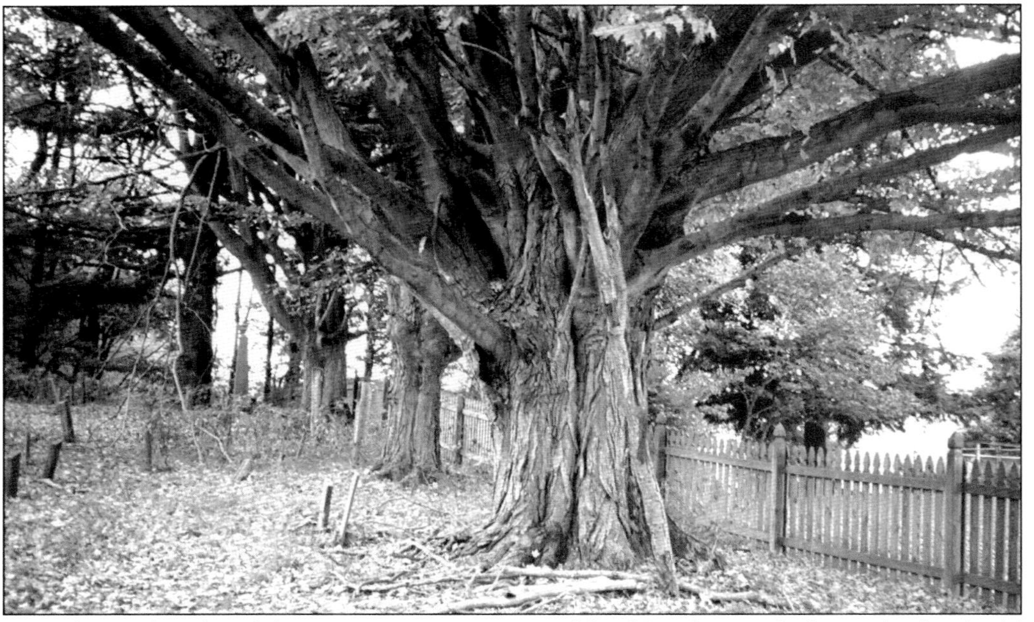

Rooted in at the edge of the Camp Cemetery on Marshland Road in Apalachin is this lovely old maple tree giving shade to the gravestones nearby.

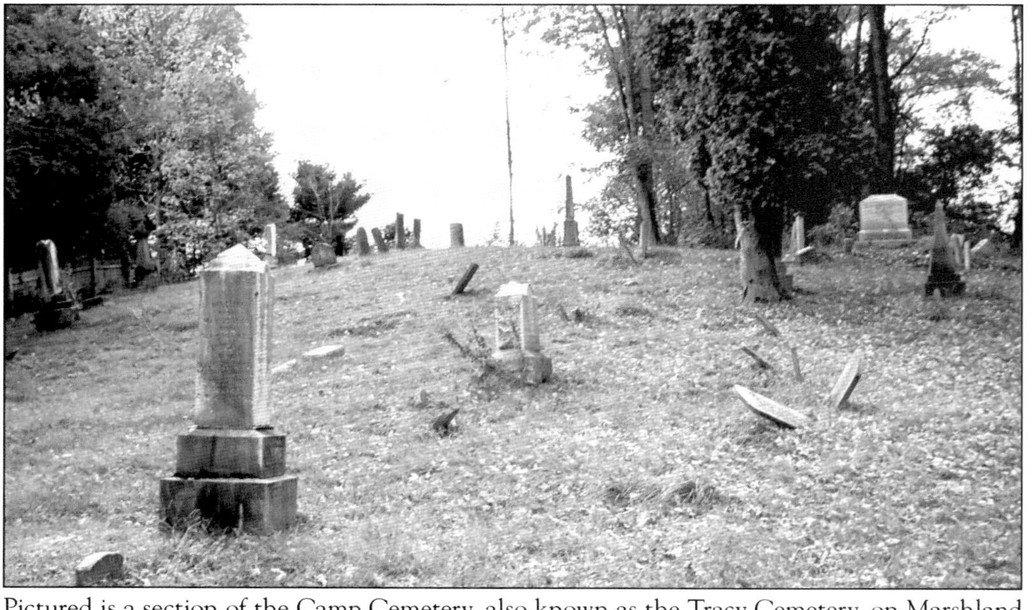

Pictured is a section of the Camp Cemetery, also known as the Tracy Cemetery, on Marshland Road in Apalachin. Burials go back to the early 1800s.

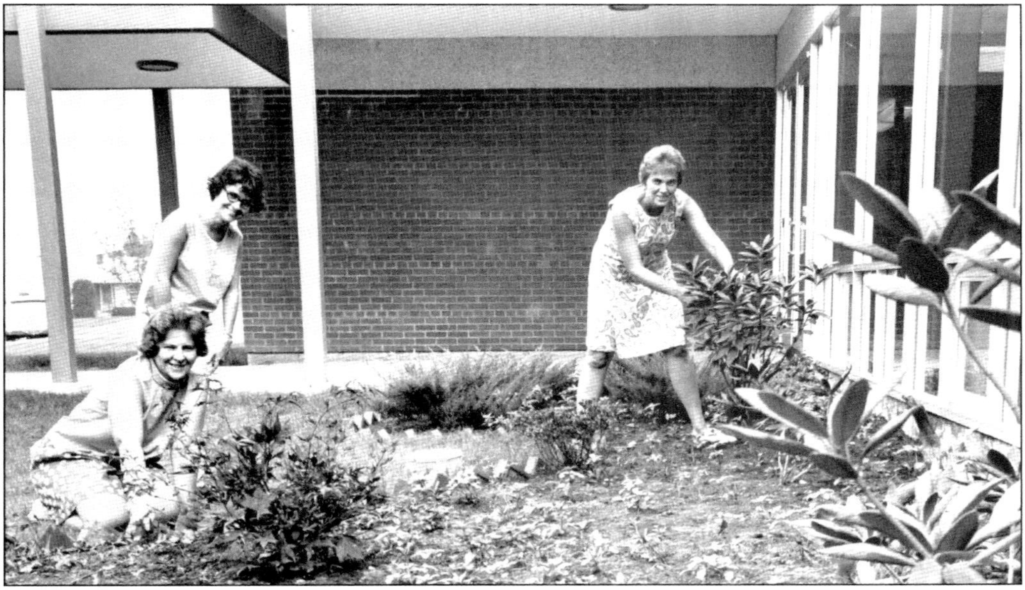

A few of the Tioga Hills Federated Garden Club members are show landscaping at the new Tioga Hills Elementary School on Glann Road in September 1969. The previous year, they planted trees, shrubs, and bulbs. Shown are, from left to right, Mrs. Bartel T. Perry, Connie Tietze, and project chairman Mrs. Eugene Marasco.

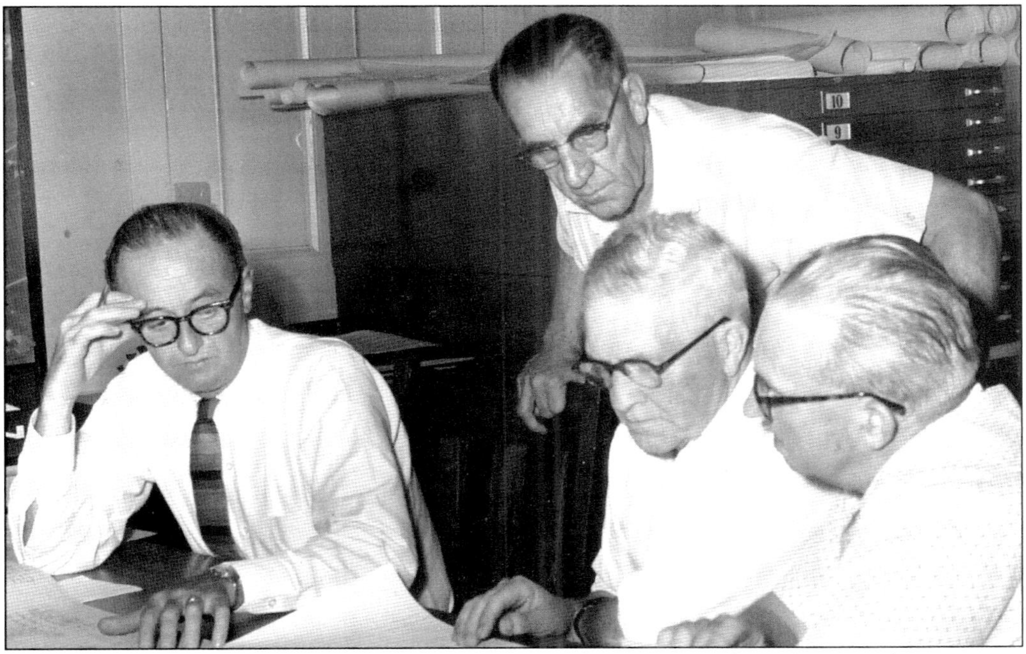

In August 1960, members of the Town of Owego Planning Board are busy studying zoning change requests to permit establishment of trailer parks in the town of Owego. Seated are, from left to right, John E. Sweet Jr., planning board chairman, and Judson Spencer and Eugene Lynch, both planning board members; standing is Eland Perry of Apalachin, who has proposed a trailer park on Shady Hill Drive, Apalachin.

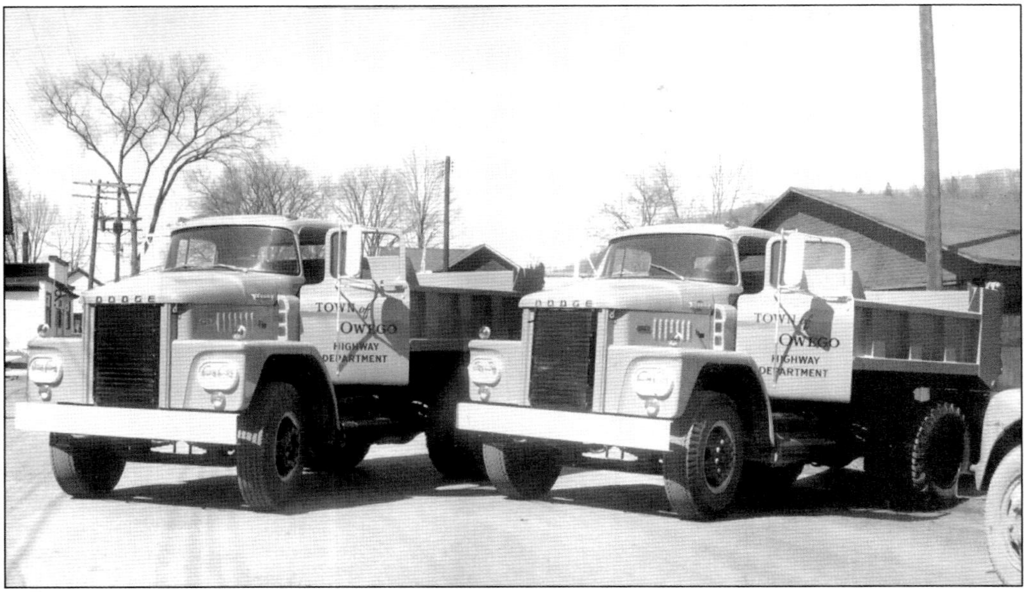

Taxpayers probably did not think so, but prices were cheap in 1963. The two heavy-duty dump trucks in this photograph were purchased by the Town of Owego for the highway department at a cost of $7,763.65 each, from Hendrick Motors of Owego, the low bidder.

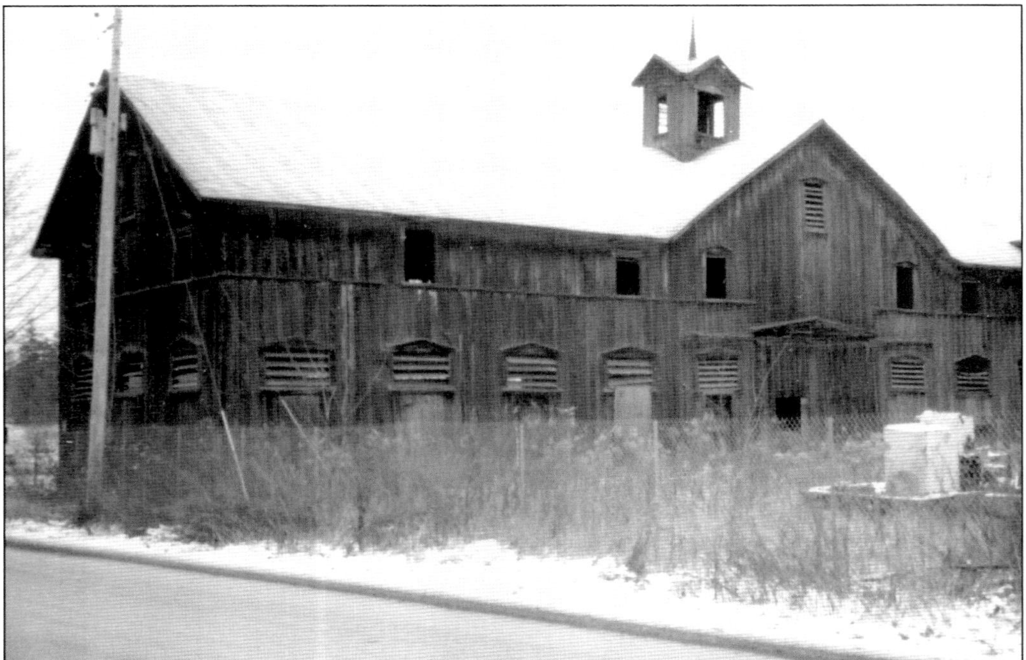

The old Tracy stock farm barns were a familiar sight on Marshland Road for many years. In this 1986 photograph, it is evident that they were deteriorating, and within a couple of years, they were razed.

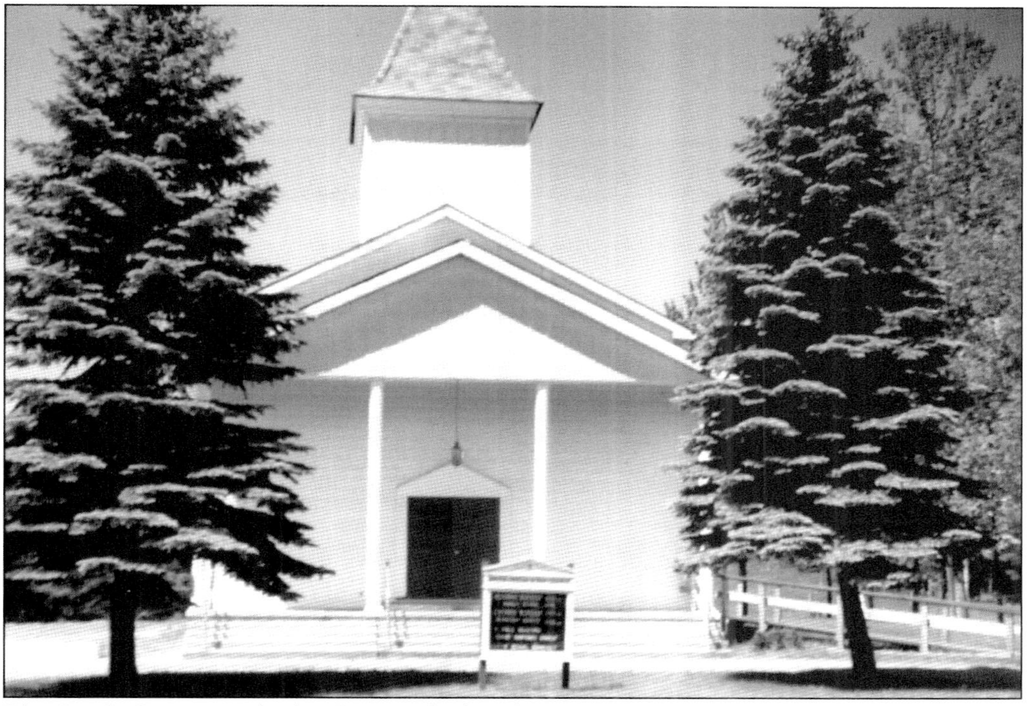

The South Owego Methodist Episcopal Church was organized as a class about 1830 and as a church society on May 20, 1856. The meetinghouse was built in 1856 and cost $1,200. Located on the Montrose Turnpike, it is now a Bible church.

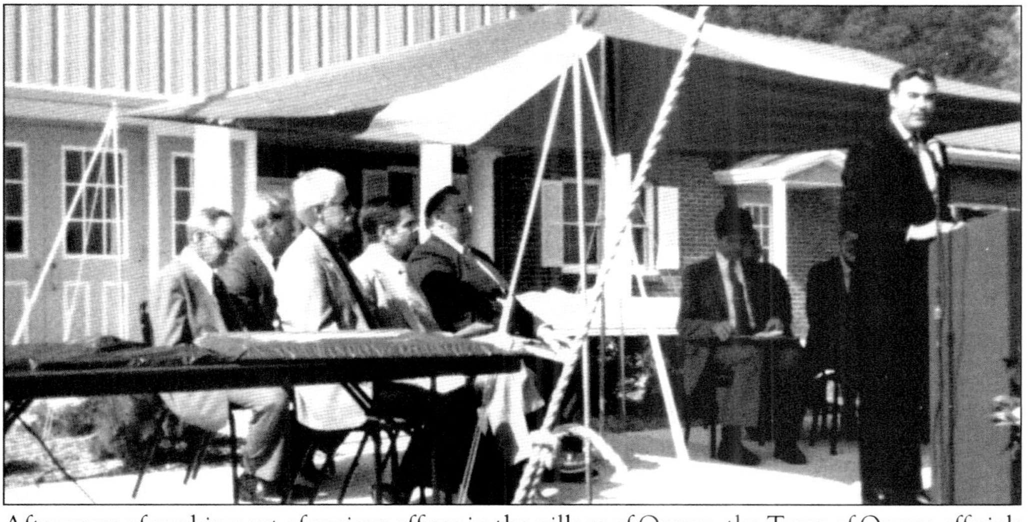

After years of working out of various offices in the village of Owego, the Town of Owego officials finally succeeded in getting their own building that housed most all of their departments. The ceremonies for the new building were held on September 10, 1988. Shown at the podium is U. S. representative Matthew F. McHugh. Sitting directly behind him is Town of Owego supervisor Thomas F. Doty. The group to the left is, from left to right, (first row) Fr. David Simon, Rev. Kenneth Simpson, and Richard Miller, assemblyman; (second row), Charles Truman and John Shumacher, both town councilmen.

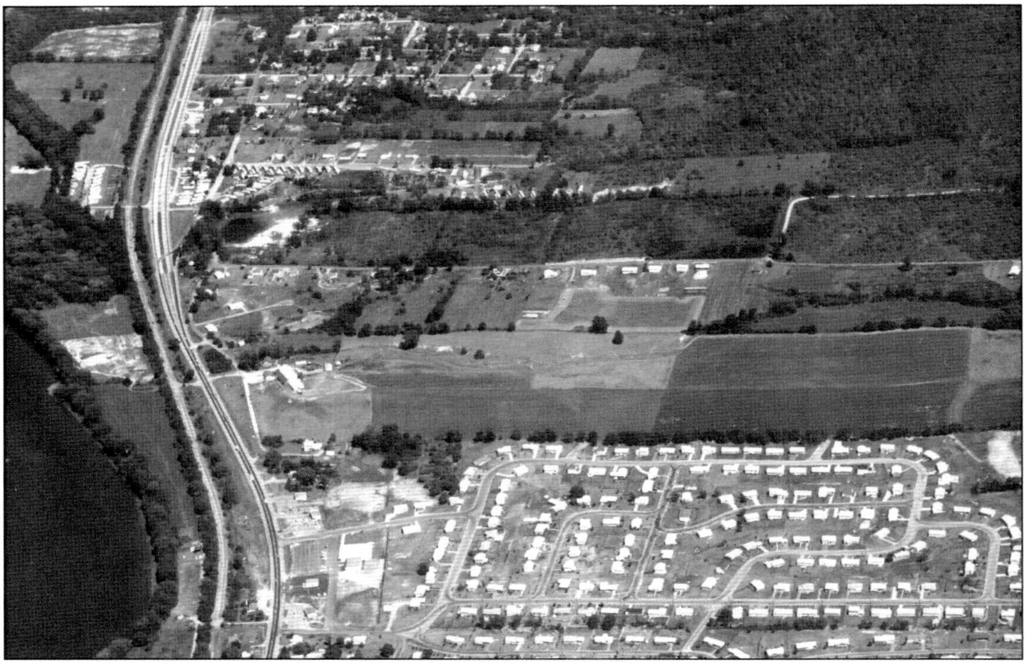

Seen in an August 1965 aerial photograph is the Tioga Terrace development in Apalachin. The Susquehanna River is on the left, and a part of the town of Vestal is pictured at the top. Because Tioga Terrace is in the town of Owego and is on the line that separates it from Broome County, a number of the students attend Broome County schools.

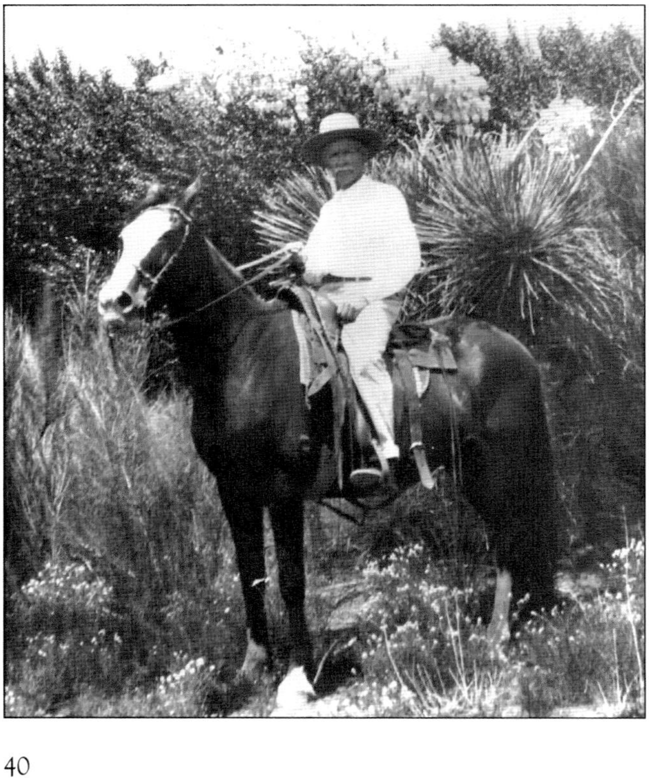

Western writer Eugene Manlove Rhodes is shown on one of his favorite horses. He died on June 27, 1934, and is buried in Rhodes Canyon, which now lies within the federal government's White Sands Missile Range. The government opens the gates one day a year to the caravan of Rhodes fans who come from all over the country to make the pilgrimage that begins in Alamogordo.

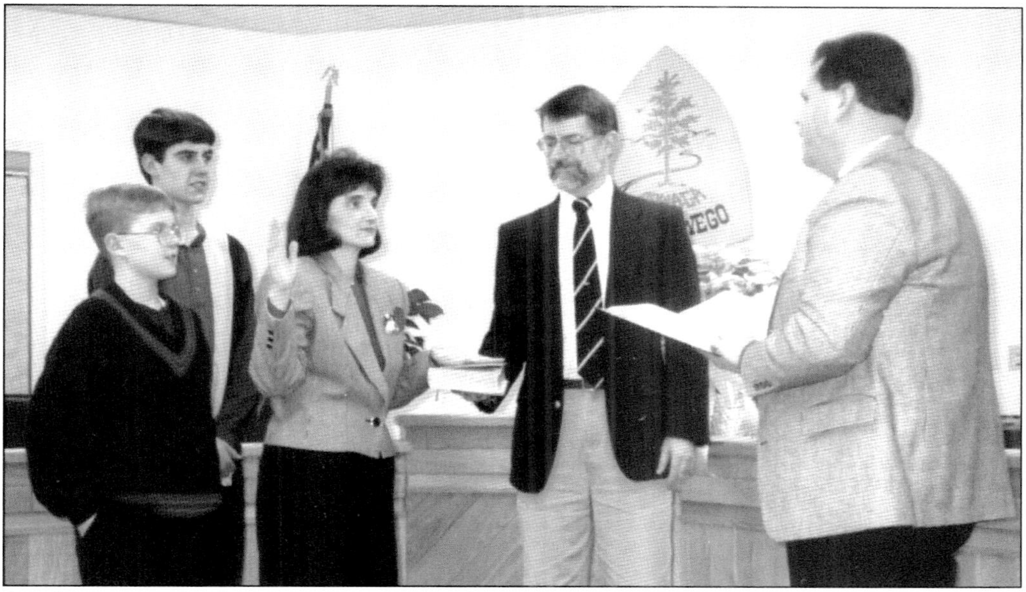

Carol Sweeney, the first woman ever to be elected supervisor for the Town of Owego, is sworn in by town clerk Michael Zimmer (right) on December 26, 1996, at the Owego Town Hall. Holding the Bible for her is her husband Stephen while her sons, Dan (on her right) and Matthew (behind Dan), observe the proceedings.

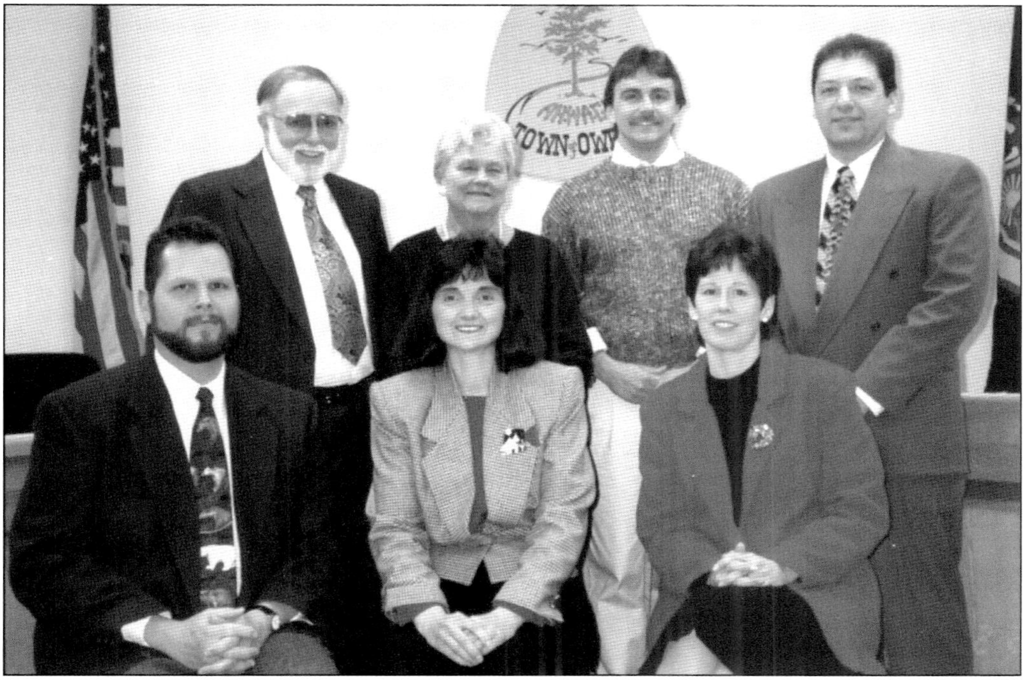

After Carol Sweeney won the post of Town of Owego supervisor, she is shown here with her first board. They are, from left to right, (first row) Michael Zimmer, town clerk; Carol Sweeney, supervisor; and Judith Melville Quigley, town attorney; (second row) trustees Bruce Brent, Doris Scott, James Hamlin, and Donald Castellucci Jr.

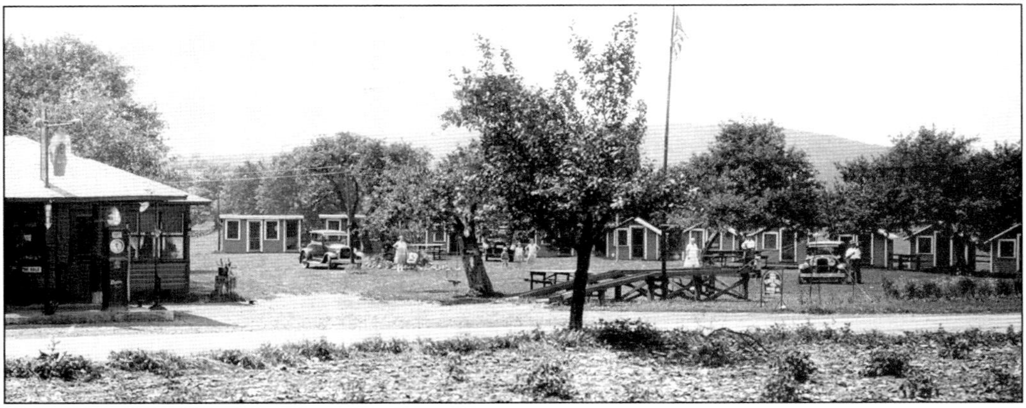

After a long drive, finding an attractive motel was a relief to travelers. Liberty Cabins was located about three miles east of Apalachin, and the people in the photograph appear to be satisfied with the accommodations. This image dates to the 1940s.

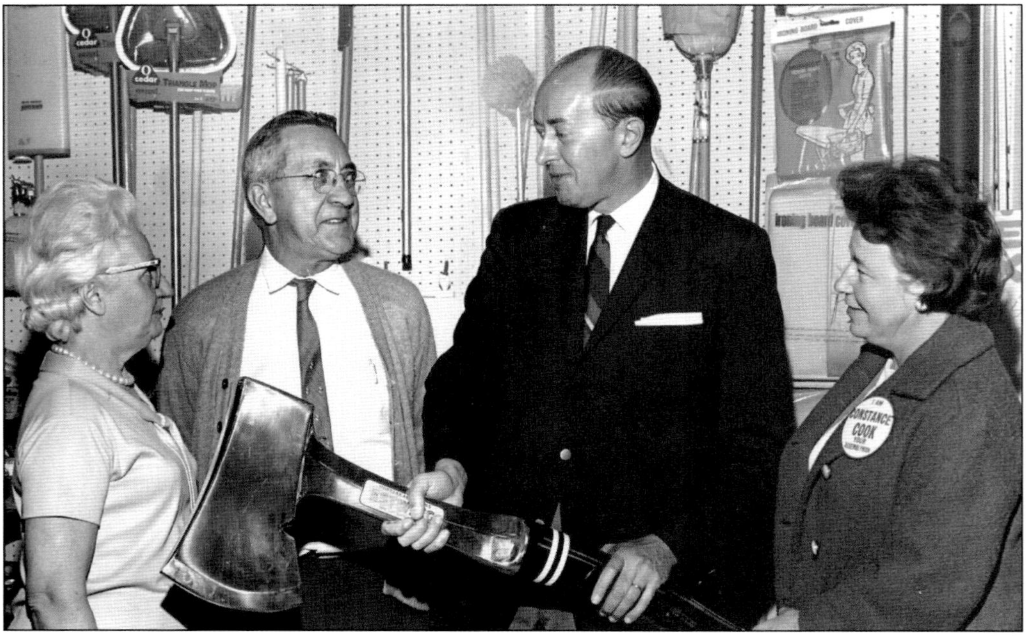

While Rep. Howard W. Robison was on a campaign tour in October 1966, he made a stop at the hardware store of Harmon Seymour in Apalachin. He jokingly grabbed a display ax that he said the GOP might use to "cut the Dems down to size" in the upcoming election. Shown are, from left to right, Lucille Seymour, Harmon Seymour, Rep. Howard W. Robison, and assemblywoman Constance Cook of Ithaca.

A June 26, 1961, newspaper article shows Phyllis Smith of Crestview Heights in the town of Owego. She was the first woman ever to seek a seat on the Owego Town Board. She won the election and served from January 1962 through December 1965.

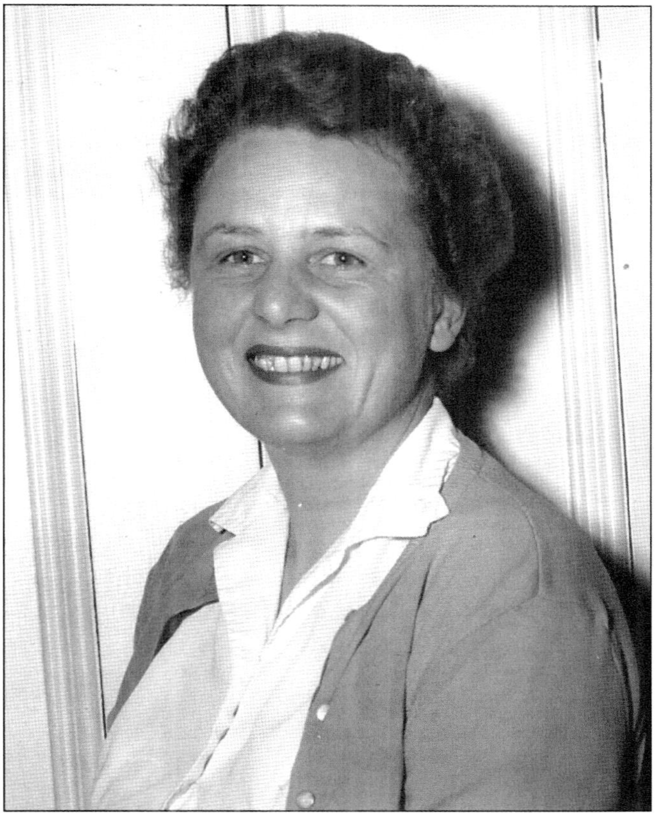

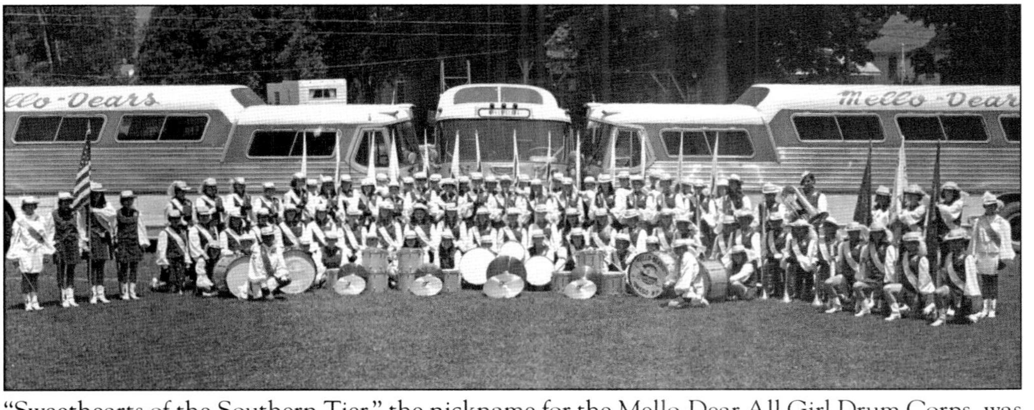

"Sweethearts of the Southern Tier," the nickname for the Mello-Dear All Girl Drum Corps, was a good one, because the corps was the favorite choice in many competitions and parades from 1961 through the 1980s. Its motto was *Contendimus pro sucessu* ("we strive for success"). What began as a simple activity for Apalachin girls blossomed into national-caliber competitions over the years that took them to many states and to Canada.

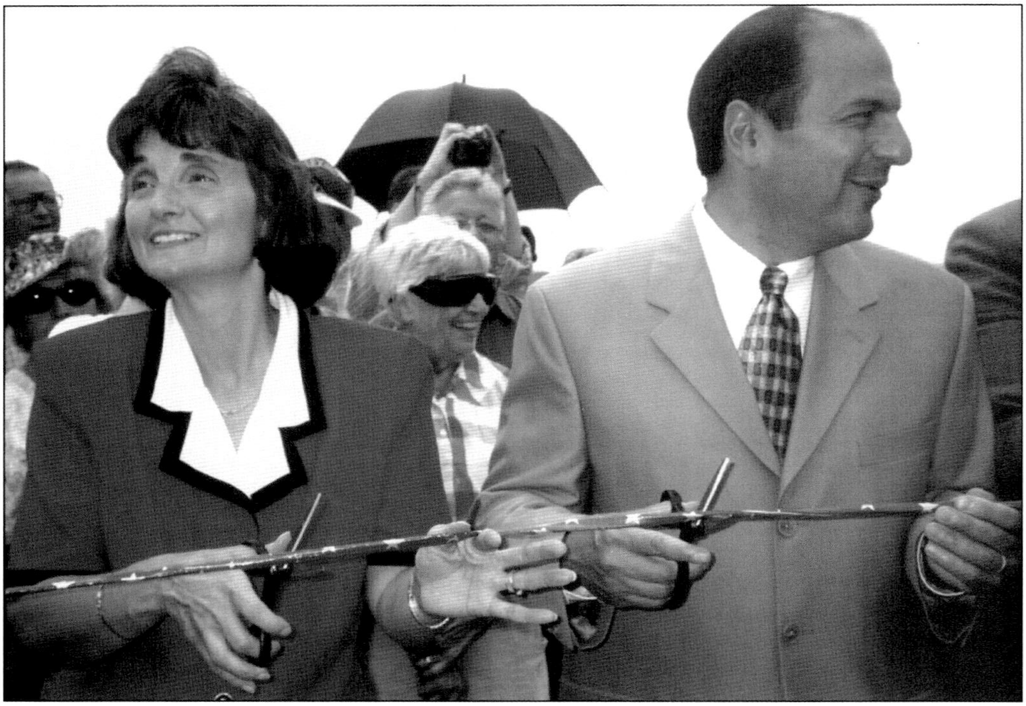

The weather cooperated, the crowds showed up, and the officials all made speeches on June 28, 2002, as part of the ceremonies for the opening of the Apalachin-Campville Memorial Bridge. Shown here about to cut the ribbon are Carol Sweeney, the Town of Owego supervisor, and New York State senator Thomas Libous.

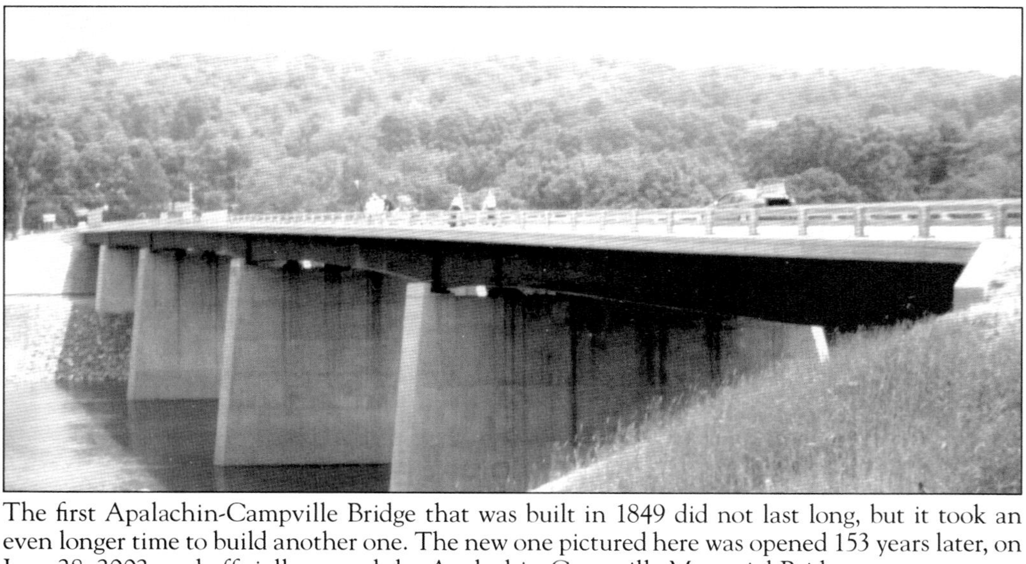

The first Apalachin-Campville Bridge that was built in 1849 did not last long, but it took an even longer time to build another one. The new one pictured here was opened 153 years later, on June 28, 2002, and officially named the Apalachin-Campville Memorial Bridge.

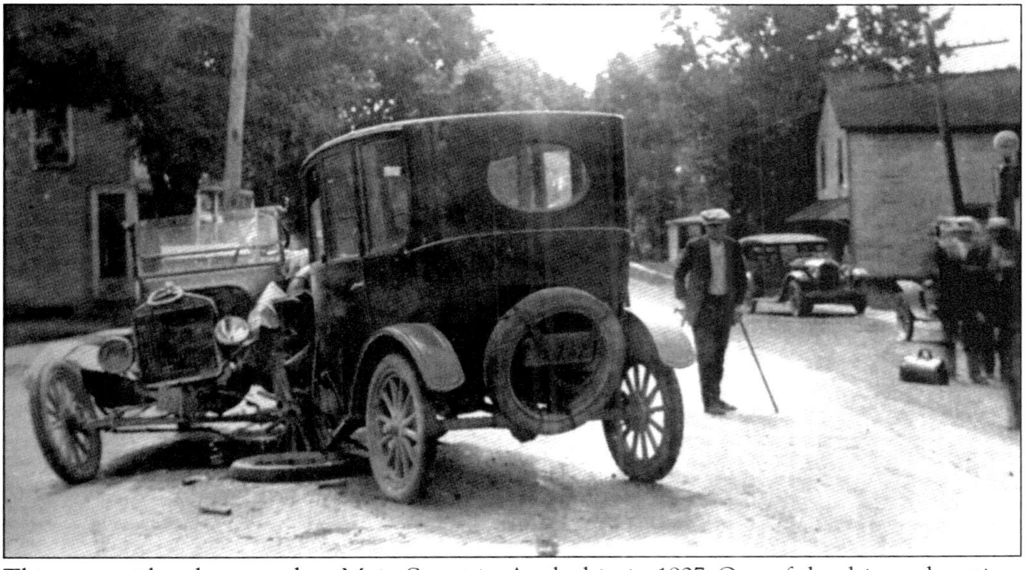

This car accident happened on Main Street in Apalachin in 1927. One of the drivers, longtime resident Gerome Drake, walks away with the assistance of two canes. It looks as though he will be without transportation for a while.

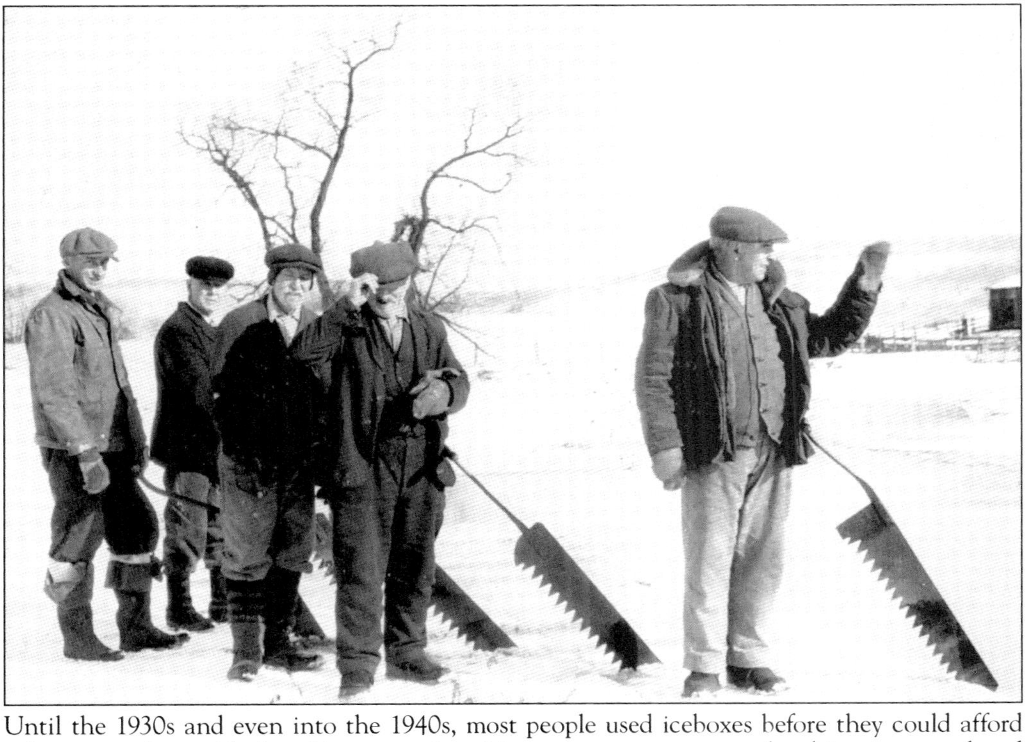

Until the 1930s and even into the 1940s, most people used iceboxes before they could afford refrigerators. Large blocks of ice were placed in one compartment and a drip pan was placed underneath to catch the water as the ice melted. Shown here on Holmes' Pond around 1930 in Apalachin are, from left to right, George Gaylord, ? Knapp, Tracy Bouton, ? Knapp, and owner Grant Holmes, taking a break.

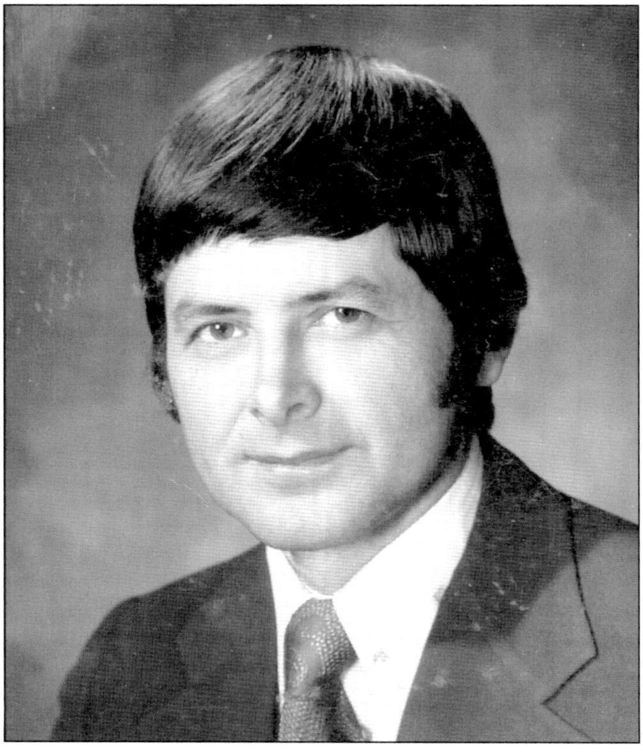

Thomas F. Doty served as supervisor for the Town of Owego for 16 years, from 1980 to 1996, when he opted not to run again. One of his major accomplishments was seeing the project of building a new town hall through to completion. It is located on Route 434 in Apalachin and was dedicated in September 1988.

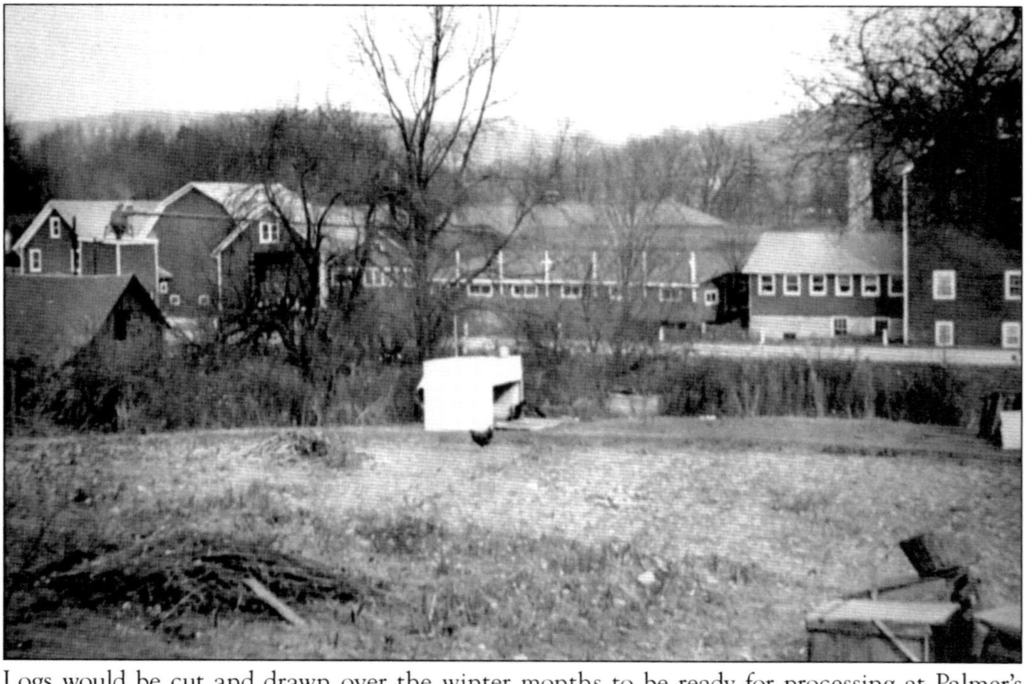

Logs would be cut and drawn over the winter months to be ready for processing at Palmer's Mill by spring. It was also a flouring mill and was located by the railroad station. This huge three-story complex burned around 1913.

Two

Campville

Located on the north side of the Susquehanna River, seven miles east of the village of Owego, Campville was first known as East Owego. The name was changed in honor of Col. Asa Camp, the first settler who came there in 1800, by Congressman Stephen B. Leonard. The Erie Railroad played a large role in its history when it came through in 1849. Stockyards were established, and businesses expanded. That same year, the first bridge was built across the river to Apalachin but was washed away in a flood in 1852. The post office was established in 1837, and Campville boasted of two hotels, a store, a school, District No. 33, and a church. The 20th century saw cars replace horses, and gas stations and motels opened to accommodate them. The Campville Fire Department was chartered in 1947, with a substation at Gaskill Corners and a fine new one in the heart of the hamlet. The Methodist church still plays an active part in the community, and although the Erie Railroad, the stockyards, and most of the old businesses are gone today, the Conrail tracks still operate, and a new bridge was finally built in 2002.

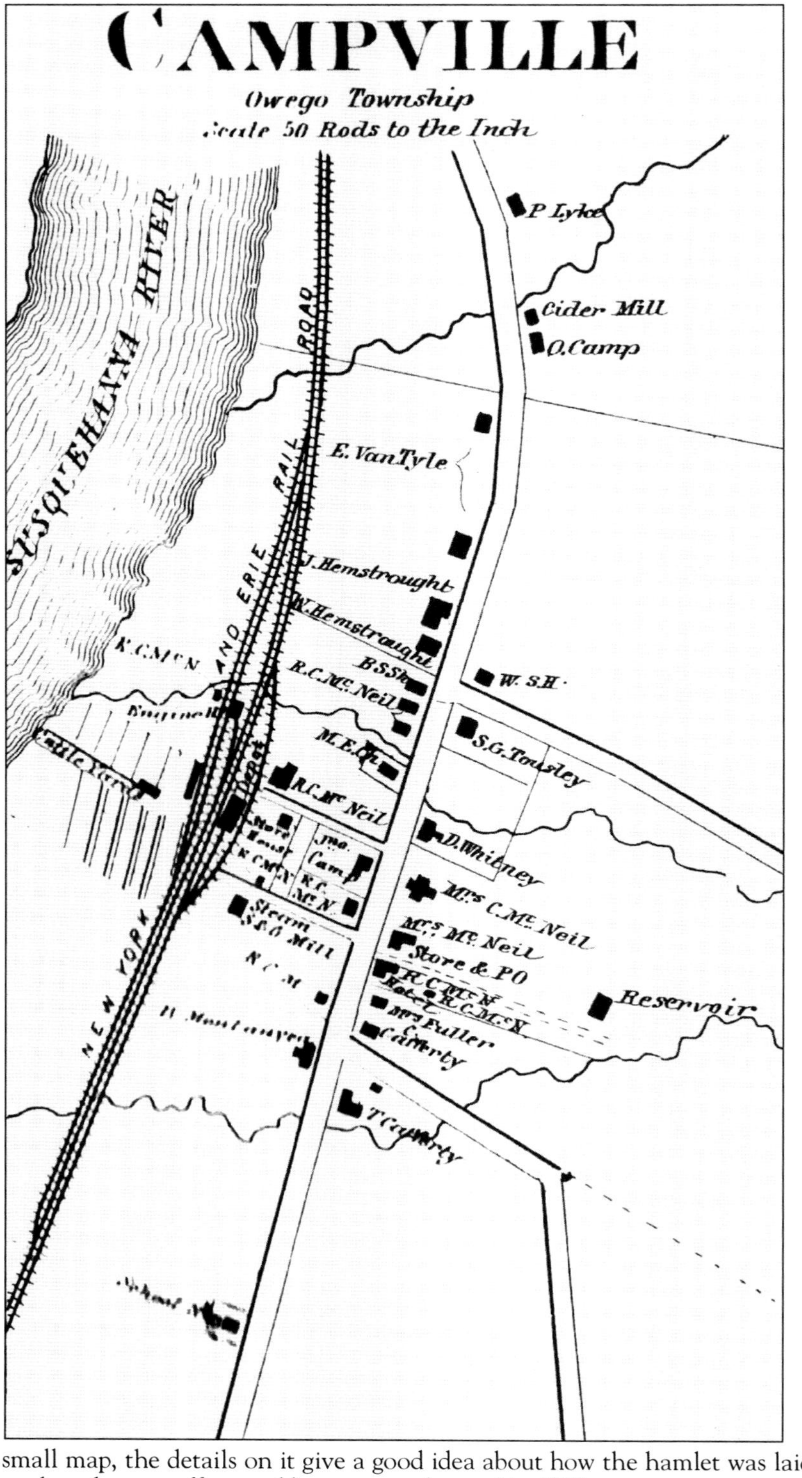

For such a small map, the details on it give a good idea about how the hamlet was laid out and where the stockyards, post office, and houses were located in 1869.

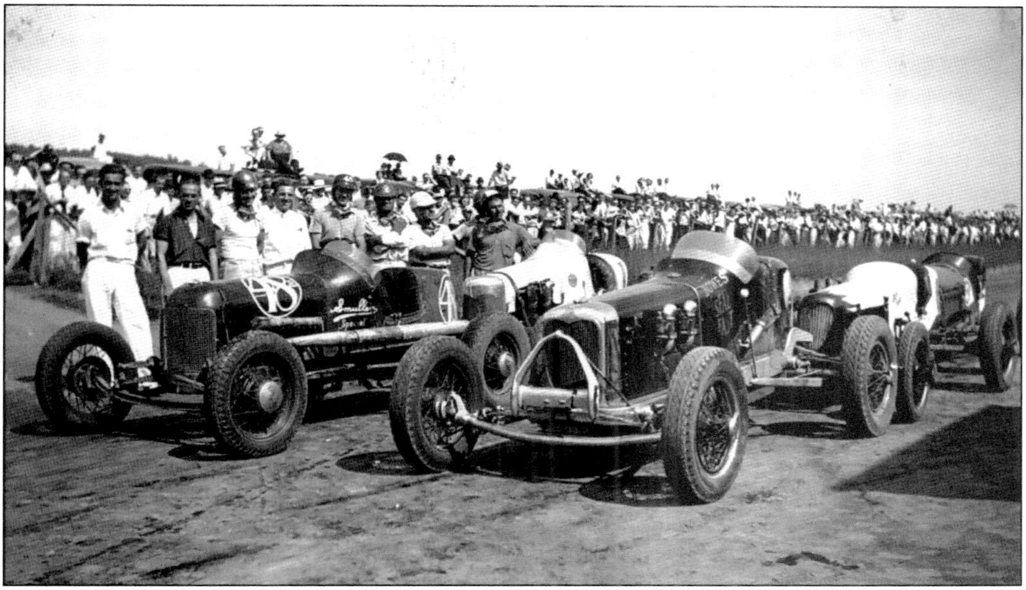

Cliff Smullen, from Binghamton, was one of the champion racers at the Campville track and even built his first car, the *Smullen Special*, No. 48. It had a V-8 engine and used benzol for gas and castor oil for lubrication.

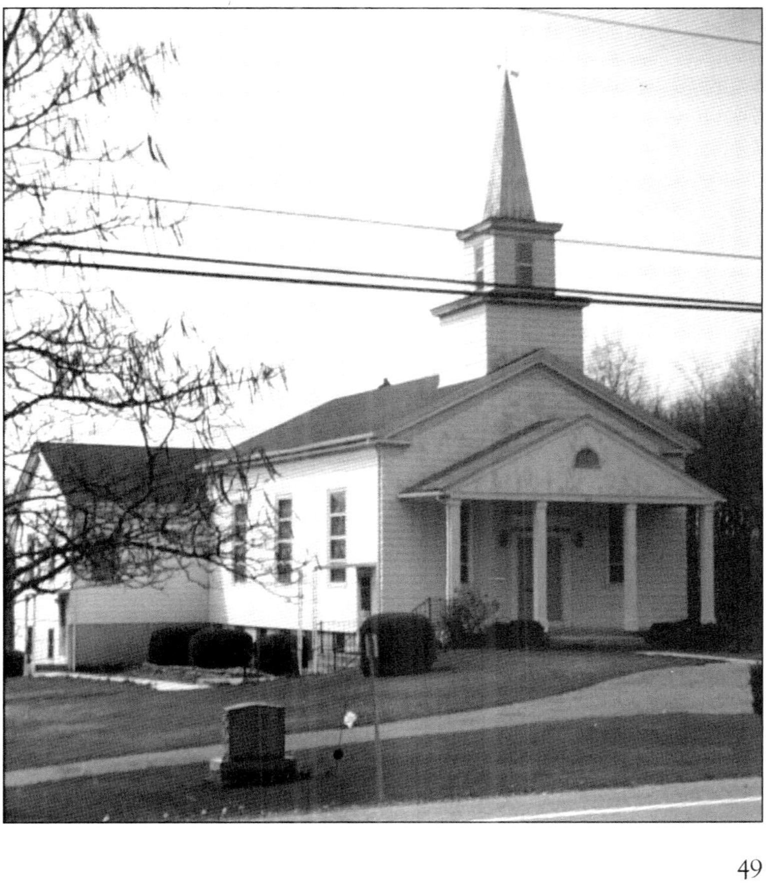

The First United Methodist Church of Campville, located on Route 17C, was organized in 1820. A church building was erected in 1854, and many changes have taken place since then. The major change took place between 1964 and 1966, when the building was moved to the center of the lot, and a full basement was dug, making space for classrooms, a kitchen, a fellowship hall, and restrooms. A new porch was erected and cement walks were installed later on. Most of the work was done by volunteers.

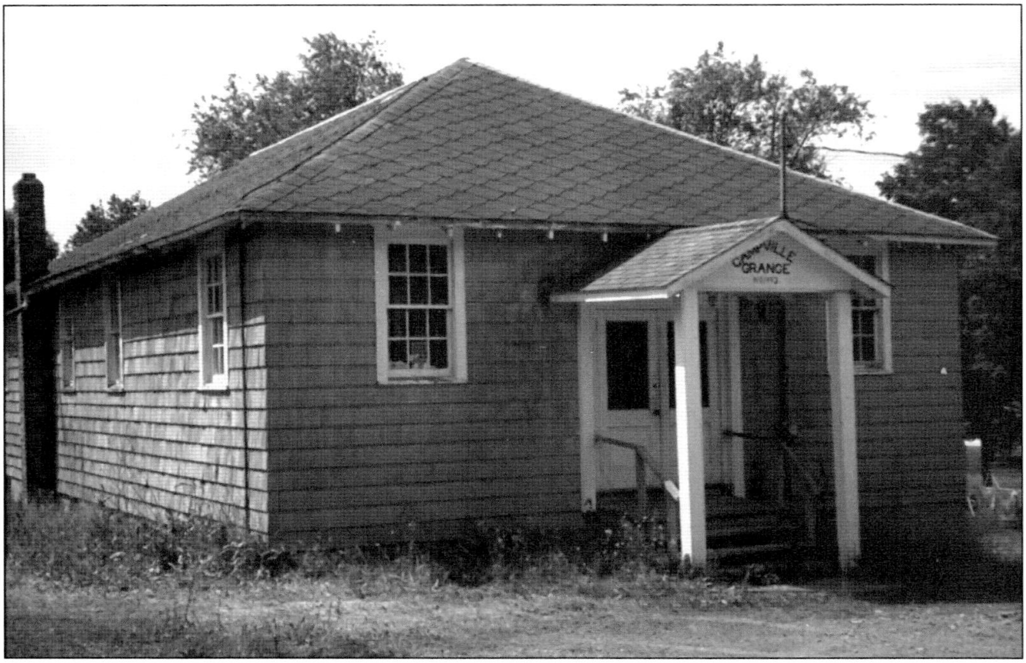

The Campville Grange, No. 1942, was an active community meeting place, located on East Campville Road. The mortgage was burned in 1946, and the building was used until the 1980s. It has since been converted into a private home.

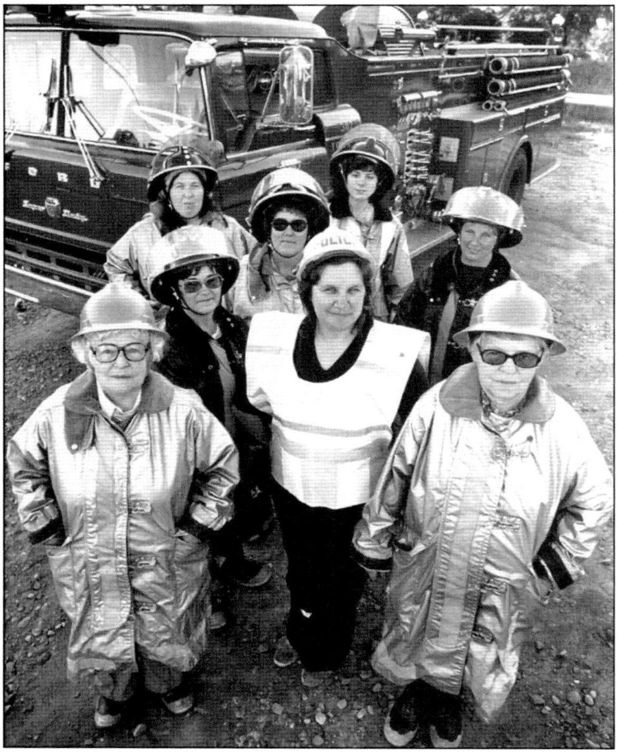

The women of the Campville Fire Department proudly pose, wearing their firefighting gear in June 1980. They are, from left to right, (first row) Ola Lindloff, Bonnie Morton, and Jean Neal; (second row) Jeannette Chernega, Ruth Ann Phelps, and Grace Ford; (third row) Shirley Sullivan and Eileen Lonergan.

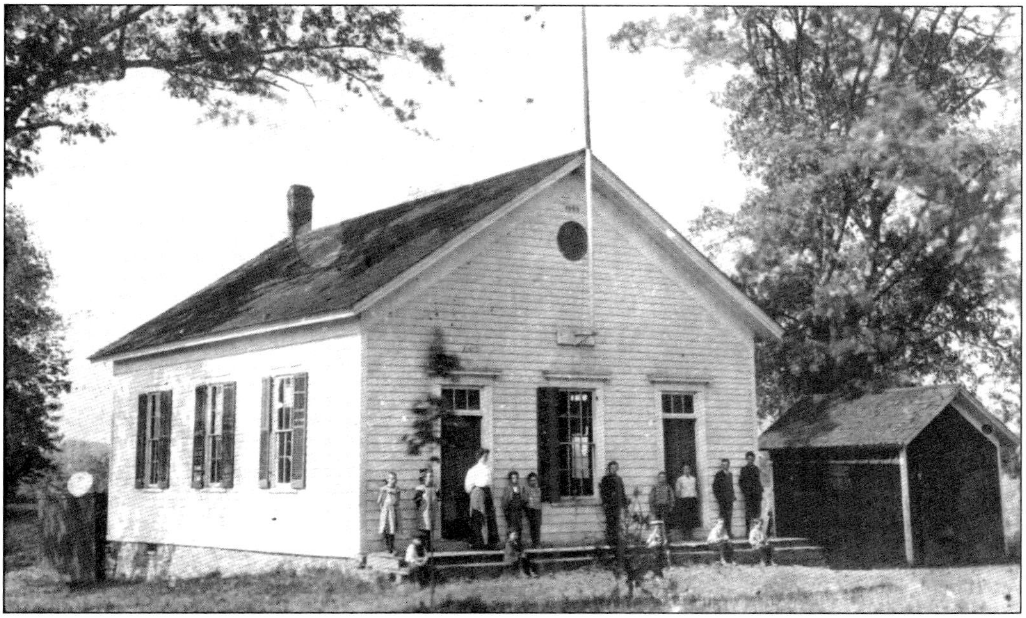

The last teacher who taught at Campville School, District No. 33, was a Mrs. McGrath when it closed its doors in 1933. After that, the children were transported by bus to Owego Central School on Main Street. What was once Campville School is now a family residence.

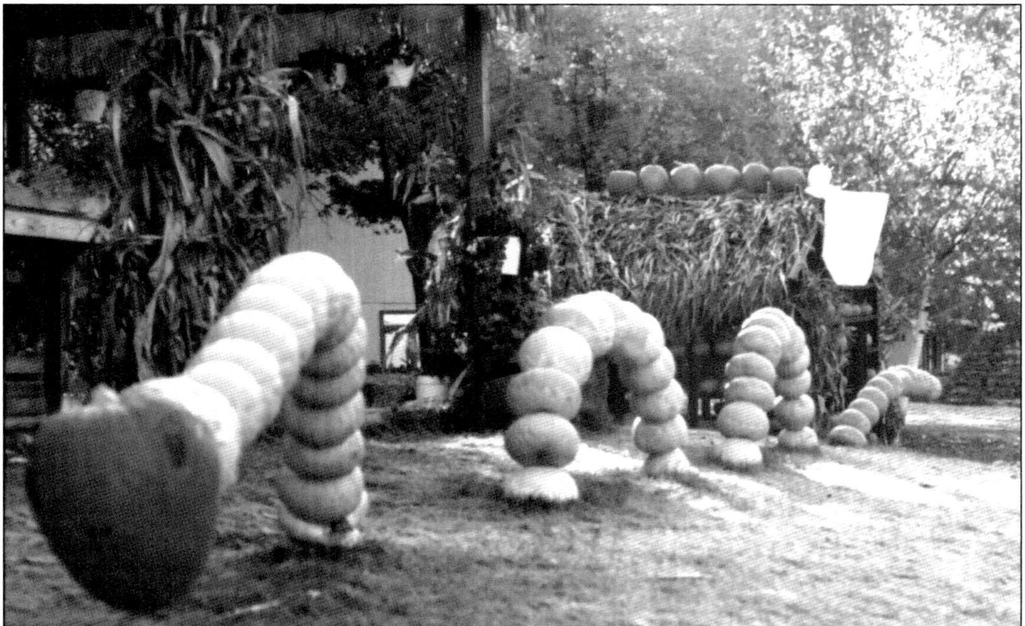

This six-foot snake that kept bobbing its head was made from gourds and pumpkins at the Jackson Pumpkin Farm Halloween display in 1990 at Campville. The display began in 1978, with a simple pumpkin house and a whimsical pumpkin man sitting at a picnic bench. Over the years, it evolved into an elaborate conglomeration of pumpkins and gourds that knew no bounds of imagination.

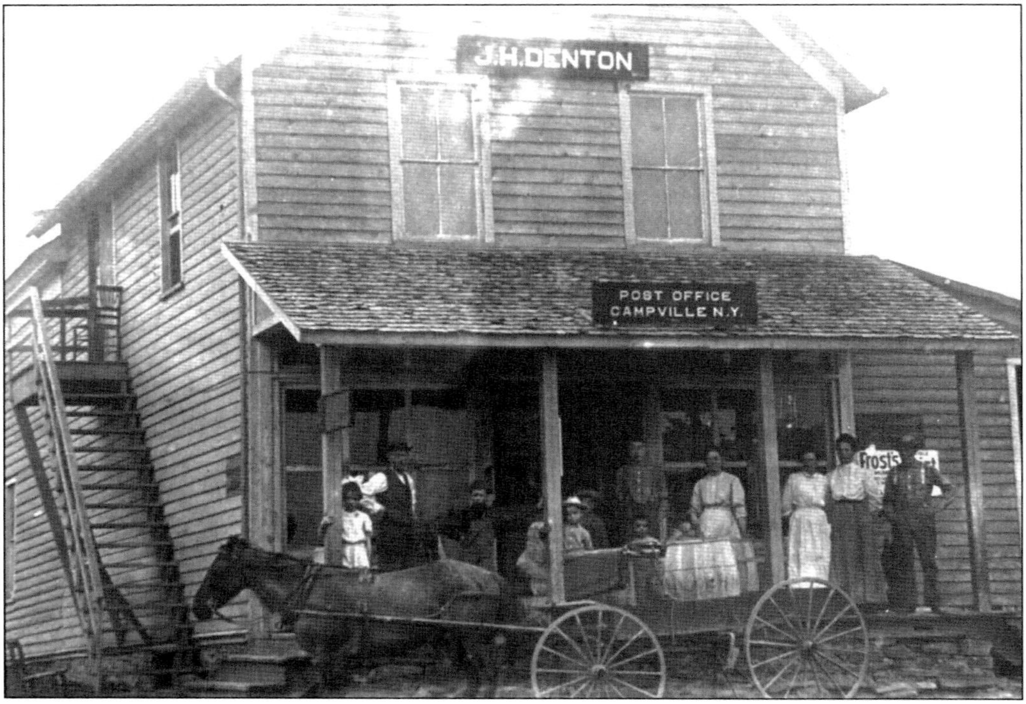

Everybody gathered to have their picture taken on the porch of J. H. Denton's store and post office around 1900. The store sold everything from canned goods to dry goods. The stairs on the left side led to a meeting hall that served as a social center and, at election time, a polling place.

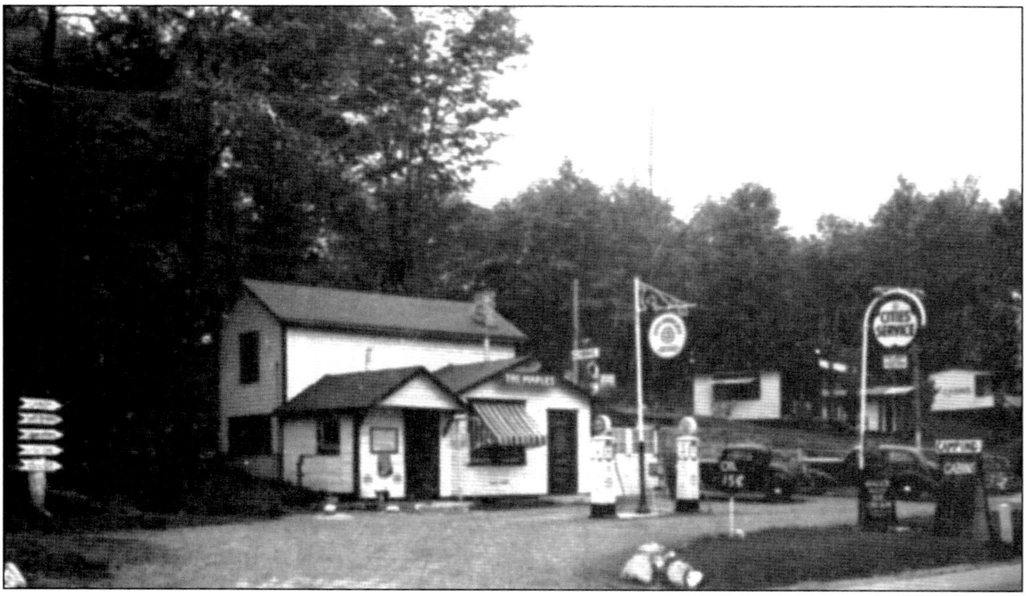

Cities Service Station was located on Route 17C, as seen in this image from the 1940s. The motel part of the business was called the Maples, which included camping facilities. Signs offer candy, soft drinks, a telephone, and oil for 15¢.

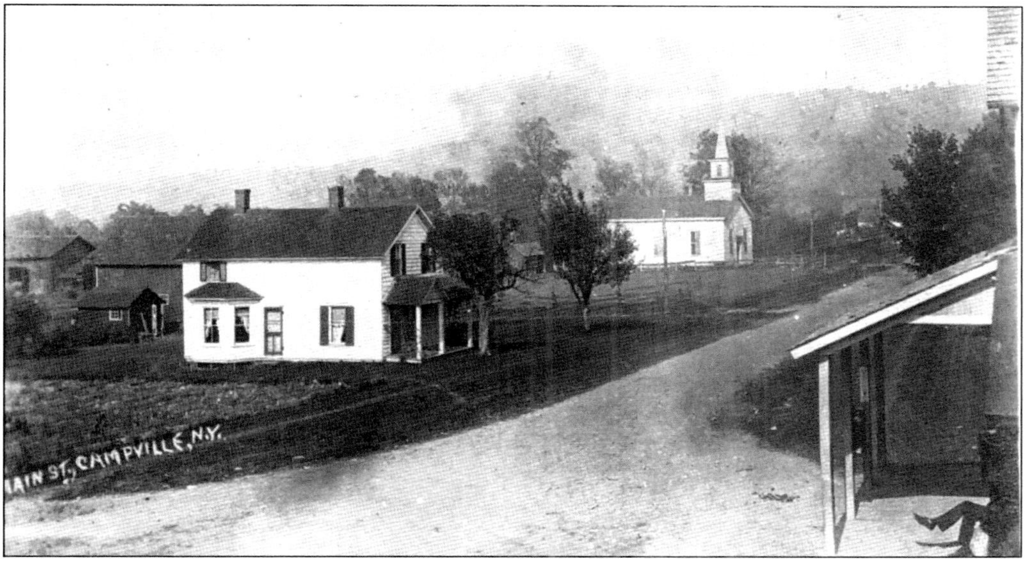

This early scene showing Main Street in Campville is probably after 1855, the year the Campville Methodist Church was dedicated. The building to the right, with someone sitting on the porch, was probably the McNeil Hotel, built around 1835.

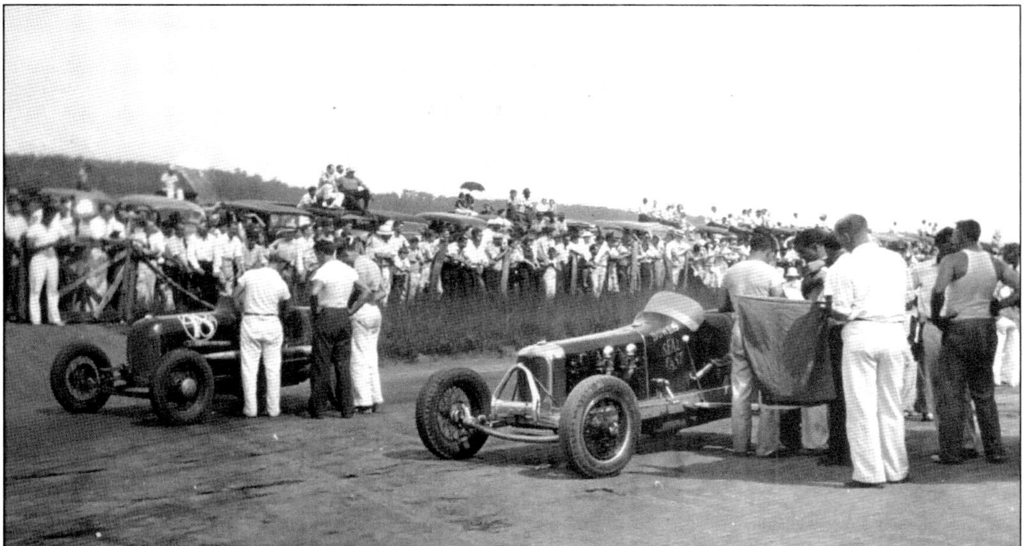

Officially known as the Triple Cities Speedway, a half-mile oval track operated from 1937 to the early 1940s and was located next to the river. Every Sunday, as many as 1,500 spectators would converge on Campville to stand behind a wire fence or sit on the roofs of their cars to watch. Today the Jackson Pumpkin Farm has replaced it.

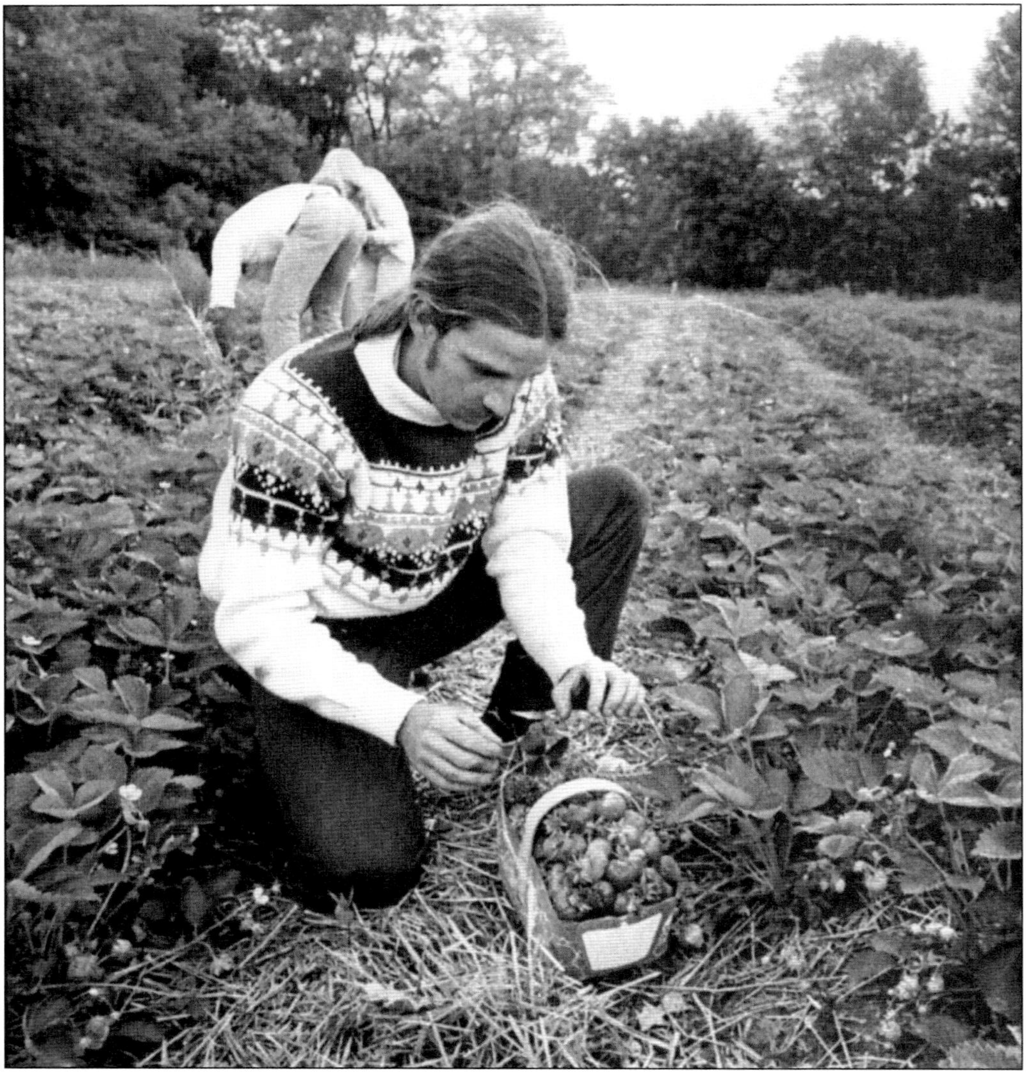

People love strawberries, and the Jacksons knew it. Their strawberry farm in Campville was crowded with pickers as soon as the berries got ripe. Jack Jackson is shown filling his basket in June 1980.

Three

FLEMINGVILLE

This rural community is located in the northwest corner of the town, approximately five miles from the village of Owego. Although the earliest settler in Flemingville was probably Asahel Pritchard, coming there around 1780, the small hamlet is named after Capt. David Fleming, who settled there from Newton, New Jersey, in 1808. Other early settlers were Daniel Ferguson, around 1790; Jeremiah Brown, around 1796; Richard Searles, 1795; Charles E. Truman, 1816; and Elizur Talcott, 1802. Some of their descendants still reside here today. The Southern Central Railroad came through Flemingville in 1869 and was later conveyed to the Lehigh Valley Railroad, which built a train station there in 1902. Businesses included a post office, general store, feed mill, creamery, stockyard, and coal shed. The post office closed about 1932, but the train passenger service, railway express, and Western Union made the station a necessity. The station finally closed in 1935. The social center was the Grange hall, dedicated in 1920 and closed in the 1960s. In the 1970s, James G. Mead operated Tioga Central Railway Excursions and a railroad memorabilia museum. Flemingville is a quaint, nostalgic place where, as Charles (Charlie) Truman, one of the descendants of the early settlers, used to say, "There are four cows to every person."

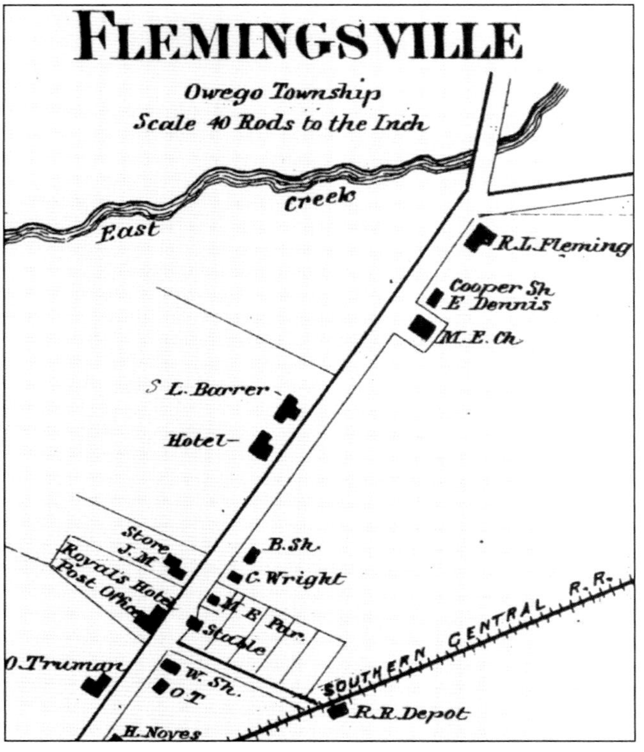

The spelling for the name of this hamlet should be Flemingville, without the *s*. In 1869, it had a store, a post office, and two hotels.

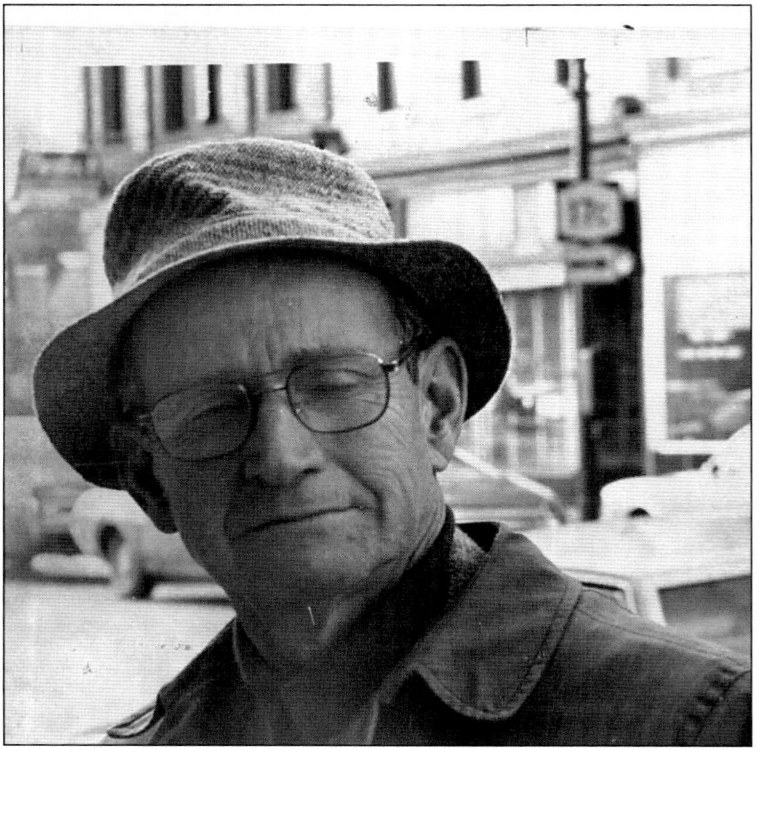

A lifetime farmer, born in Flemingville on a fourth-generation farm, gregarious Charles (Charlie) Truman graduated from Cornell and had a career as a high school teacher in the Owego Apalachin Schools and served 12 years on the Owego Town Board. Born in 1920, Truman passed away in 1998.

The scaffolding on this church is the result of two transient boys who broke into the United Methodist Church of Flemingville on a cold February morning in 1970. In an effort to keep warm, they lit candles, which started a fire that led to extensive damage. However, by the following year and after many delicious dinners, donations, and insurance money, the lovely old 1834 building was restored.

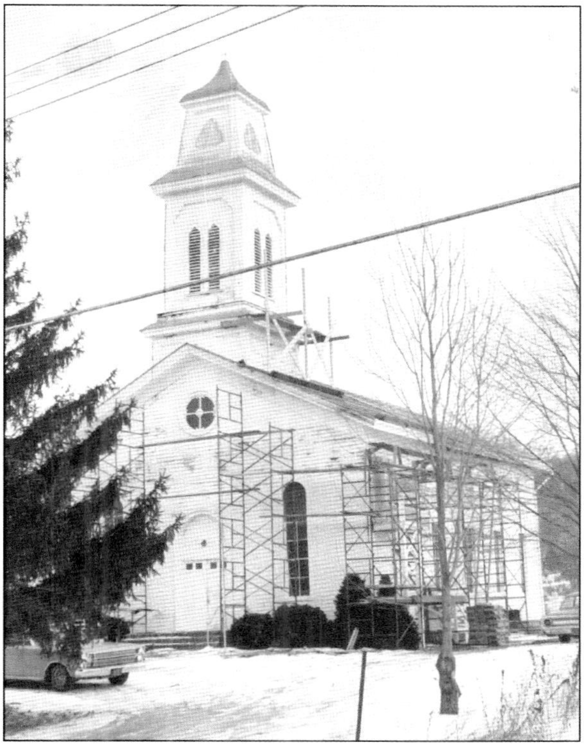

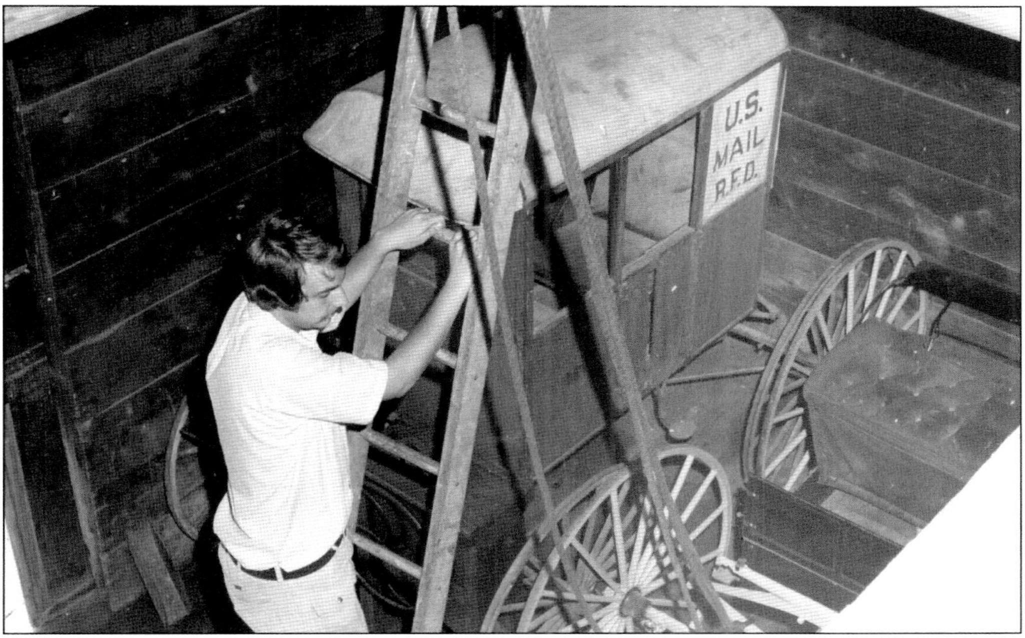

James G. Mead operated Tioga Central Railway Excursions on the old Lehigh Valley Railroad tracks in Flemingville in the 1970s. He also used the station as a museum, featuring over 50 carriages, antique automobiles, bicycles, and a gift shop. He is pictured checking a relies mechanism on an antique mail wagon in September 1972.

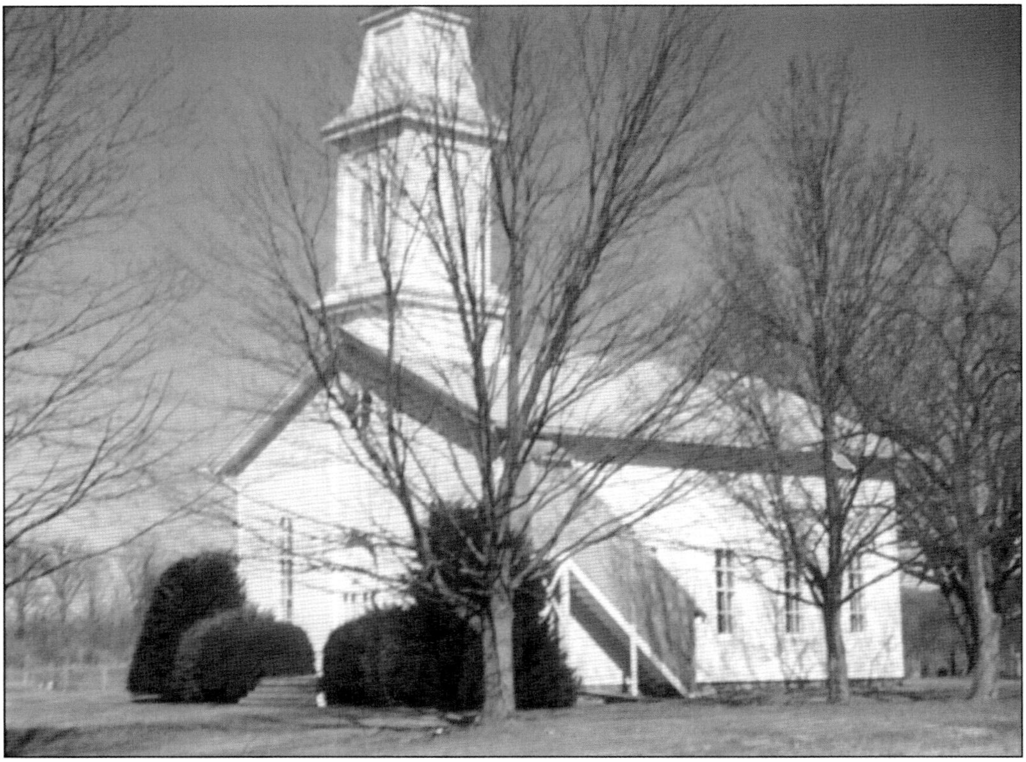

The United Methodist Church of Flemingville began when a Methodist Episcopal society was organized as a class in 1811 with 15 members. The church organization was fully completed several years later, and a meetinghouse was built in 1834.

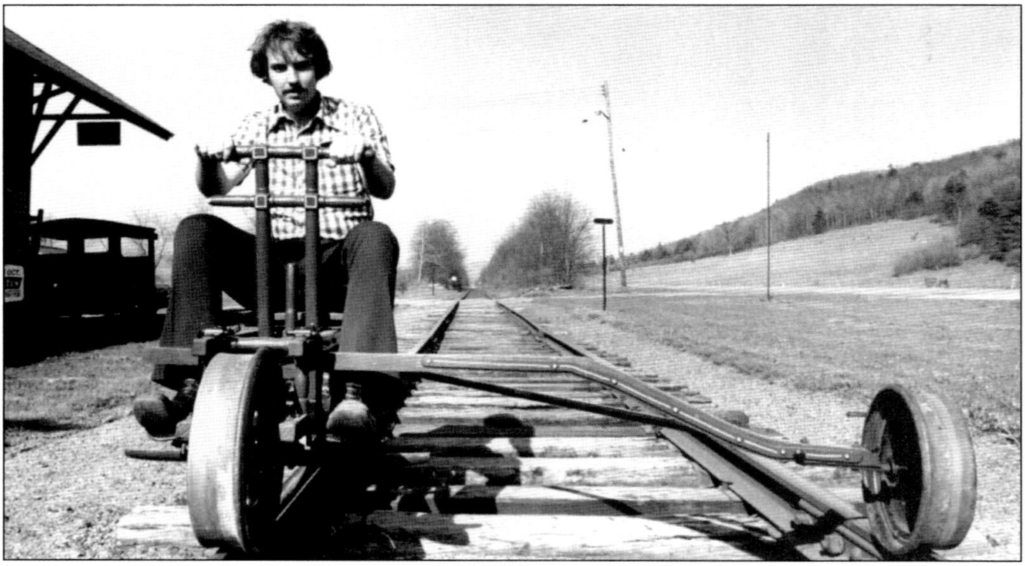

In April 1976 at Flemingville, James G. Mead shows how to operate an 1887 velocipede, among the many antiques at his Tioga Central Railway Museum. It is a type of handcar, peddled like a bicycle.

Four

Gaskill Corners

Located on the Little Nanticoke Creek, five miles east of the village of Owego, Gaskill Corners takes its name from Joseph Gaskill, who settled there in 1822 from New Hampshire. Nathaniel Spencer came in 1826, and his descendants still live on their original land. Gaskill Corners began as a small farming community and grew with the opening of lumber mills, a creamery and a cheese factory, and, at one time, a large tannery that was operated by Lewis C. England. It was also a stagecoach stop, and in 1866, a post office was established. The District No. 37 school was built near the little cemetery, and in 1907, the Gaskill Telephone Company was established with 17 subscribers. The 1920s saw an influx of immigrants to Gaskill Corners, such as Albert Rudin, Adolph Gradel, Otto Wagner, and William Rypkema. Today Wagner's grandson Les Wagner is the owner and operator of the Wagner Companies. It is one of the largest hardwood lumber manufacturers in the Northeast. The Rudins ran a popular rodeo from the 1930s through the 1950s. They are still drawing crowds today with Rudin's Old Tyme Farm Days, displaying and demonstrating antique farm machinery and keeping the spirit of Gaskill Corners alive.

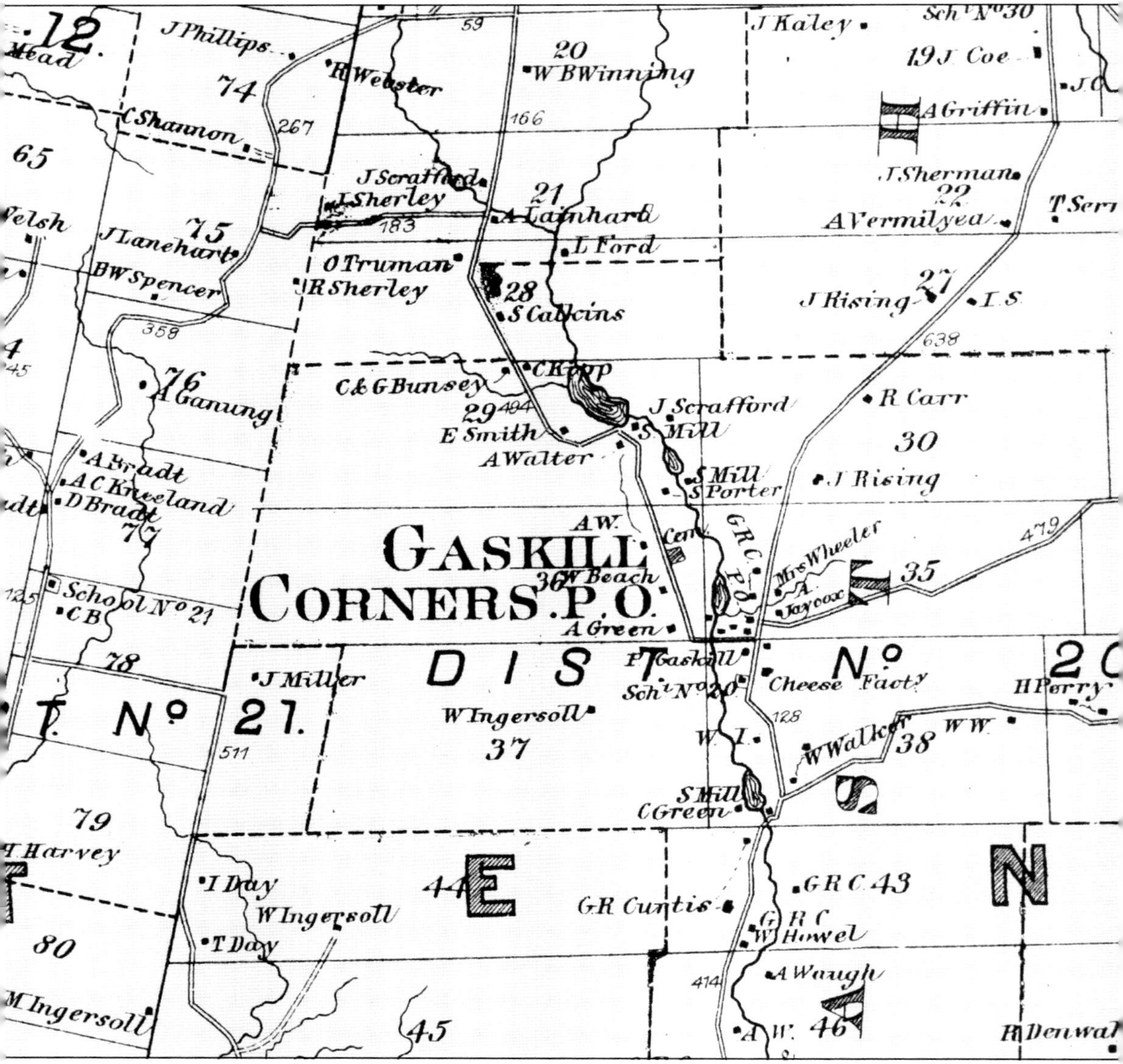

This 1869 map of Gaskill Corners really gives a good overview of what used to be there in its early years, including a cheese factory, a post office, and its school.

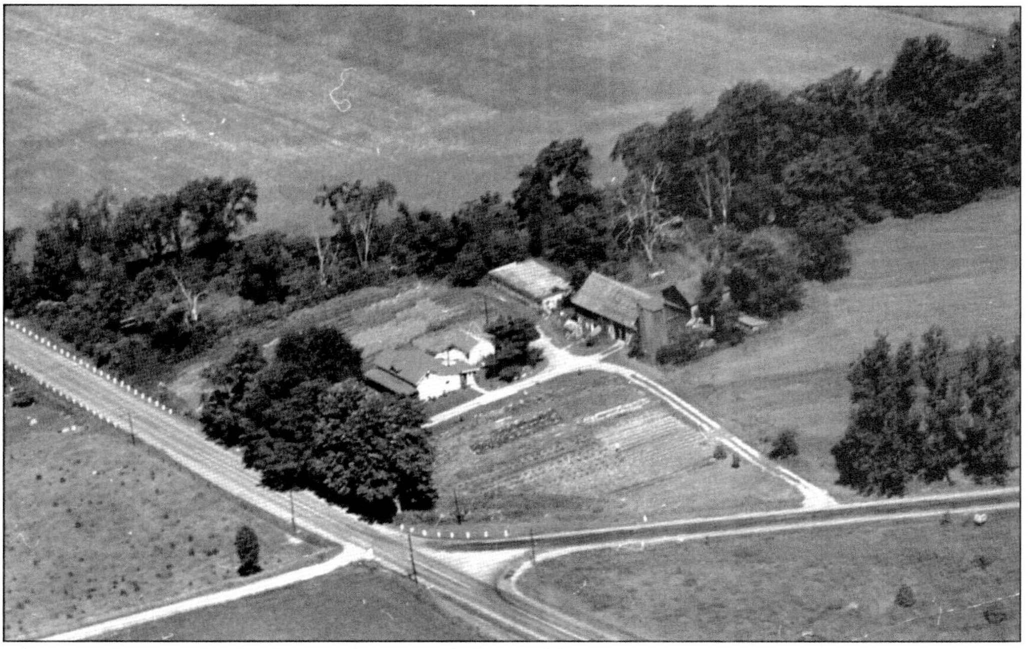

This aerial view clearly shows where Gaskill Road branches off to the right from Day Hollow Road, and Spencer Lane branches off to the left. Cutler and Jeannette Spencer Baldwin live in the house near the trees, closest to Day Hollow Road. The old barn was moved from the corner of the roads back to where it is today.

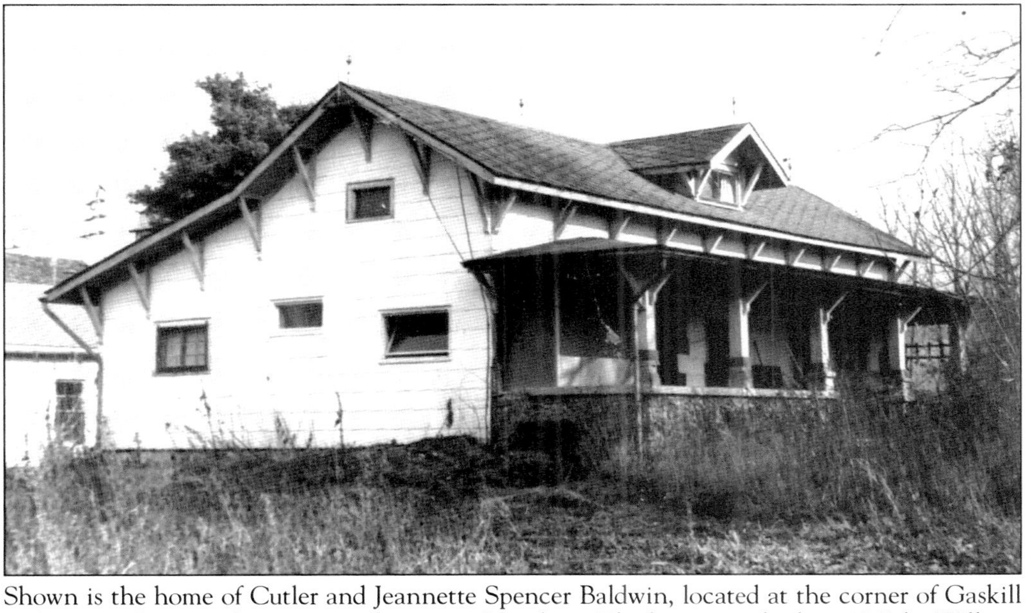

Shown is the home of Cutler and Jeannette Spencer Baldwin, located at the corner of Gaskill and Day Hollow Roads, in an area known as Broadway. The house was built in 1862 by William Ingersoll, Cutler's great-great-grandfather. From 1913 to 1921, the house was owned and used as a summer residence by Gen. Henry Martyn Robert, author of *Robert's Rules of Order*. After he moved in, he had the windows cut down to a smaller size to lessen the noise from the road.

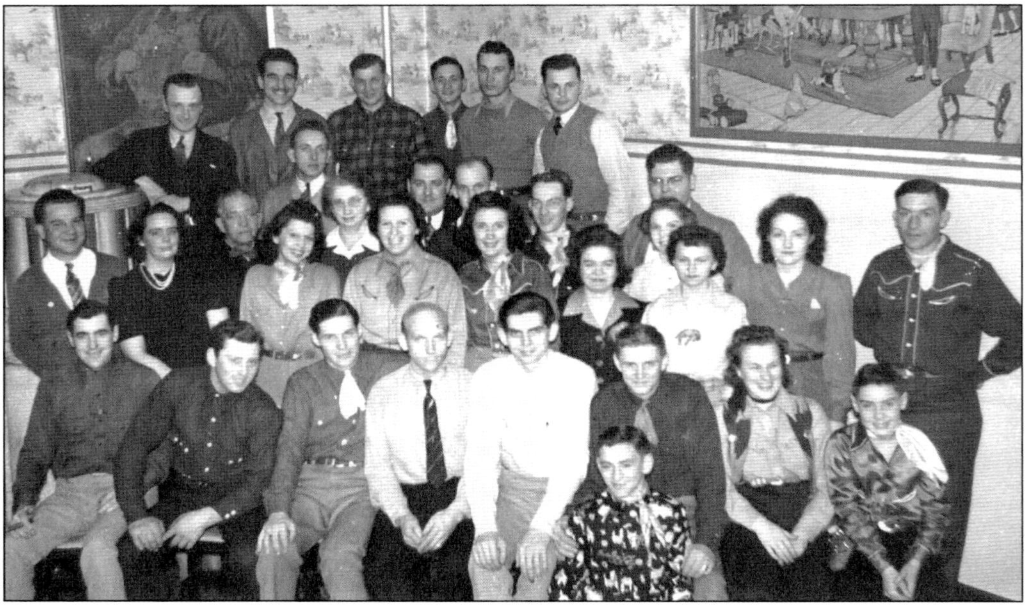

The Bar-O-Corral gathered for a group picture at the Owego Hotel around 1940. They were a talented riding group who starred in the rodeos at the Rudin farm at Gaskill Corners. This well-known group also rode its horses in most of the local parades. Among those pictured are Paul Steele, Albert Rudin, Ed Pickard, Ralph Berry, Paul Taylor, Louie Rudin, Fritz Rudin, Jessie Rudin, Nick Moraitis, Lena Berry, Alice Rudin, Ruth Jenkins Cotton, Hilda Saddlemire, Mary Bryant, Margaret Bryant, Ernie Rudin, Al Dodge, Jerry Bryant, and Lacy Clark.

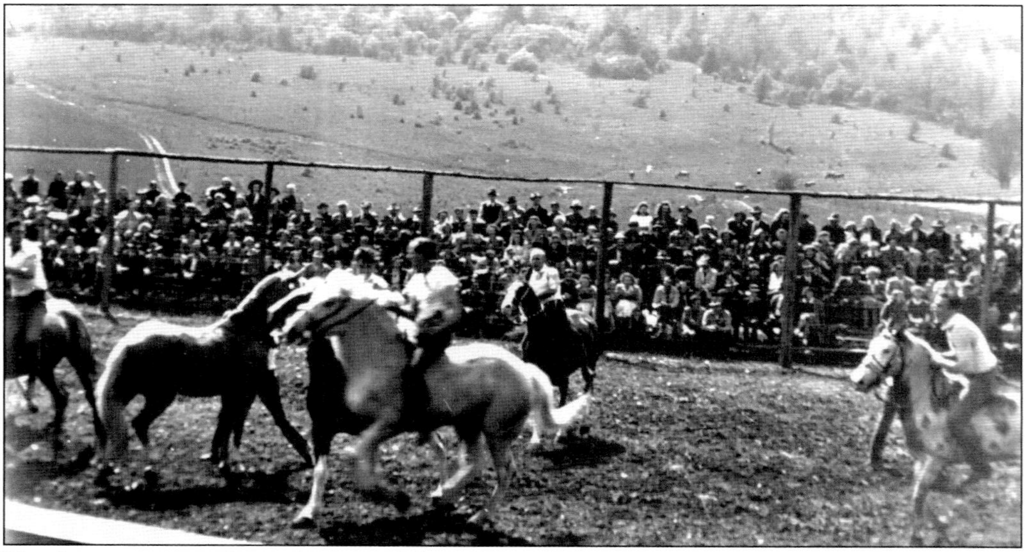

The farm was just a few miles east of the village of Owego, and this would have been a typical action scene at the Rudin Rodeo Days in the early 1940s. Crowds of fans filled the bleachers to cheer and clap for their favorite cowboys and cowgirls who performed daring stunts. Today things are more subdued, and the name has been changed to Rudin's Olde Tyme Farm Days. Old-fashioned farm equipment is the main attraction, with demonstrations throughout the day in late summer.

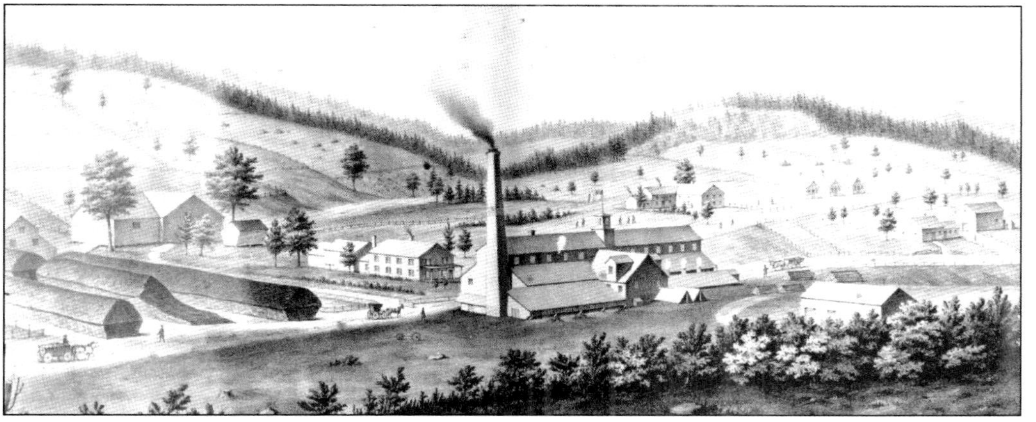

Englandville is an unlikely name for a business, but that is what Lewis C. England called his tannery near Gaskill Corners around 1840. In this advertisement, he claimed that the tannery was capable of tanning 25,000 sides of sole leather a year.

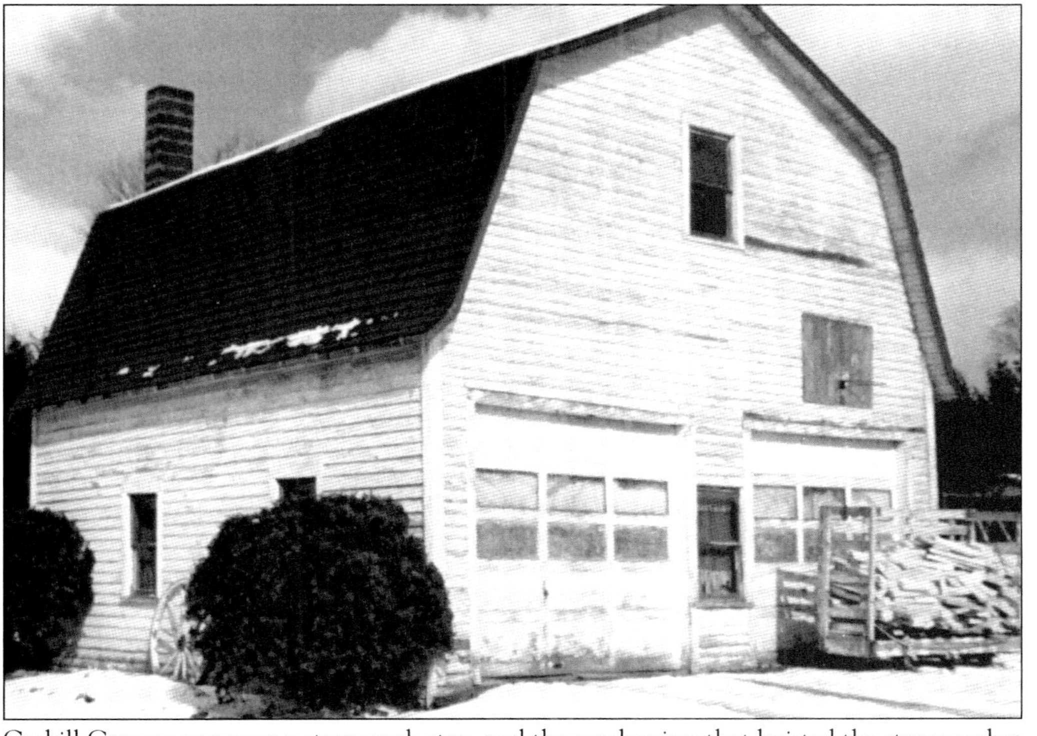

Gaskill Corners was once a stagecoach stop, and the mechanism that hoisted the stagecoaches up for repairs is still in the upper level of this barn.

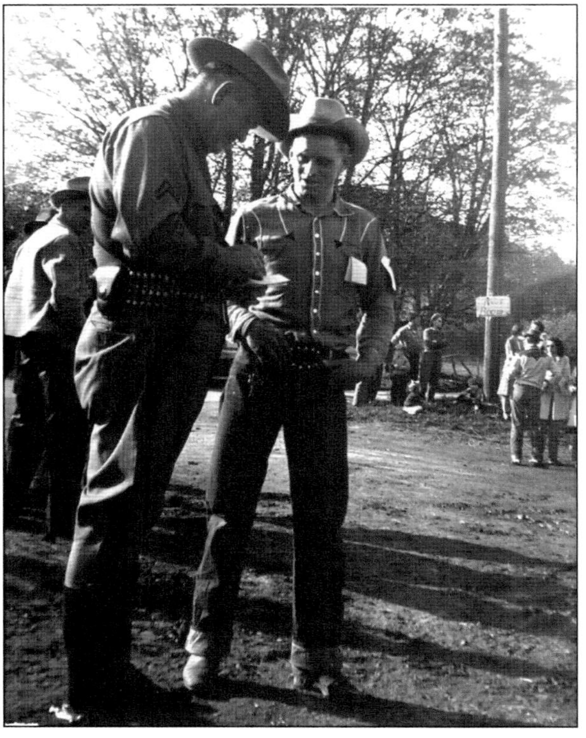

The Rudin Rodeo Days on Sundays were so popular that hundreds of people came to enjoy them. The only place to park their cars was along the side of Gaskill Road, which sometimes caused a problem for other cars trying to drive past them. This was the case in the early 1940s when a policeman had to write up a ticket and give it to Louie Rudin, who does not look too concerned.

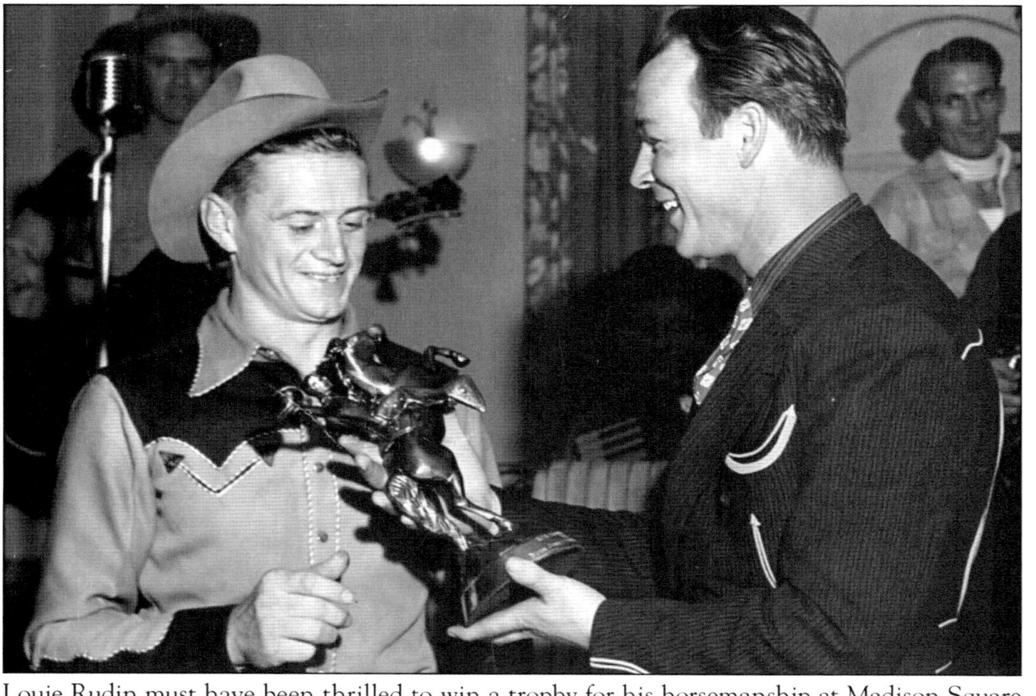

Louie Rudin must have been thrilled to win a trophy for his horsemanship at Madison Square Garden in New York City in October 1942. The famous Roy Rogers is shown presenting it to him.

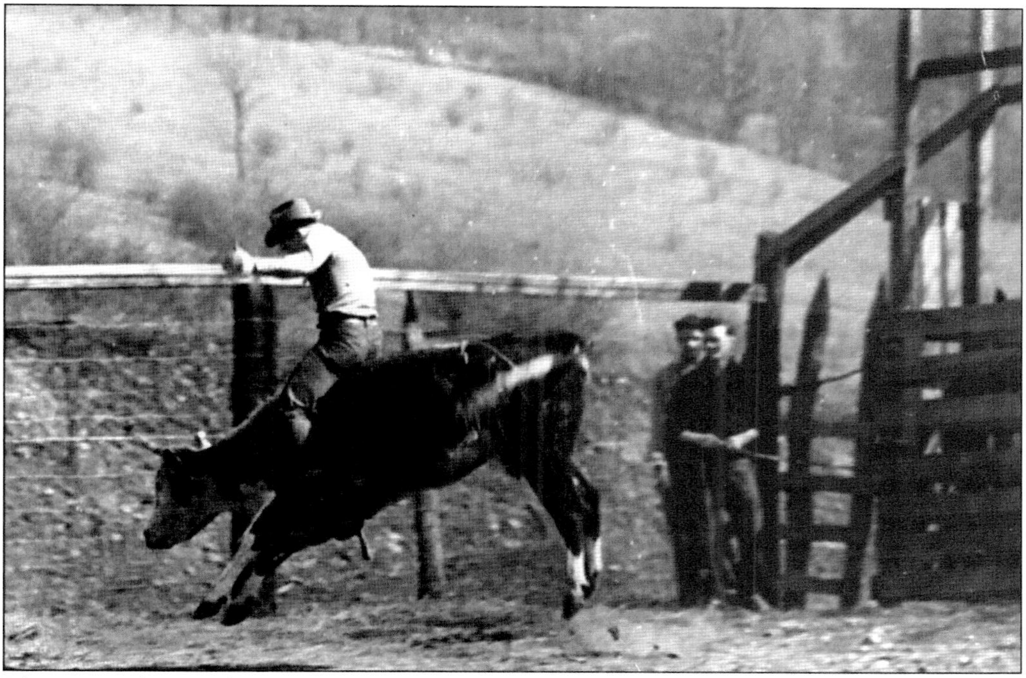

The steer is doing its best to throw Albert Rudin off its back, but he is holding his own. Brothers Louie and Ernie are watching from the sidelines at their Gaskill Corners ranch in the town of Owego, perhaps waiting for their turn to give it a try.

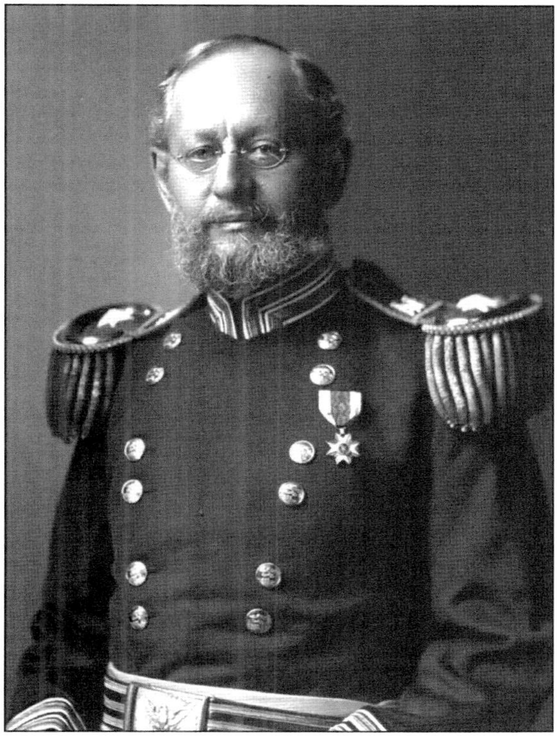

Looking very official, Gen. Henry Martyn Robert is well known in the town of Owego. He married Isabel Hoagland in Owego on May 2, 1901; she was a schoolteacher who lived in a small farmhouse at the corner of Day Hollow Road, in the area called Broadway. They met while she was teaching in Hawthorn, New Jersey, and after their marriage moved to Owego, where they lived for more than 20 years.

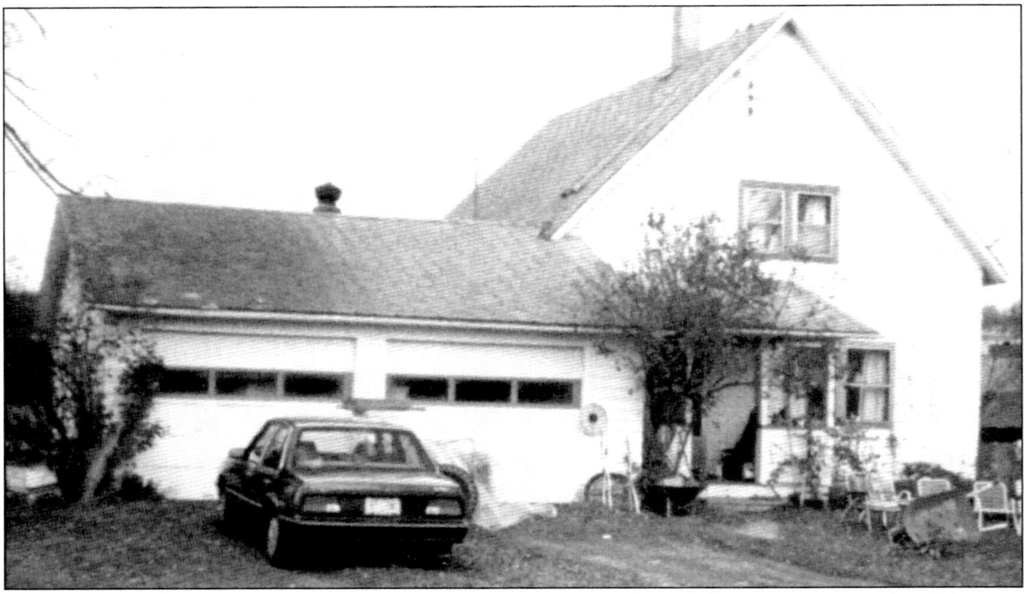

Today this private home with a garage attached does not look like a one-room school, but up into the 1950s, it was a pretty lively place. The children all lived within sight of the school, and it was no secret that if any of them misbehaved they would be reprimanded when school was dismissed.

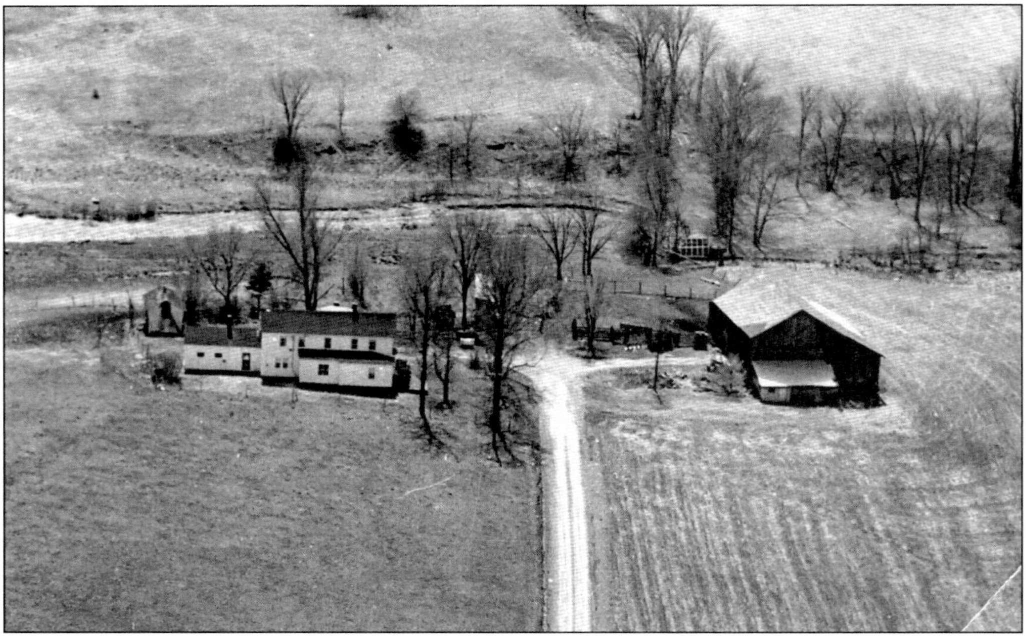

Spencer Lane leads to the old farmhouse that Nathaniel Spencer built in 1826. The home used to be on the same side as the barn but was moved across the road, and since then, the barn has been removed. Today the eighth generation of Spencers still occupies the farm.

Five

Waits and Gibson Corners

Waits is located in the southwest corner of the town of Owego, about five miles from the village. The name is derived from one of its earliest settlers, Henry Wait, who came from Saratoga County in 1819. Today it is a prosperous dairy community. In its early years, it had a grocery store, a post office, a creamery, a church, and a school. The school was in District No. 3, and when it closed, it was auctioned off in 1957. The quaint little Methodist Episcopal church is the last remaining historic structure of the Waits community. It was built in 1853 and was placed on the National and New York State Registers of Historic Places in 2000. A group of residents, known as the Waits Cemetery Corporation, is working to preserve it. Funds have enabled them to restore the steeple and replace the roof.

Located on the south side of the Susquehanna River, Gibson Corners is four miles from the village of Owego and was named after Eli Gibson, a surveyor who came from Stowe, Middlesex County, Massachusetts, in 1812. He and his wife, Betsy, traveled by an ox-drawn wagon and built their home directly opposite from where the United Methodist church stands today. The church was built in 1902; a cemetery is just above the old schoolhouse, which was once called the "Red School House," in District No. 18. As with most of the one-room schools, it closed in the 1950s due to the centralization of school districts. Today the church is the hub of activity with religious services and social functions.

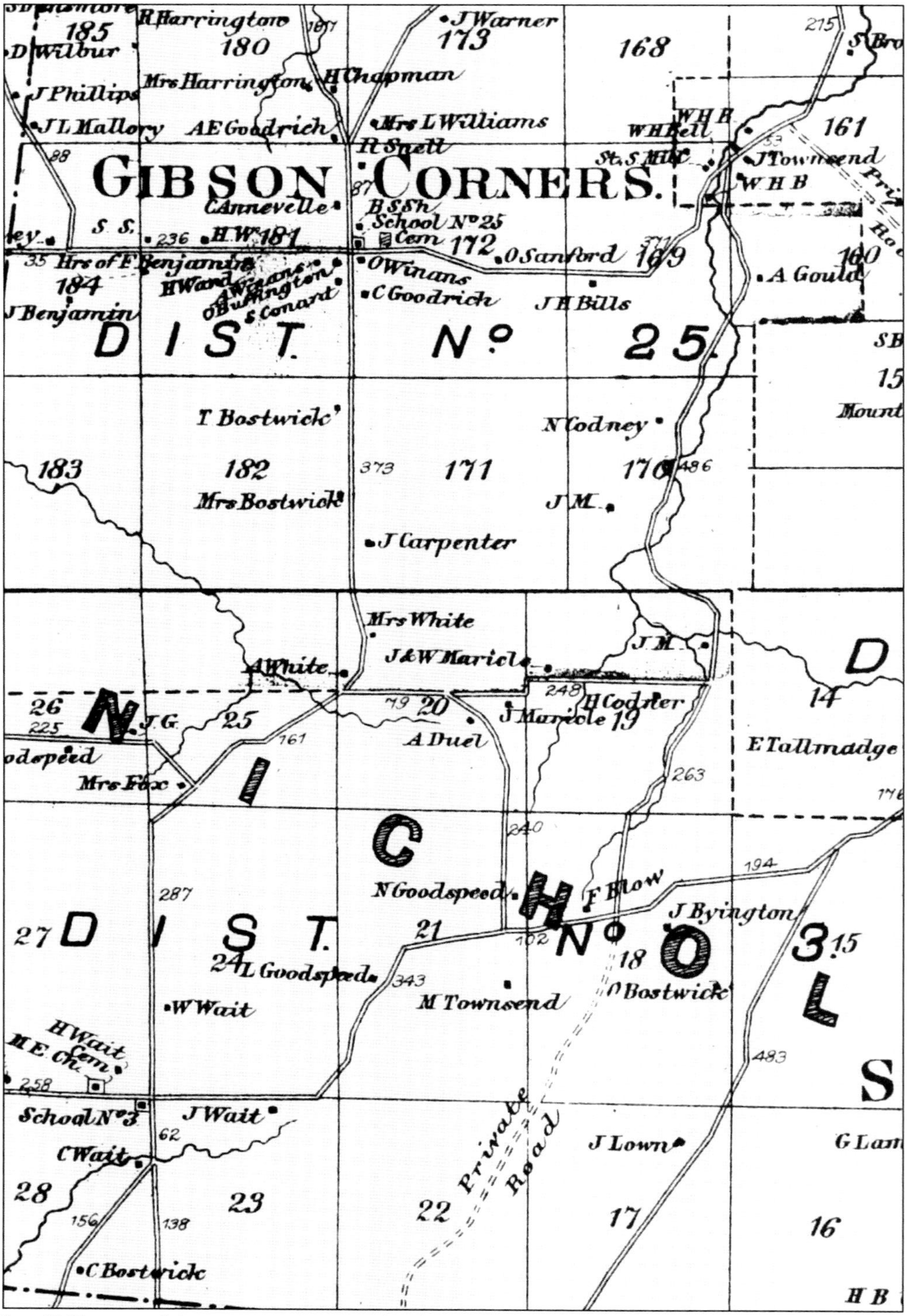

This 1869 view of the areas in Waits and Gibson Corners shows the schools, the churches, and many of the early family farms.

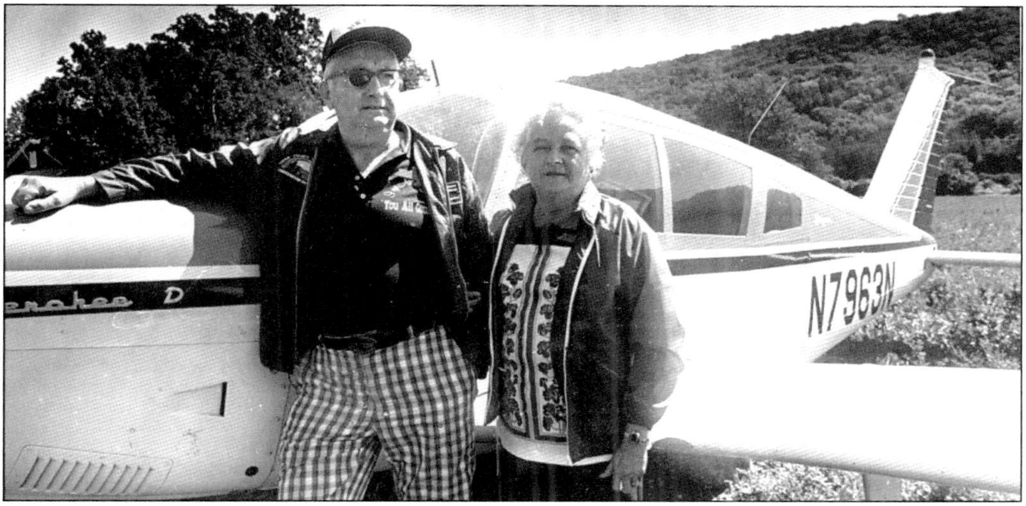

Gerald Mead was a Flying Farmer at the time this picture was taken. He belonged to the New York State and International Flying Farmers Association. Shown with him in August 1982 is his wife, Helen, standing next to his Cherokee airplane. Together they flew to many states and even as far as Alaska.

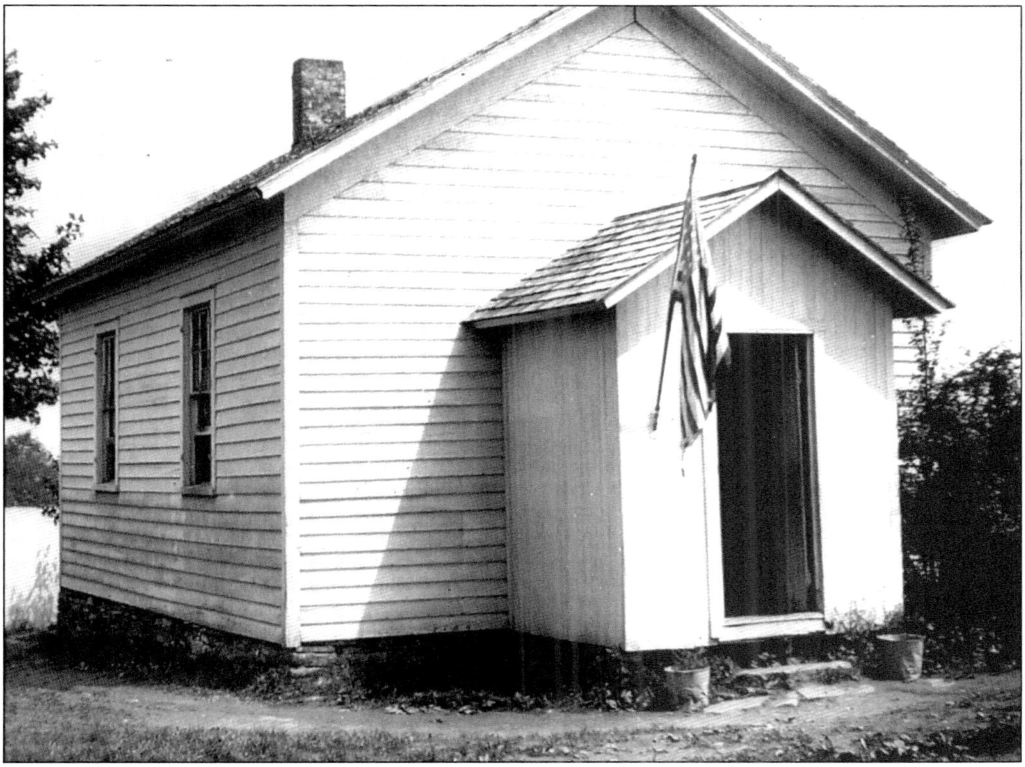

The Arbor Glade schoolhouse, No. 16, located in south Owego around 1930 was about as typical as a one-room schoolhouse could be. There were no frills, unless the two potted plants at the entrance counted. Children came to learn, but extracurricular activities were limited to games at recess.

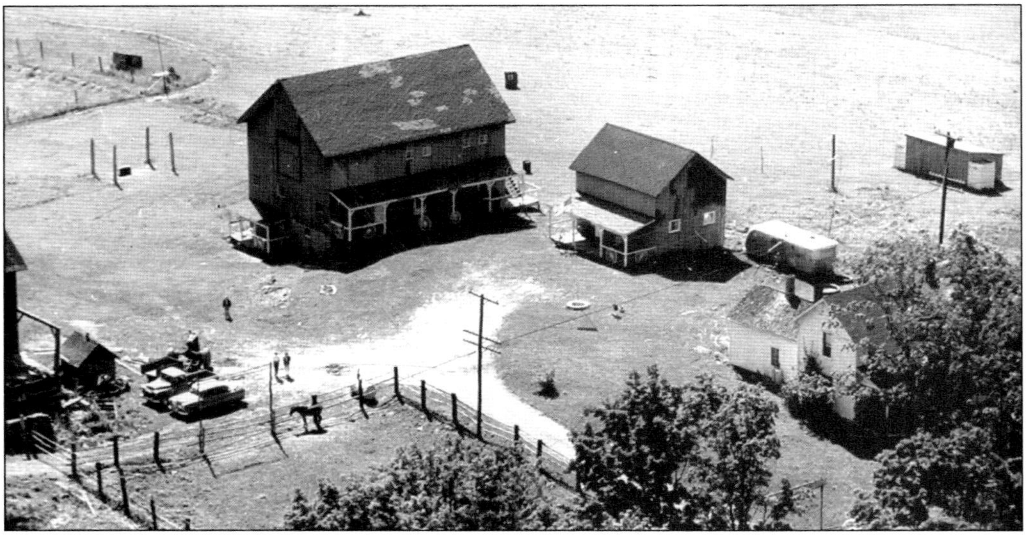

El Rancho de Paz, the "ranch of peace," is located on the Montrose Turnpike, about five miles south of the village of Owego. It began in the 1950s as a Christian youth camp from an idea that Dale Linebaugh and Bob Monell came up with. It started out by using converted chicken coops for bunkhouses, washrooms, and even an outhouse. Today there are new and improved facilities that offer everything from summer camps, horseback riding, retreats for young and old, and even paintball.

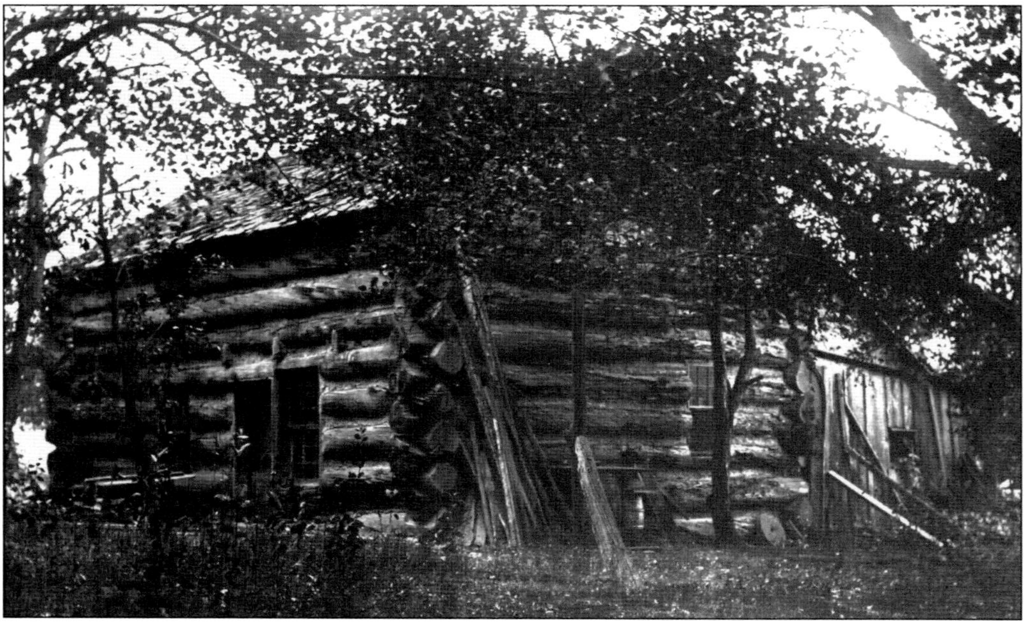

Ira Fox's family was one of South Owego's earliest settlers when the forest was still dense with virgin trees. It must have been so from the size of the logs in his house. It stood about a quarter of a mile east of Gibson Corners, away from the main highway.

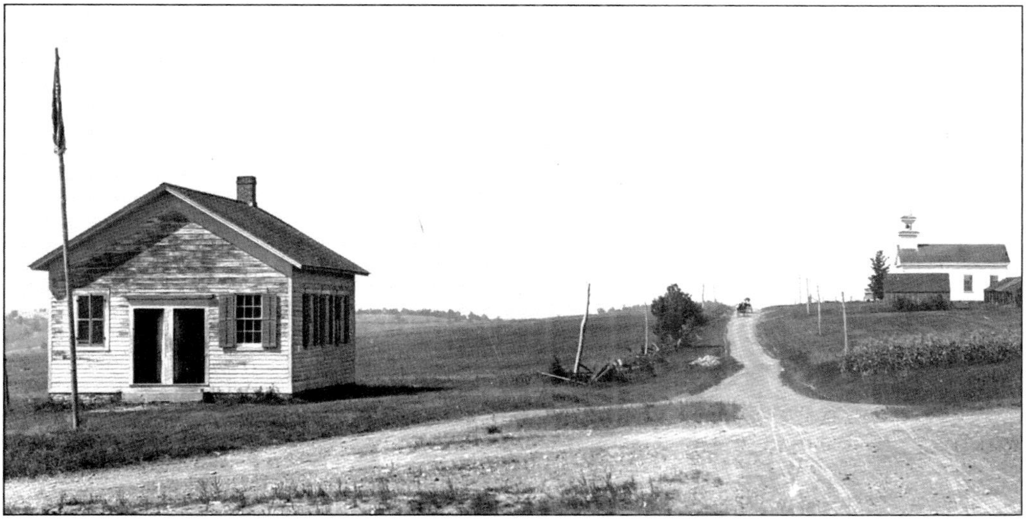

Looking somewhat stark in this photograph, the schoolhouse and church can be seen clearly, but the Waits area was once described as "a little bit of heaven" because of the scenery and hills. Before the school was auctioned off in 1957, it was a hub of activity and housed all of the grades at one time. A stove often doubled as a barbecue, because the children would bring hot dogs and roast them on a stick over the fire at lunchtime.

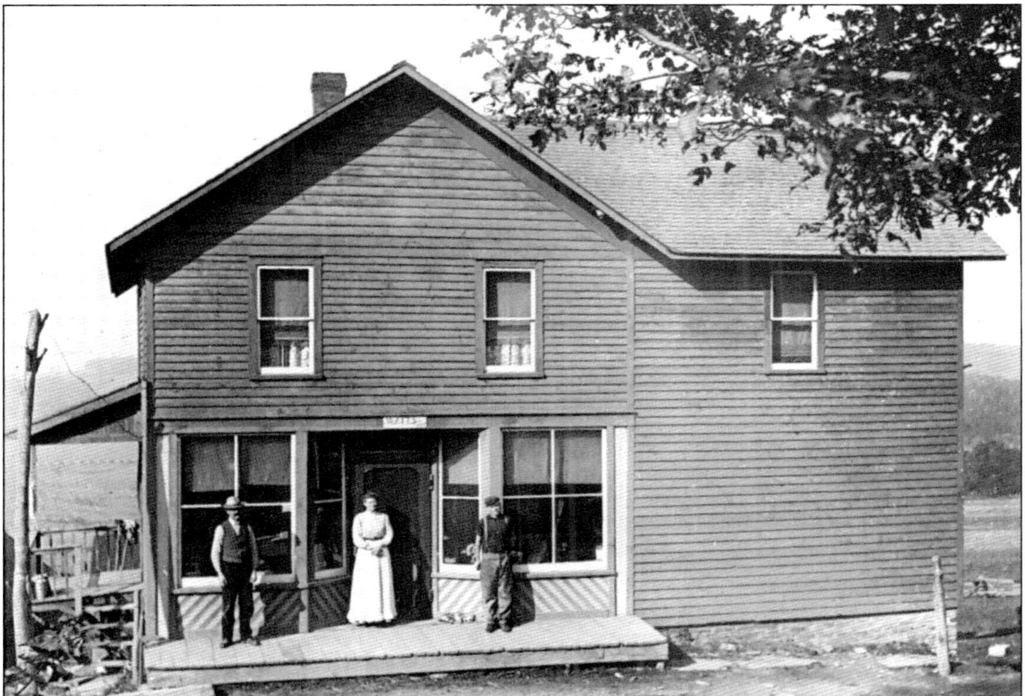

Standing out on a rural road, the Waits Store was built in 1896 by Clarence Dunham and included a post office. It changed hands eight times, finally closing in 1934. A fire finished off the building in 1948.

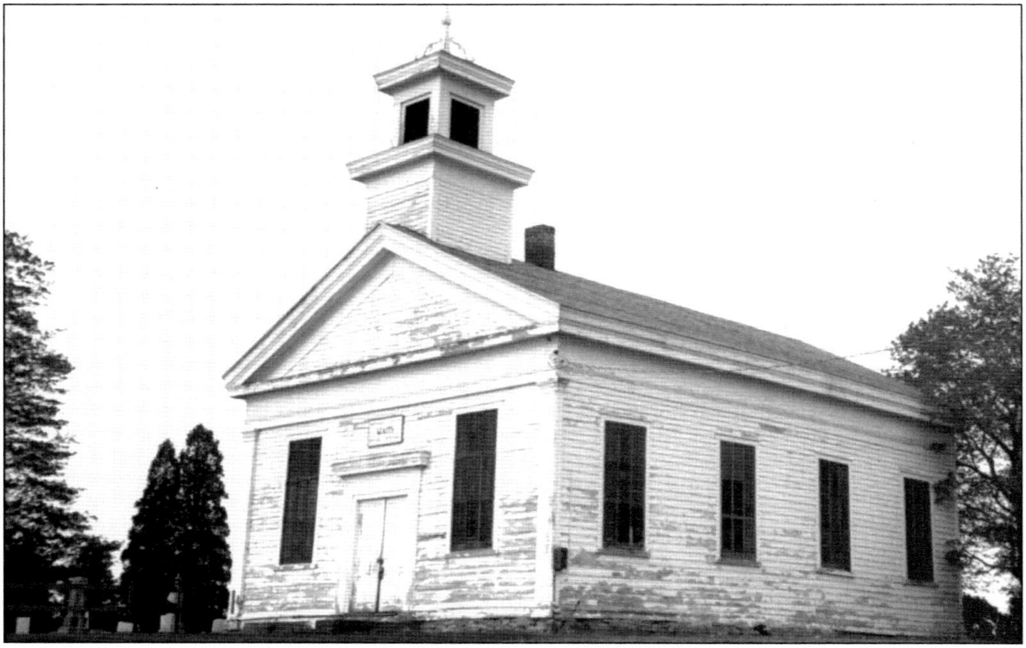

Incorporated in 1837 as the Waits Settlement Methodist Episcopal Church, this building did not get built until 1853. When it closed in 1973, the Waits Cemetery Association bought it to keep it from possibly becoming a chicken coop. It was placed on the National and New York State Registers of Historic Places in 2000, and a group of concerned people are working to restore it.

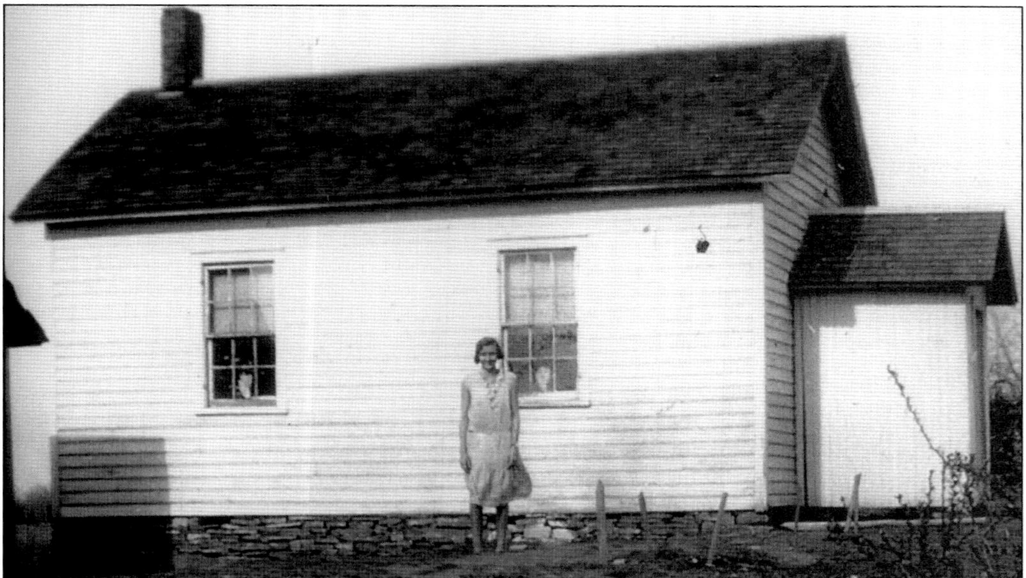

The young, pretty schoolmarm in this photograph is Edith Race (Meyermann), posing in front of the Arbor Glade schoolhouse in South Owego, District No. 16, in the early 1930s. She told stories of how she used to ride a horse to school and sometimes fell off. After she bought a car, she would drive it over the snow as far as she could, then park it at a friend's house and ski the rest of the way. Those were the good old days.

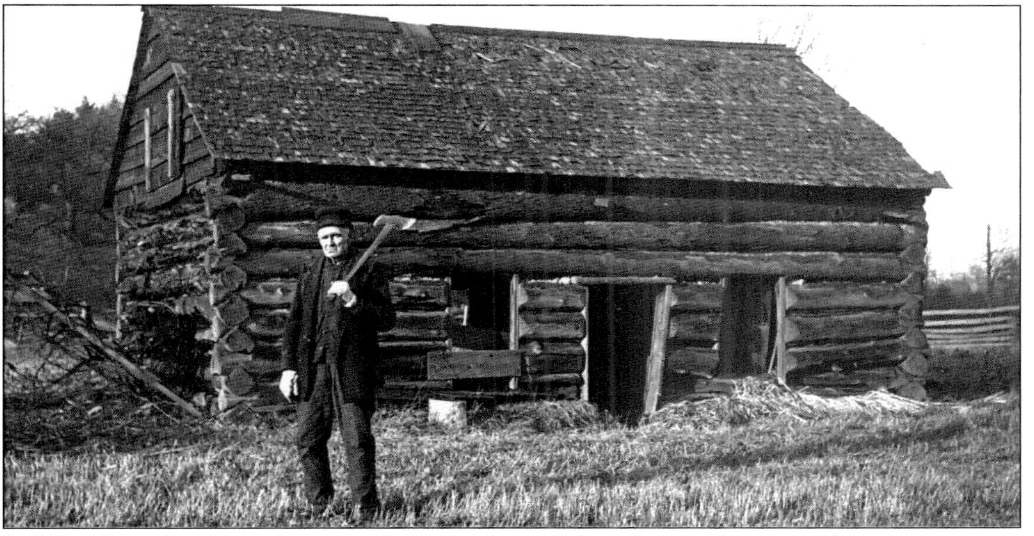

Joel Goodspeed built this log cabin for his bride in 1848, and it stood for several generations near east Nichols. After Joel's death, his brother James G. Goodspeed (shown posing with his ax) owned the property, to be followed by his son Earl Goodspeed.

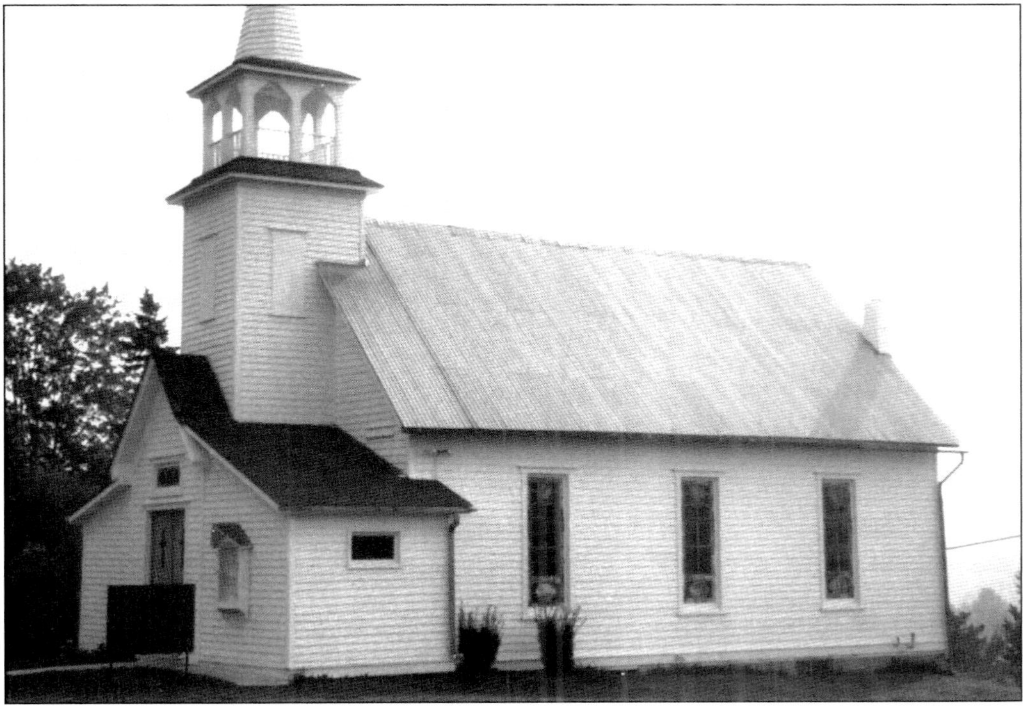

The Gibson Corners United Methodist Church, located on Waits Road in the town of Owego, was organized in 1855 and early services were held in the schoolhouse. The church was built in 1902 on land donated by Charles Anvil. Over the years, improvements were continually being made, such as painting the exterior, installing cushions on church pews, putting in a parking area, as well as acquiring an organ and furnace. A basement was later dug and is used for Sunday school classes and church activities.

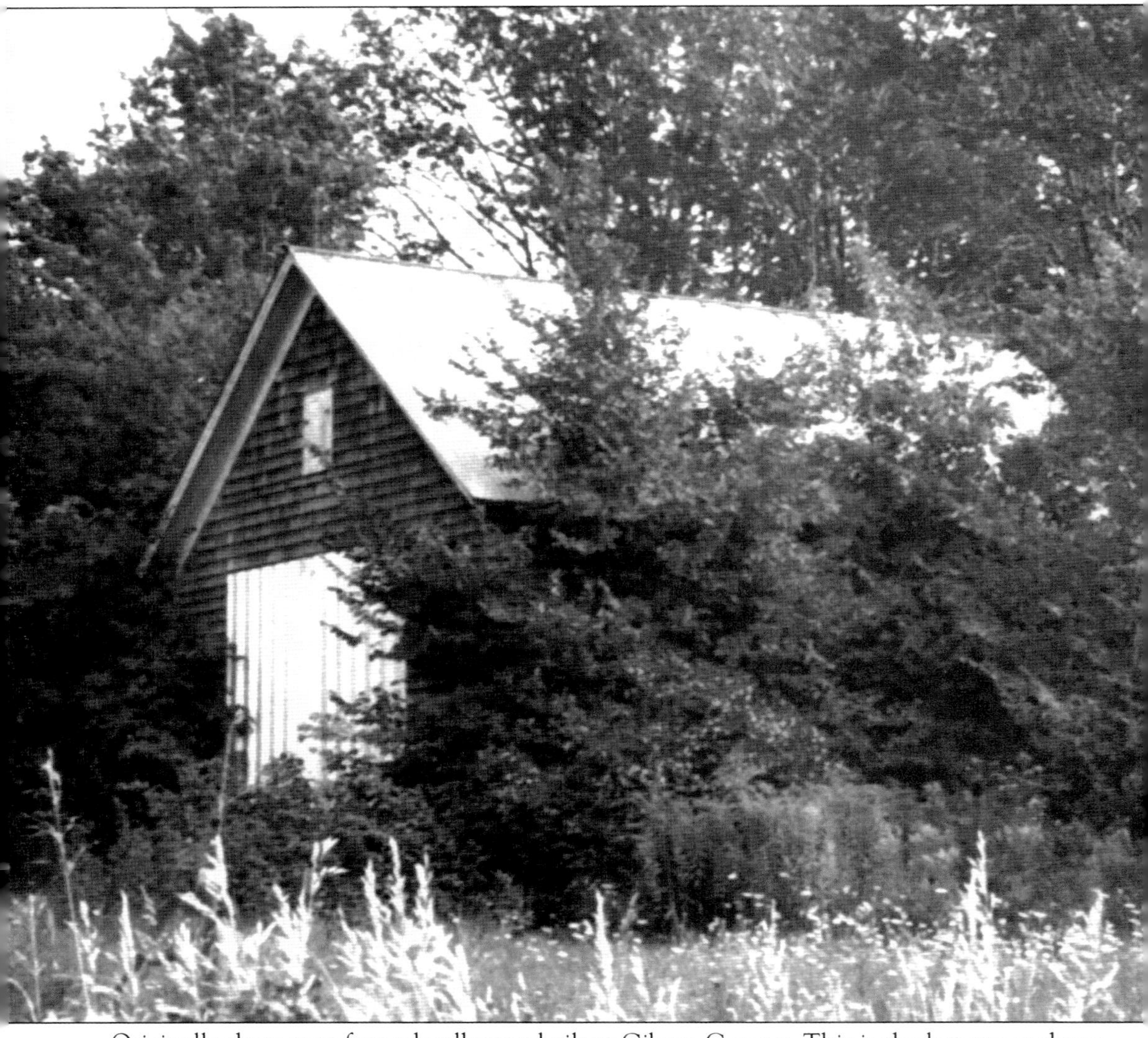

Originally there were four schoolhouses built at Gibson Corners. This is the last one and was known as the "Red School House." After the schools consolidated in the 1950s, it was sold and a large door was cut into the back of it, as seen in this photograph, and the building was used for storage. Nature has taken over, and the overgrowth obscures most of it.

Six

NEIGHBORHOODS

Because the town of Owego is so large, the six hamlets are separated by miles of roads. History abounds in those miles, in separate little communities or neighborhoods. A few of them have churches still in use, old cemeteries, and former one-room schoolhouses that have been converted into private homes. The areas include the south side of the Susquehanna River, along Route 434, and the north side of the river includes Taylor Road, Ivory Foster Road, Day Hollow Road, Broadway, Whittemore Hill Road, East Beecher Road, and Hullsville Road. Many of the names of these important little neighborhoods are from the families who settled there in the 1800s. The section known as Broadway runs less than a mile on Day Hollow Road, but it contains the former schoolhouse, built in 1847, where Rev. Washington Gladden, famed American clergyman and author, attended as a child. Across the road from it is the former home of Isabel Hoagland, who married Gen. Henry Martyn Robert, and at the corner of Day Hollow and Gaskill Roads is the quaint little Broadway Cemetery that has been nestled there since the early 1800s.

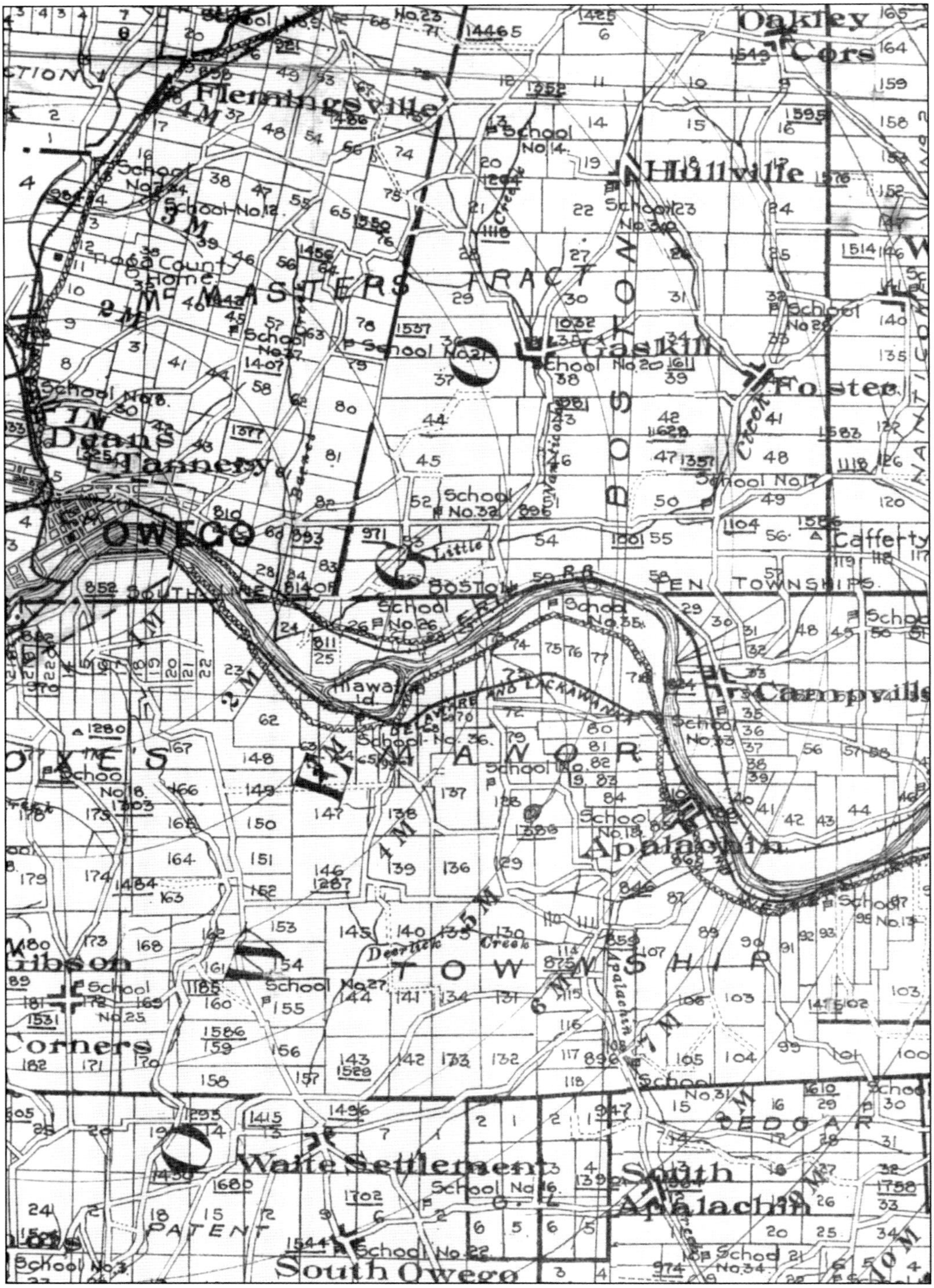

The date of this map of the town of Owego is estimated at about 1900. It shows the Delaware-Lackawanna Railroad, which came through in 1882. Some of the neighborhood areas named after early settlers are also shown.

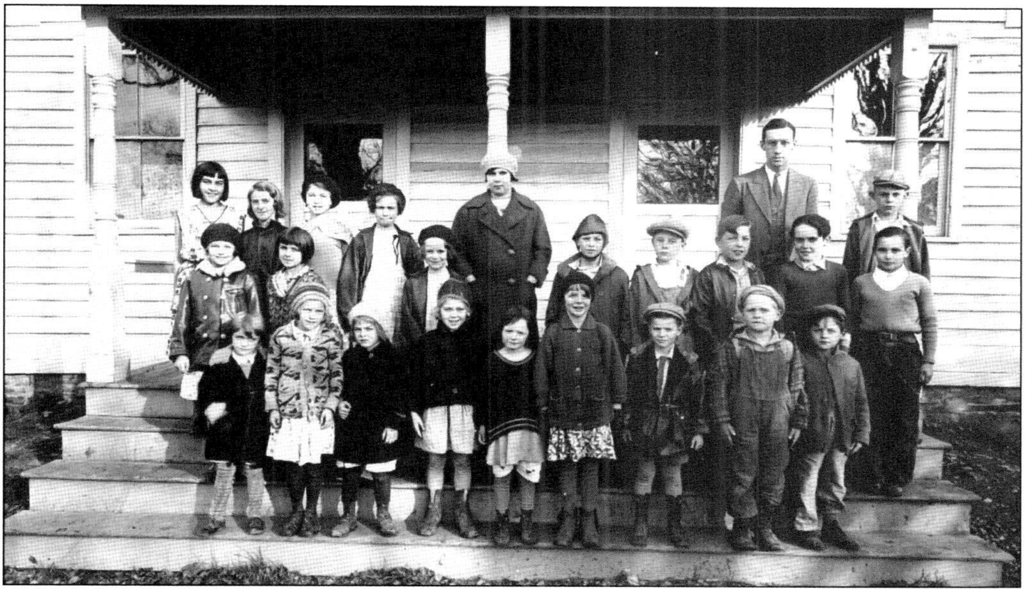

The Broadway district's school No. 32, located on Day Hollow Road, was built in 1847. The children in this 1933 photograph are, from left to right, (first row) Geniveve Jennings, Melinda Maasen, Gertrude Maasen, June Spencer, Fern Jennings, Frances Jennings, Charles Arnold, Richard Keene, and James Keene; (second row) Margaret Cronk, Anita Maasen, Royce Arnold, Donald Haus, Milton Cole, Raymond Maasen, Robert Keene, and Donald Cronk; (third row) Elsie Maasen, Mary Jennings, Jeannette Spencer, Jennie Arnold, June Bruner (teacher), Elwood Stone, and Robert Cole.

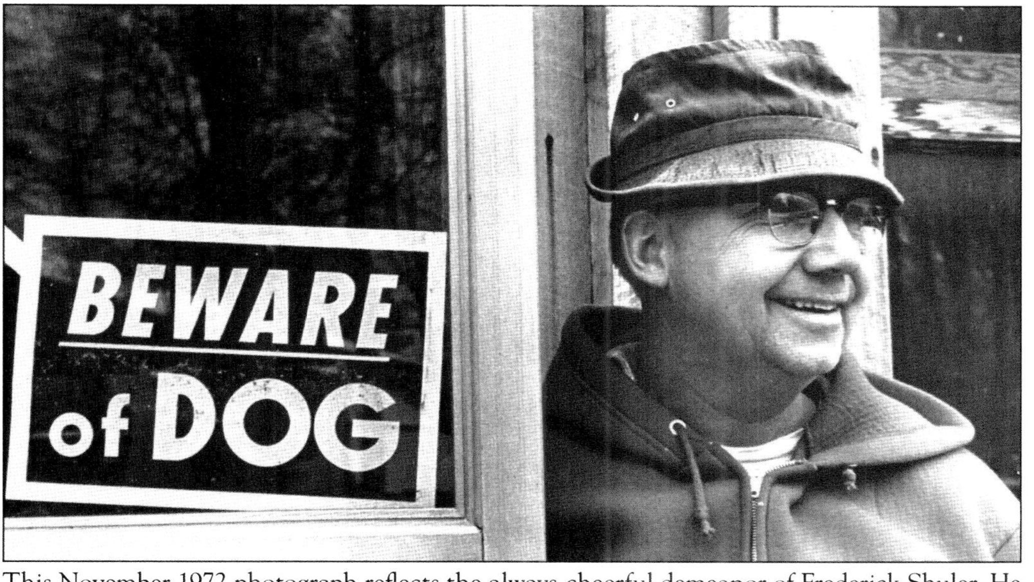

This November 1972 photograph reflects the always-cheerful demeanor of Frederick Shuler. He served with the 10th Mountain Division in World War II as a medic. His war history includes heroic acts while facing intense action in Italy in the famed battle at Montecassino. After he returned home, he was best known for operating dog kennels and also served as dog warden for the Town of Owego. Shuler passed away in 2006.

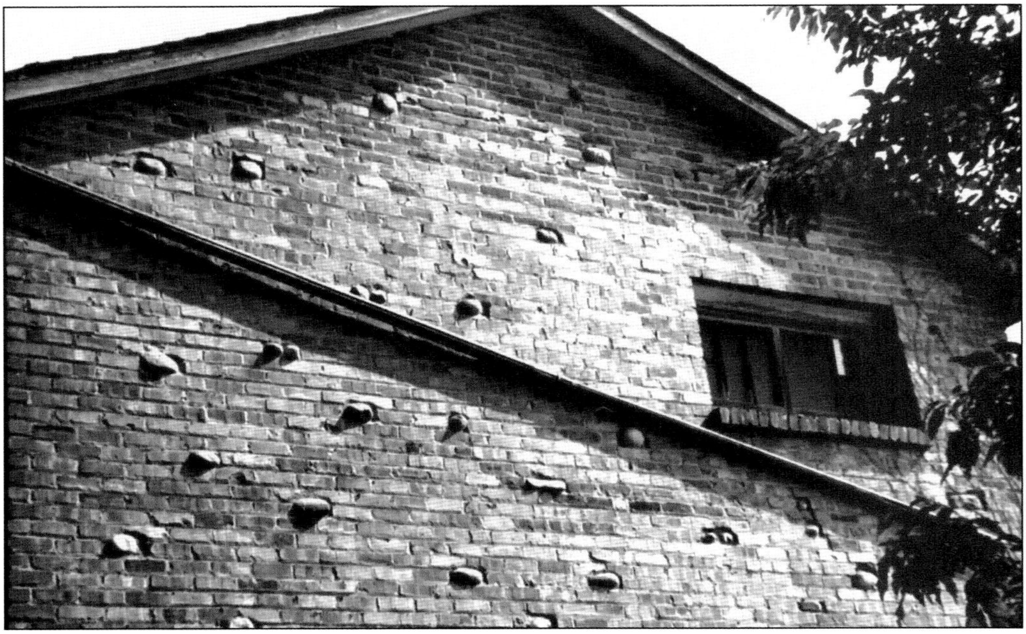

Because there were so many hickory trees on the land, the name Hickories was adopted. The house was built before 1850 by its first owner, George Young, an enterprising farmer from England. It was constructed of brick veneer, using this unusual design with fieldstones to give it interest. The house had 12 rooms and was sold numerous times over the years. The Town of Owego purchased the property in 1963, and by 1996, the building was in such need of repairs that it was razed.

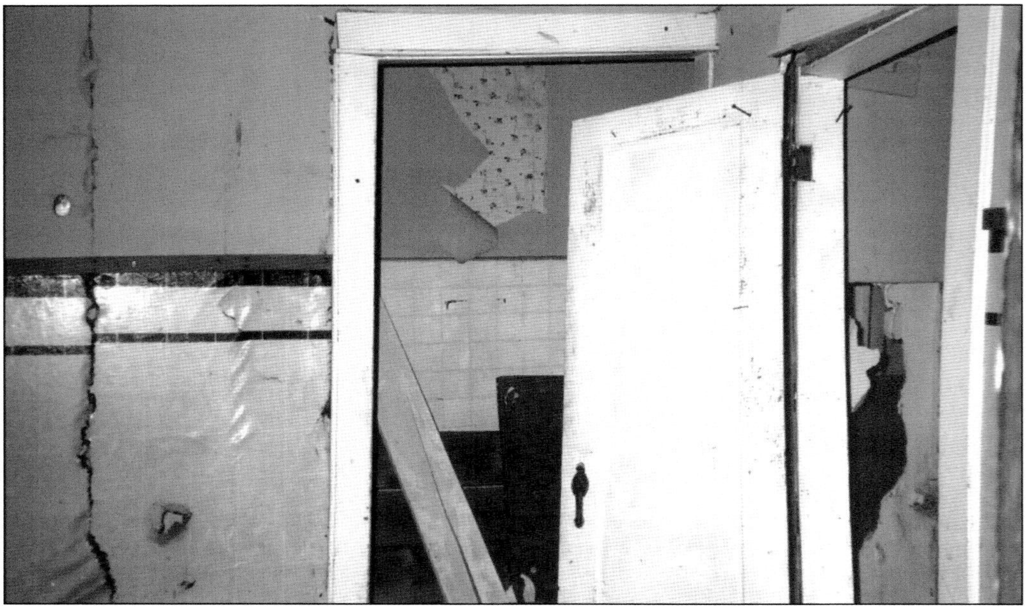

The Hickories homestead is shown in its final hours before being razed in September 1996. This peek into the remains of the kitchen shows few reminders of days past when it was a warm place, with the aroma of home cooking inviting one in.

The backhoe takes a big bite out of the bricks of the Hickories homestead on September 19, 1996, and down it goes forever. After years of abandonment, rotting floors, and boarded-up windows, the only living creatures in it were field mice and a lot of large wasp nests. Its time was up.

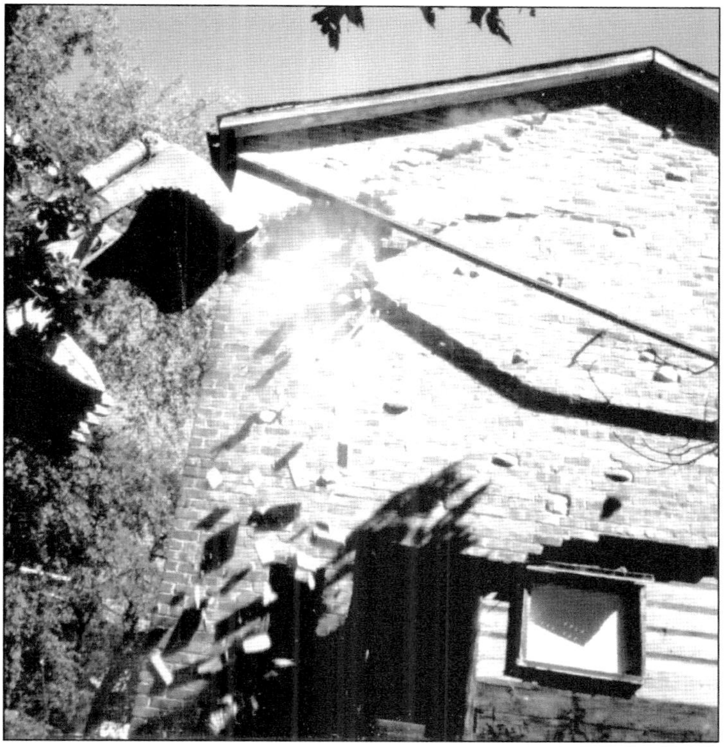

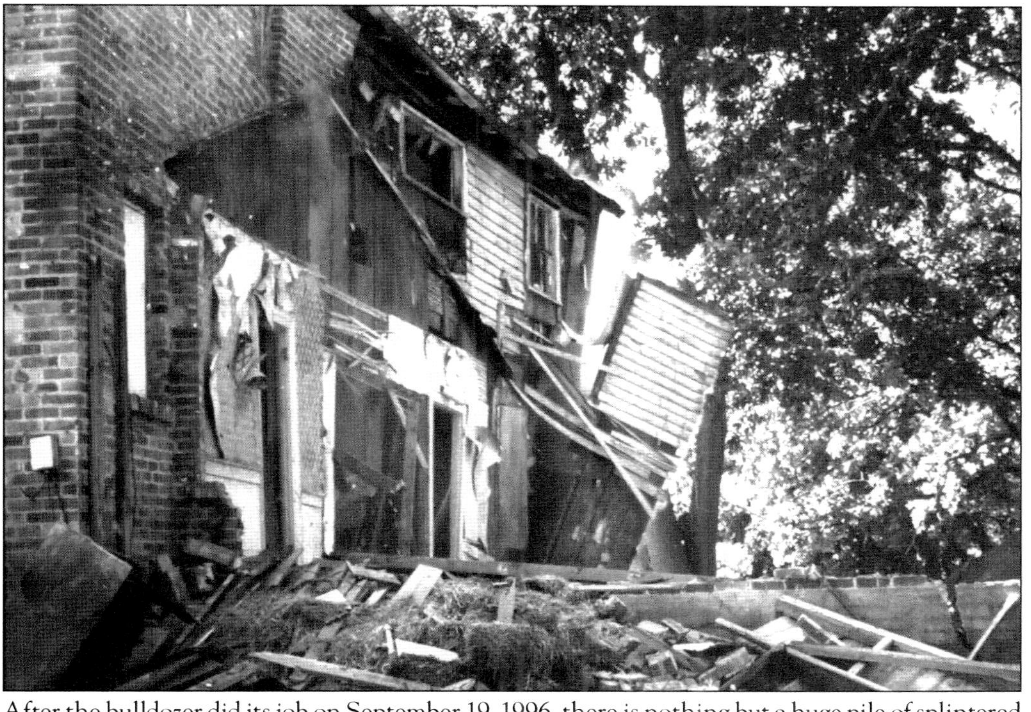

After the bulldozer did its job on September 19, 1996, there is nothing but a huge pile of splintered wood and bricks left of the old Hickories homestead.

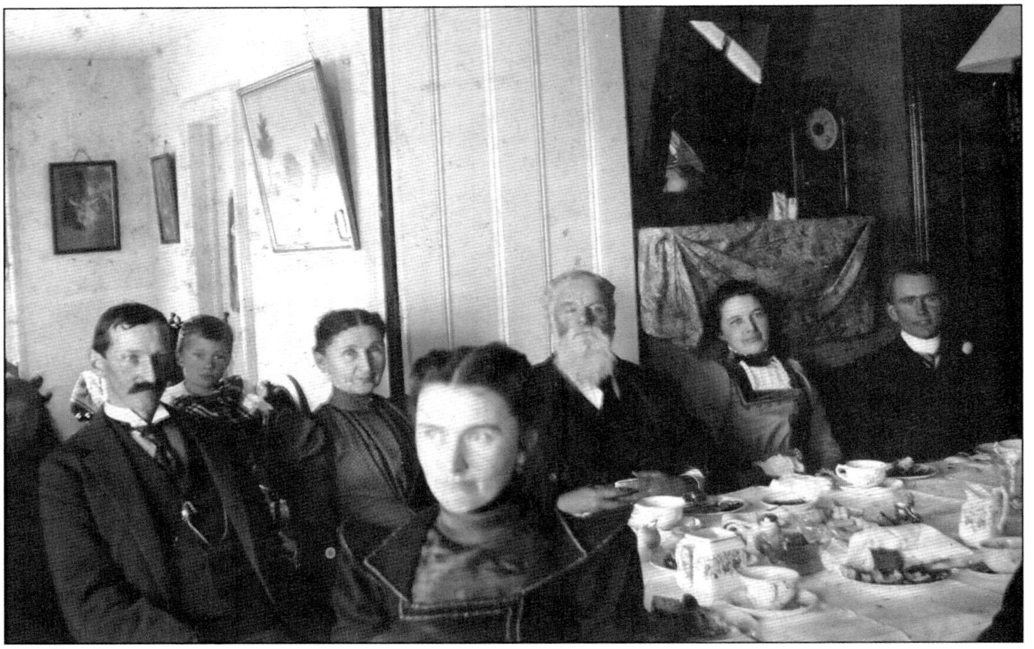

Virgil "Pete" Whittemore and his wife, Ruth, celebrated their 50th wedding anniversary at their home with a lovely dinner. Pictured at the extreme right are Ruth and Burt Pitkin, and to the left of them are Virgil and Ruth Whittemore. In the foreground are Mary W. Keeler and her husband, Grant.

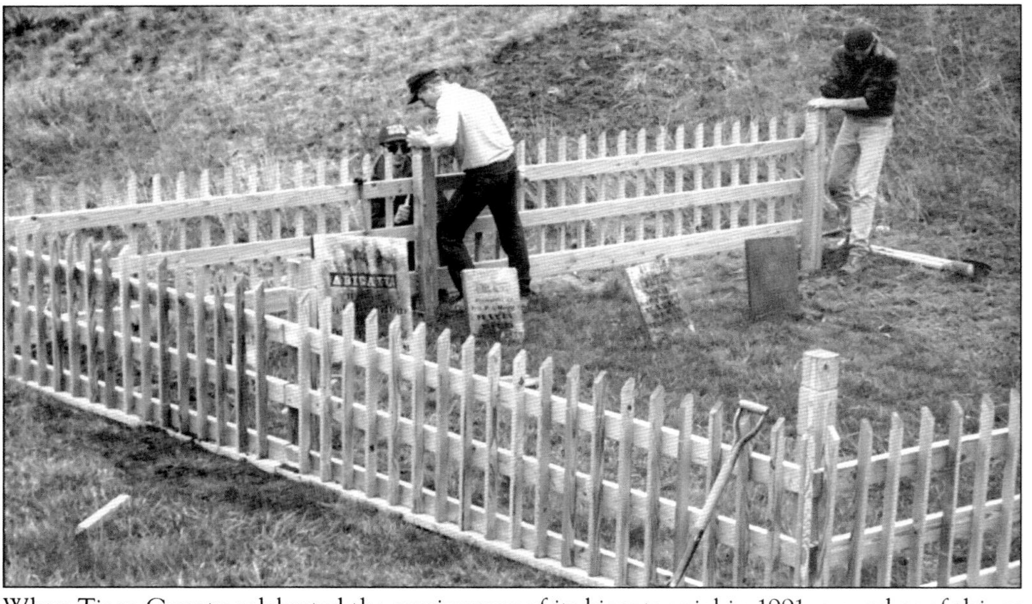

When Tioga County celebrated the anniversary of its bicentennial in 1991, a number of things were done to improve the towns. One of the projects completed in the town of Owego was to refurbish an abandoned cemetery on Route 434, just east of the Court Street Bridge. A three-foot-high fence was constructed and installed by the parks department. Shown putting it in place are workers Dave Chase (white shirt) and Kurt Weed.

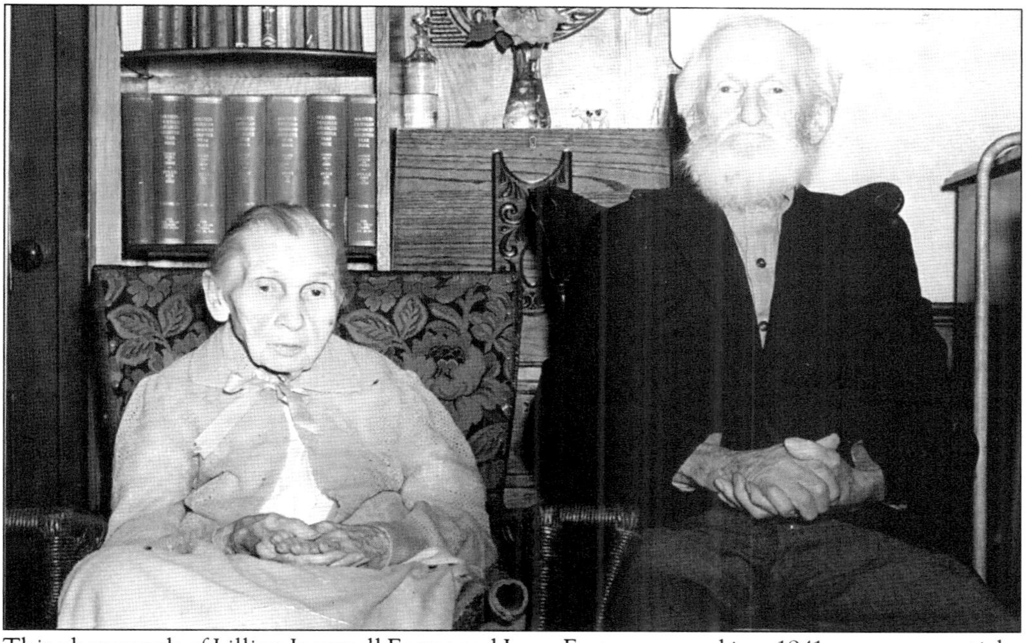

This photograph of Lillian Ingersoll Foster and Ivory Foster was used in a 1941 newspaper article. They had been married 64 years and lived on the family's 150-year-old farm in the town of Owego, on a road now named after him, Ivory Foster Road.

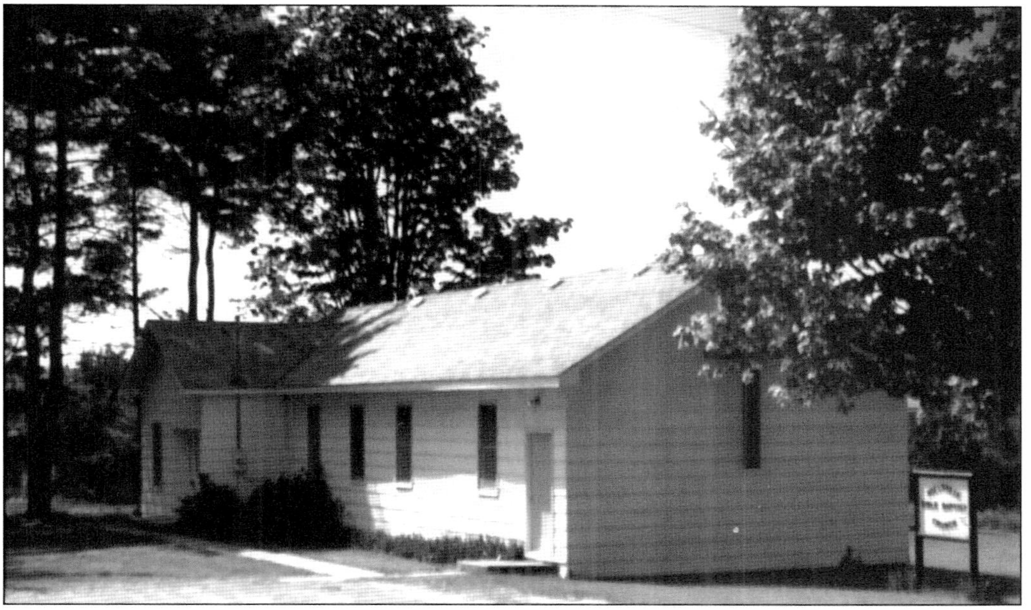

The Hullsville Bible Church was a former schoolhouse, north of Gaskill Corners. One of the students who attended the school was Henretta Whitney, who became a well-respected teacher in the town of Owego and remembered that Ruth Whittemore was the district superintendent in 1932. After the consolidation of the schools in the 1950s, the building was sold to the church, which at first was Methodist and later changed to Baptist. The largest, most active congregation was in the 1960s. By 1995, a steeple was installed.

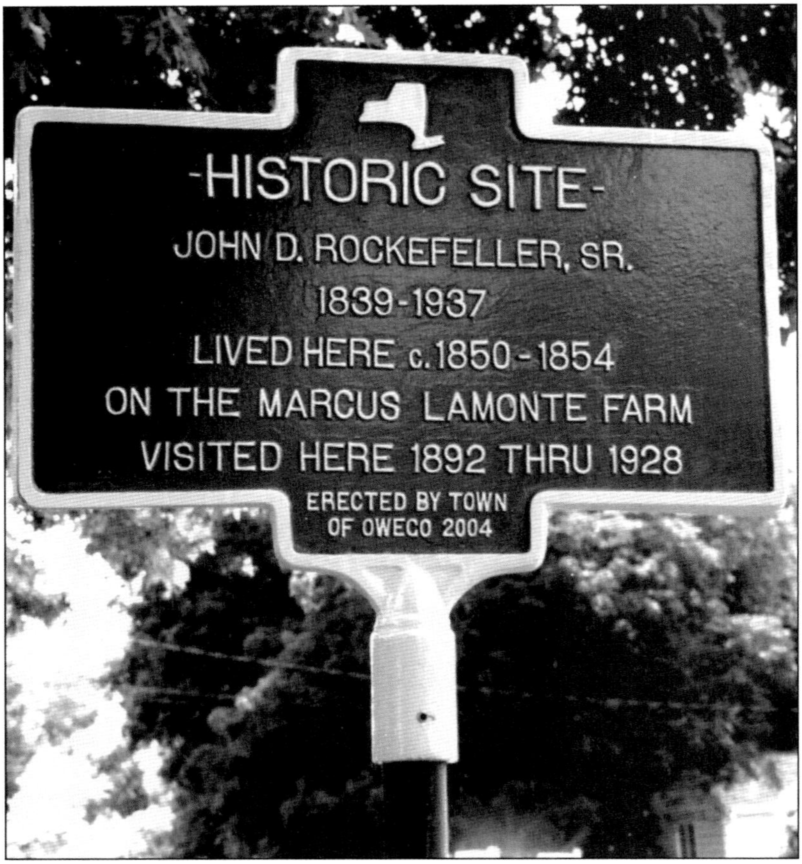

This historical marker was installed in 2004 at the site of the house where John D. Rockefeller Sr. and his family lived for several years. They moved to the town of Owego, on what is now Route 17C, from Moravia in 1849.

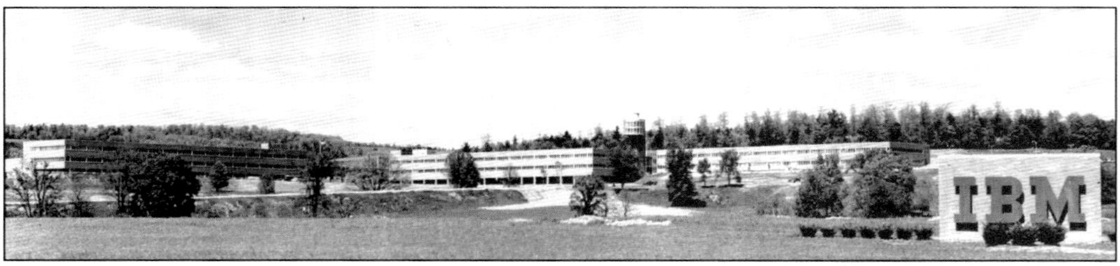

When groundbreaking took place in November 1955 for the military products division of IBM, it was like striking gold for the local economy. Thousands of people were hired, roads were improved, schools were built, and almost everything along with it changed. The dedication ceremonies were held on June 20, 1958, and included famed opera stars Rise Stevens and James Melton. Almost 40 years later, in 1994, it was sold to the Loral Corporation and two years later was sold to Lockheed Martin Corporation.

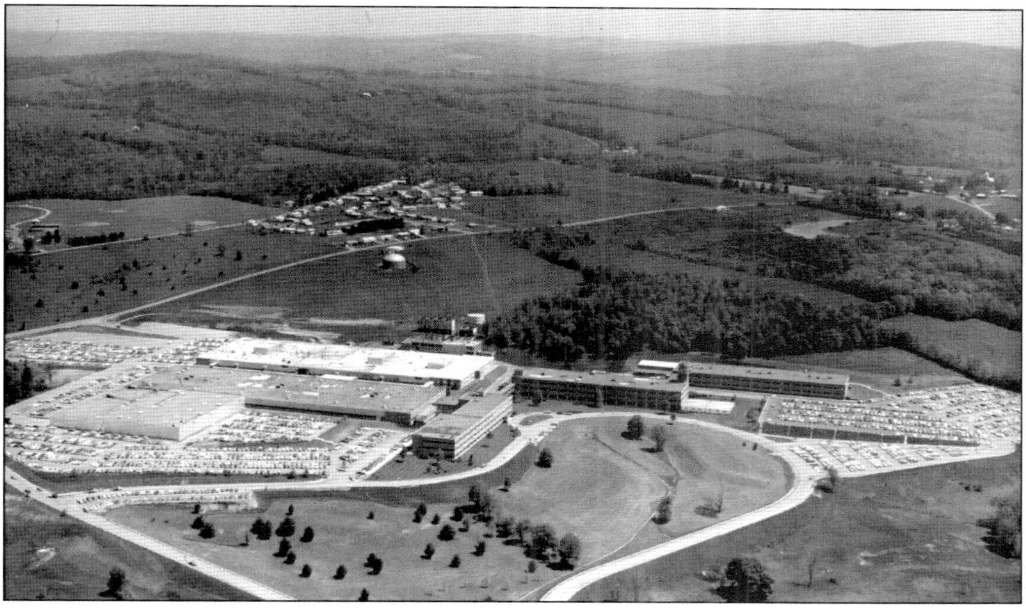

Pictured is a great aerial shot of the IBM plant in the town of Owego in May 1970. The homes shown at the upper left are part of the Lincolnshire subdivision, which opened in 1958 to accommodate some of the employees hired when the plant opened.

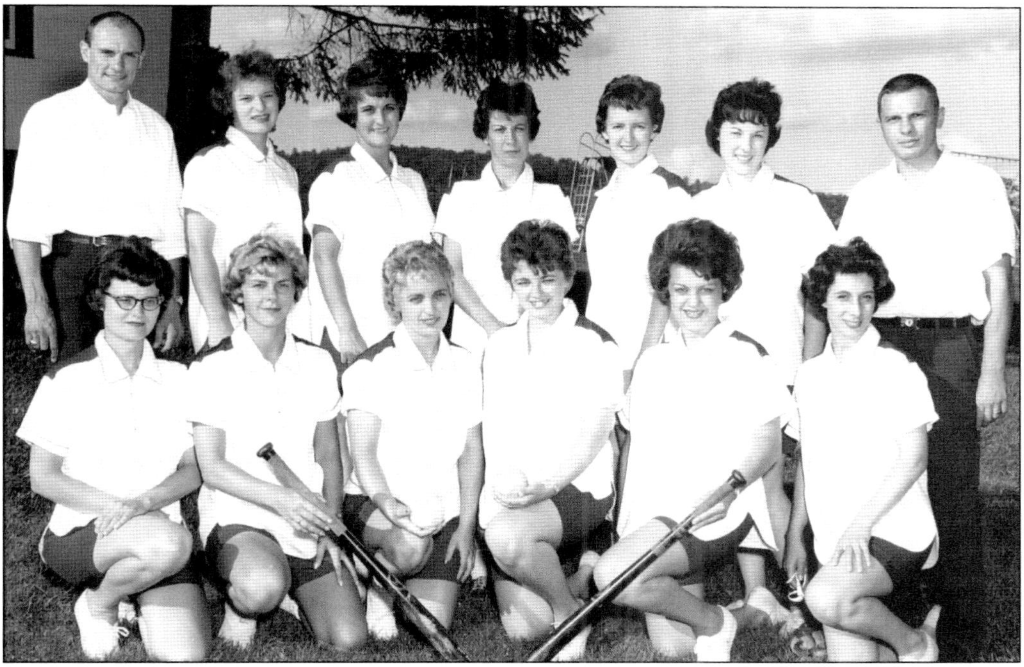

In the 1960s, IBM sponsored a women's softball team. The photograph shows the champions of the Women's Industrial Softball League of the Triple Cities. Pictured are, from left to right, (first row) Phyllis Richards, Pat Valabek, captain Frances Rompala, Miriam Kocik, Pat Kizale, and Emma M. Sedore; (second row) assistant manager Bob Lasker, Ellen Sorochinsky, Joanne Lubert, Pat Barta, Mitzi Manning, Betty Woodcook, and manager Dick Barta.

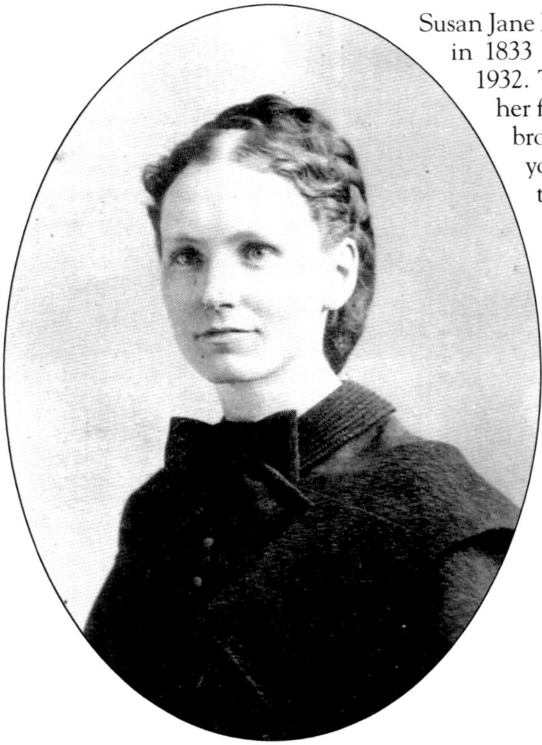

Susan Jane LaMonte Life was born in the town of Owego in 1833 three miles east of the village and died in 1932. The Rockefeller family resided in a house on her family's farm, and she tutored John D. and his brother William in her home when they were young. Their friendship continued throughout their lives. She first became a teacher and taught at local schools. In 1856, she married Rev. William Life, and they lived in Muncy, Pennsylvania, where in 1857 she opened a small school for girls. From there, they moved to Rye, New York, and in 1869, she founded the Rye Seminary, which became one of the leading private schools in the state.

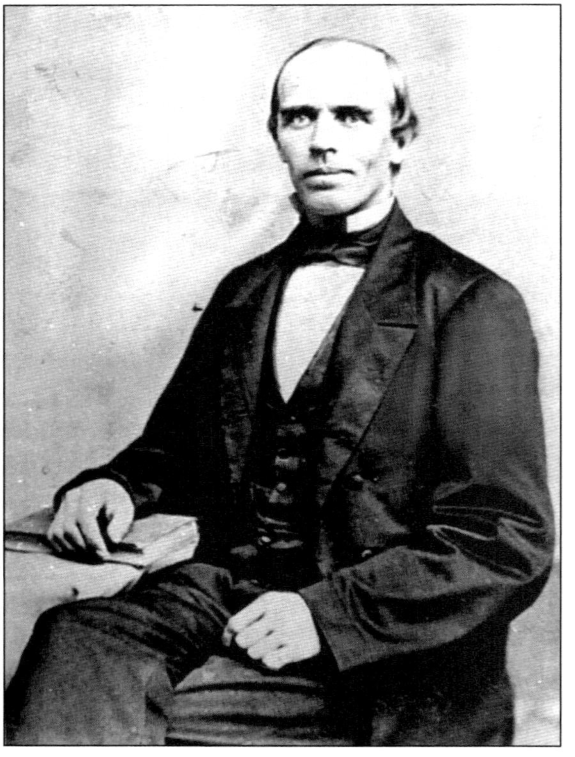

Rev. William Life was the husband of educator Susan Jane LaMonte Life of the town of Owego. They married in 1856 and lived in Rye where she was headmistress of the Rye Seminary. Reverend Life died in 1898 and is buried in Rye.

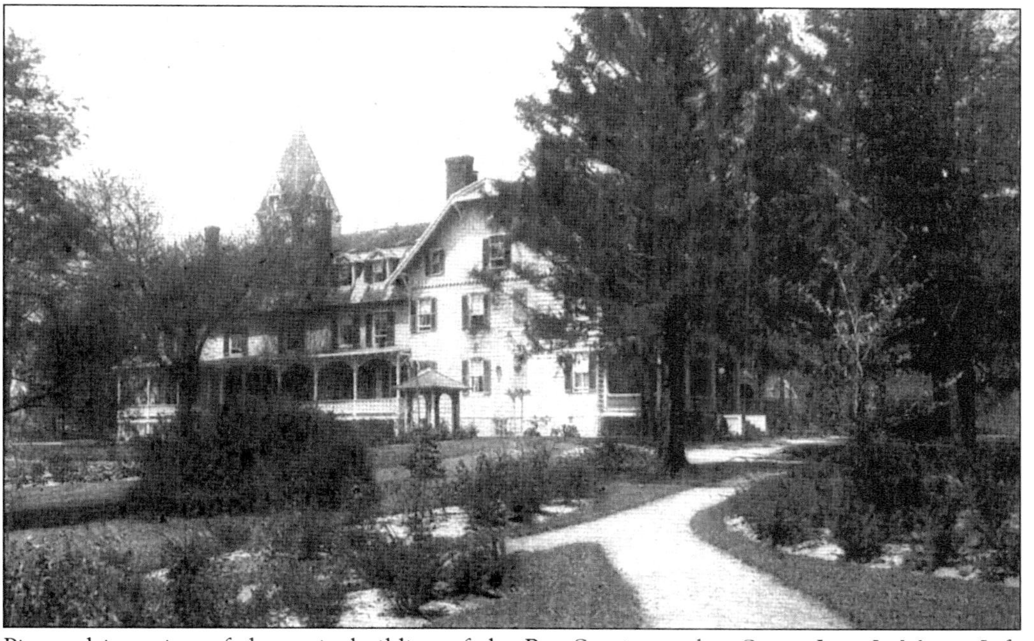

Pictured is a view of the main building of the Rye Seminary that Susan Jane LaMonte Life founded in 1869 and of which she became headmistress. The school is now called the Rye Country Day School and continues to be a leading private school.

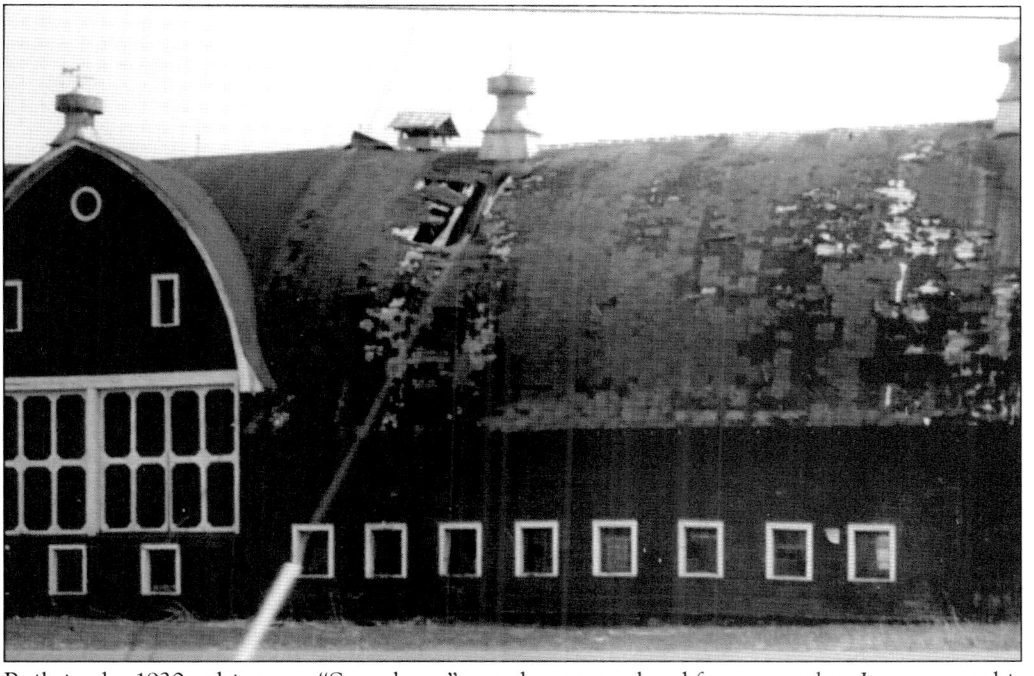

Built in the 1930s, this was a "Sears barn," one that was ordered from a catalog. It came as a kit by train and had to be assembled after it arrived. It was first painted yellow, but over time, it was painted green and was known for years as the "Green Barn." Located on Route 38, it was finally demolished in 2003.

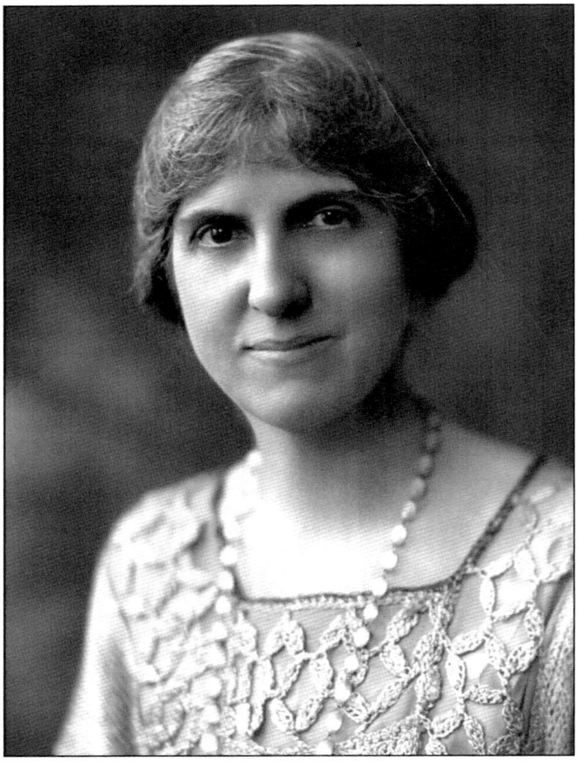

Frances Paget Price was born in the town of Owego in 1879 to Silas and Frances (Ingersoll) Paget. After she graduated from Owego Free Academy and Elmira College, Price taught modern languages in New York City and in 1922 married Dr. William Price. Dr. Price was the supervisor of modern and foreign languages for the University of the State of New York for 24 years, from 1911 to 1936. She had always maintained a summer home in Owego and after her death generously bequeathed her 32-acre farm on Ivory Foster Road to a charitable corporation to be known as the Paget Price Presbyterian Home. The home was established for retired Presbyterian ministers and their wives and is still being used as such to the present day, including several additional homes on the property.

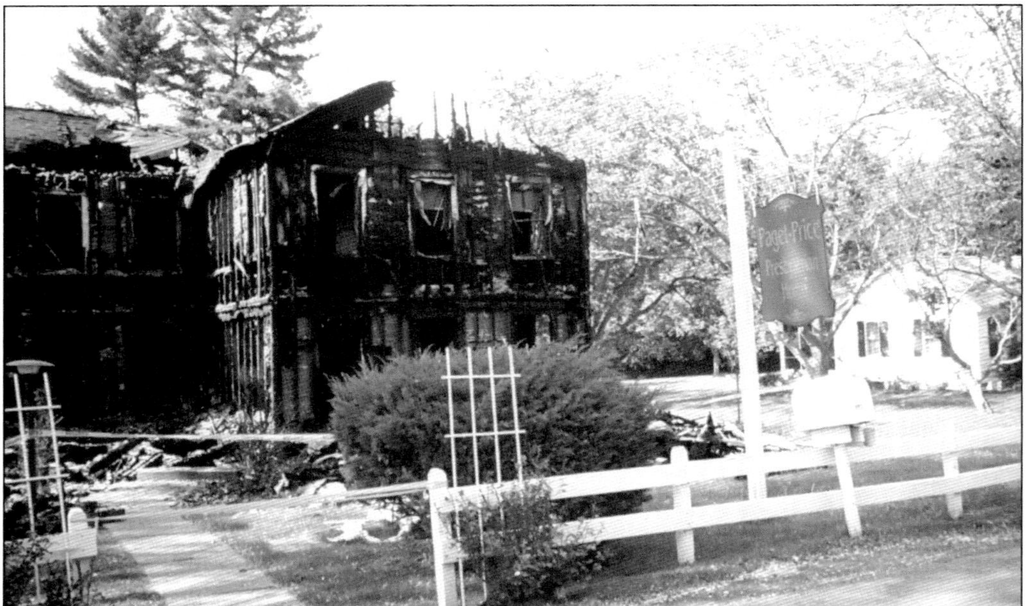

The beautiful home for retired Presbyterian ministers known as the Paget Price Presbyterian Home caught fire on May 16, 2001, and the whole front of the building was destroyed. It was rebuilt by the following year, designed as closely as possible to the one that burned. The wooden spindles on the front porch were able to be saved and were incorporated into the new building.

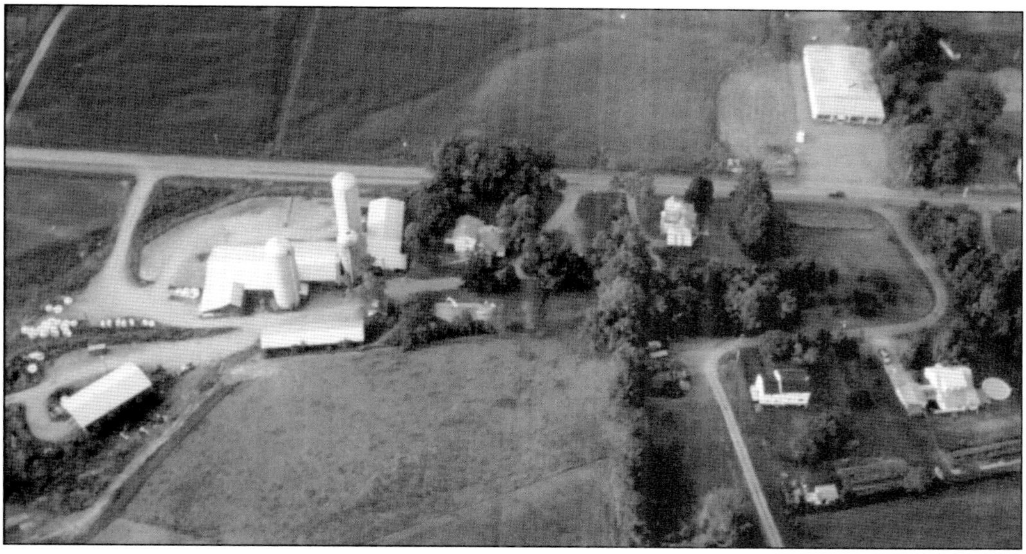

Pictured from a hot air balloon ride is the Robinson dairy farm on Day Hollow Road in the area known as Broadway.

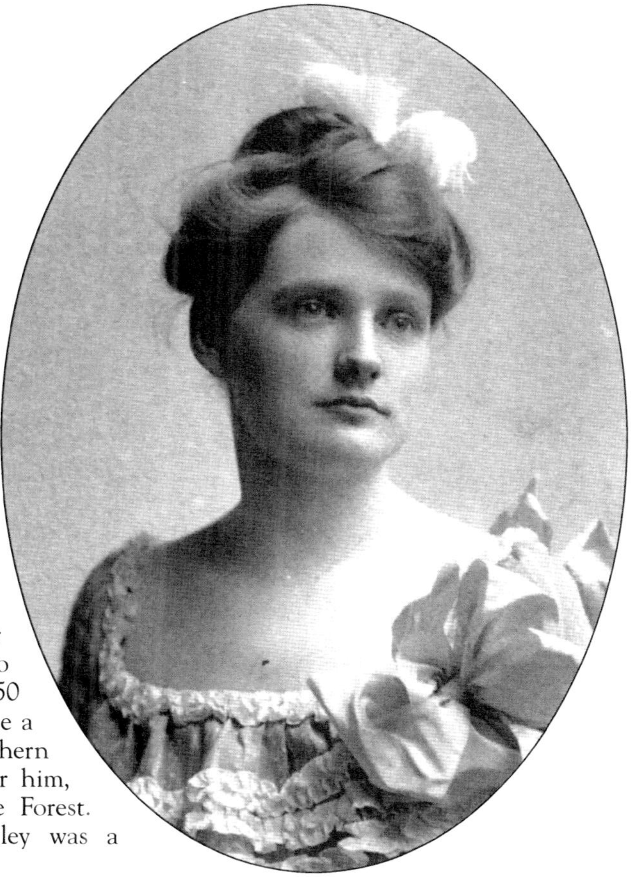

Susan Oakley was the daughter of Dr. Conklin Lewis Oakley, who came to the town of Owego in 1850 from Geneva, New York. He became a prosperous lumberman in the northern part of the town now named after him, Oakley Corners and Oakley State Forest. Susan's brother Timothy B. Oakley was a longtime, well-respected lawyer.

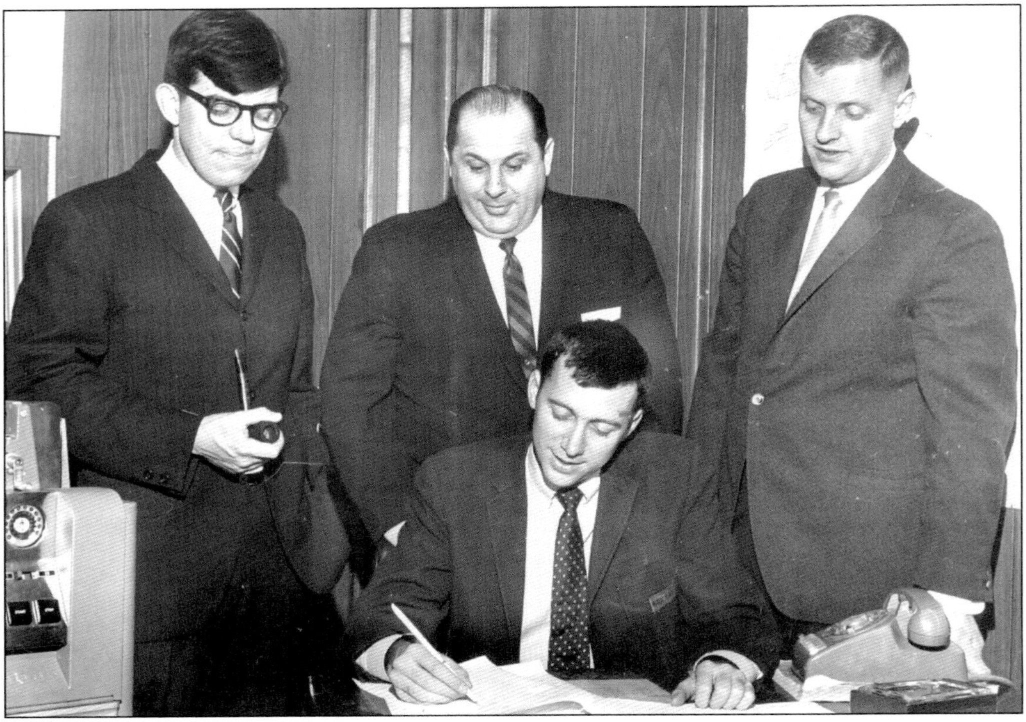

In January 1968, a pact was signed to operate a new motel to be known as the Owego Treadway Inn and construction would start within 90 days. Shown at the signing of the agreement are, from left to right, Ferguson R. Jansen Jr., MNORX vice president; Edward L. Tott of Binghamton, vice president of Owego Associates; and a Mr. Petrolawicz. Seated and signing is Thomas Garrison Morfit Jr., son of television and radio celebrity Garry Moore.

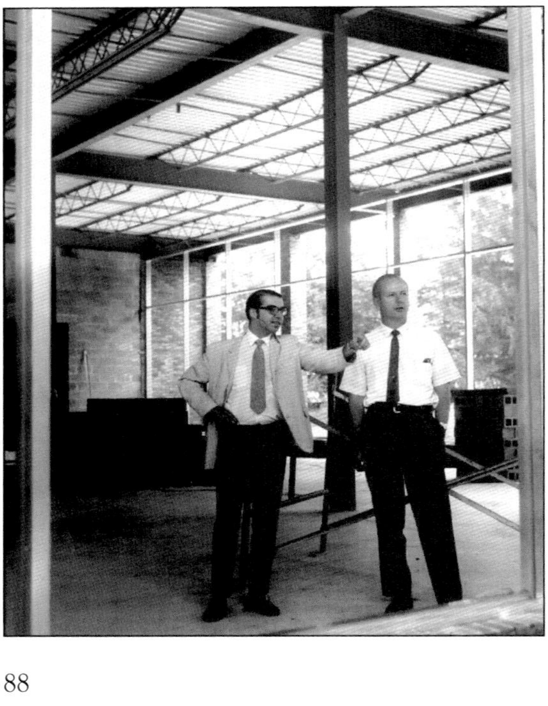

In August 1969, the Owego Treadway Inn was almost completed. Executive Joseph P. Brosnan, right, and innkeeper Teke Kilmer discuss the progress of the $1.5 million project, located on Route 17C. An addition was added later to accommodate large gatherings.

Sara J. Taylor never married and lived on the family farm on Taylor Road all of her life. She was a past regent of the Beulah Patterson-Brown Chapter of the National Society of the Daughters of the American Revolution and was well known in the community.

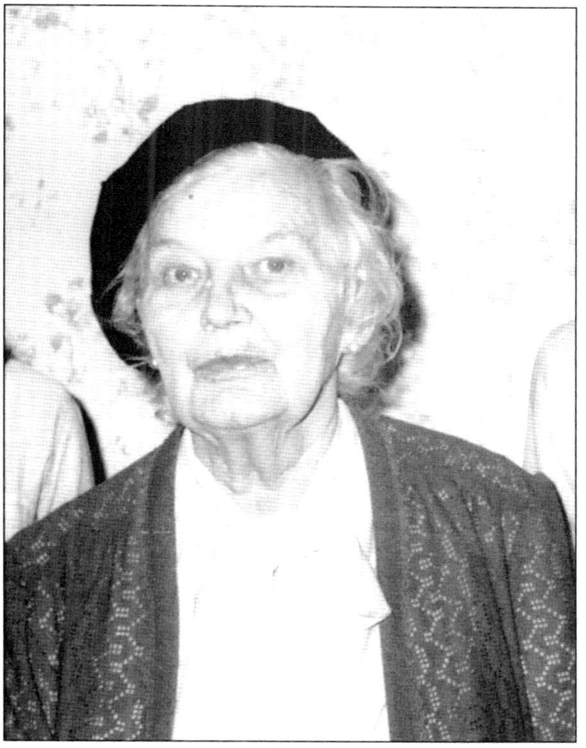

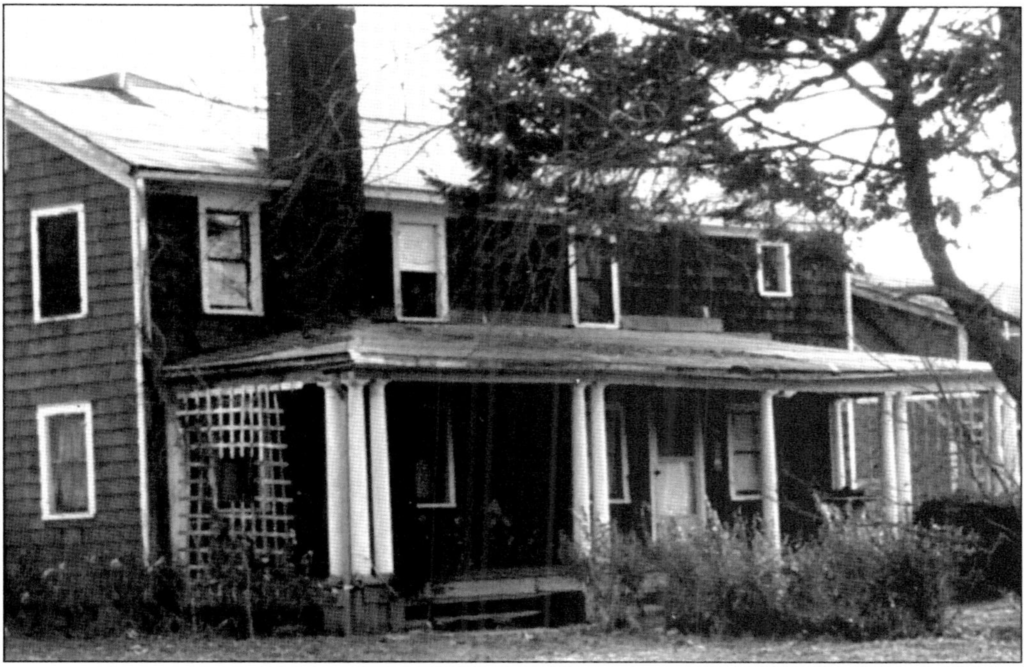

The farmhouse in this photograph was originally the home of Robert J. Taylor on Taylor Road. After the death of Robert and his wife, Estella (Storm) Taylor, their daughter Sara J. lived there for the rest of her life, passing away on August 23, 1986.

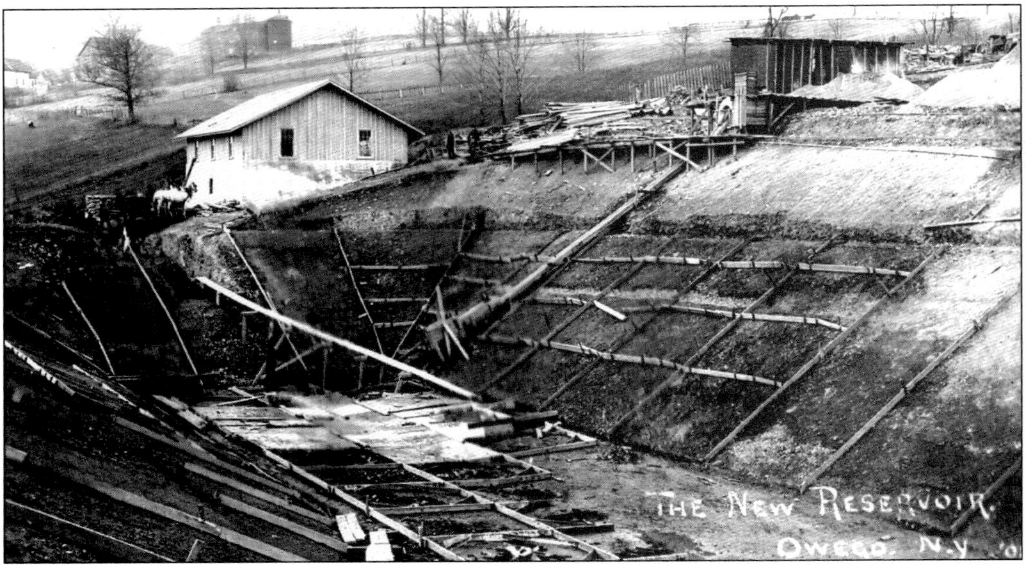

When the village of Owego had a reservoir dug near Barnes Creek in the town of Owego in 1908, many of the laborers were immigrants and worked for little pay. This is a great shot of the work in progress.

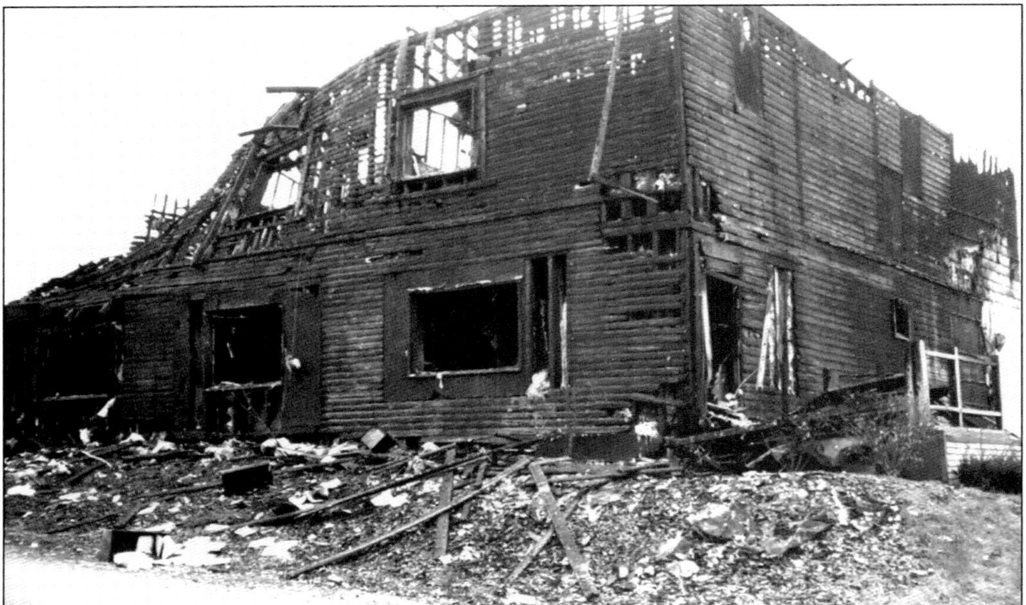

One of the barns on the old Taylor farm was converted into modern offices for an engineering firm in the 1980s, but a huge fire occurred in 1994, and this was all that was left of it.

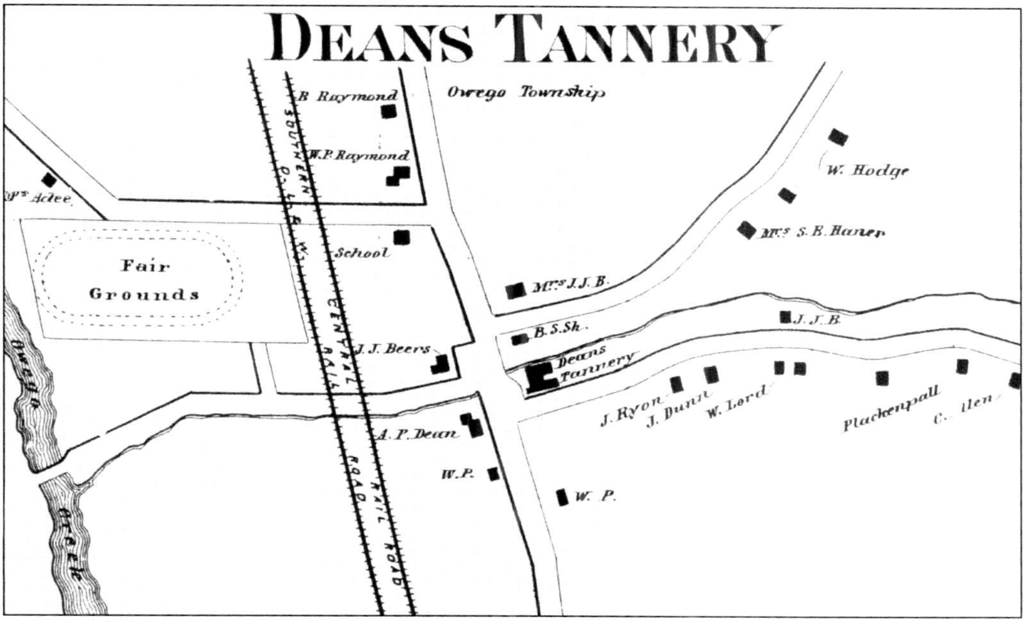

A map of the Dean's Tannery area was included in an 1869 atlas and shows the surrounding neighborhood. Notice the Southern Central Railroad that was in business on the same tracks that the Lehigh Valley Railroad ran later on.

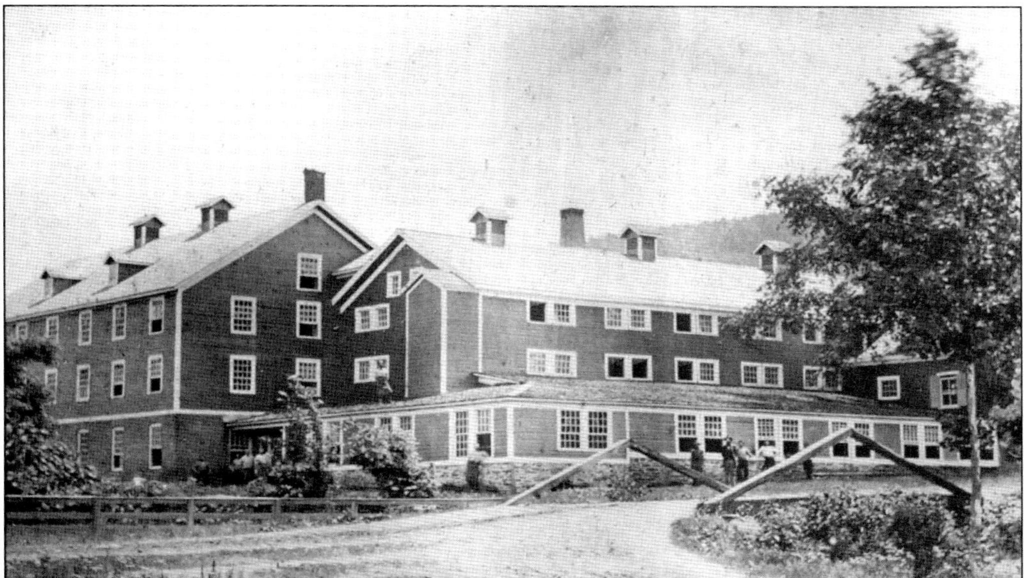

Alanson Dean first purchased the tannery property from Elihu Parmenter in 1862. The tannery was located just outside the village of Owego and was owned and operated by H. Nelson and son Ransom Dean for many years.

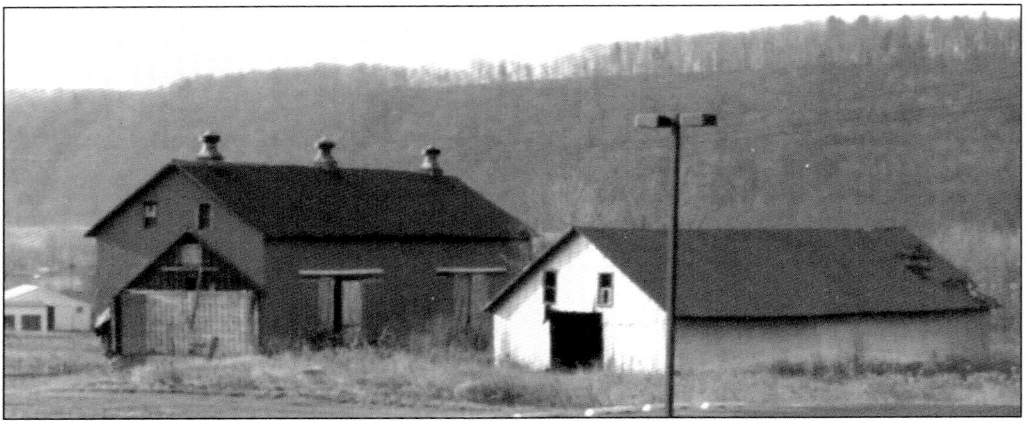

Except for the house, the Taylor barns were just about the last remaining structures of a once-prosperous farm on Taylor Road.

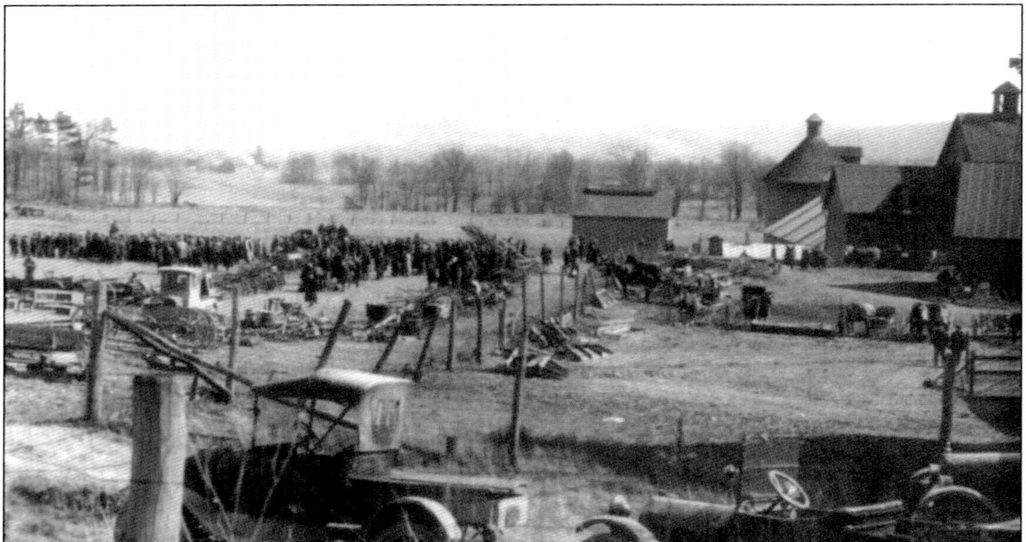

This photograph is believed to be of an auction that was being held at the Taylor farm in the 1930s. When the Depression hit, Robert Taylor was not spared and most of his farm had to be sold.

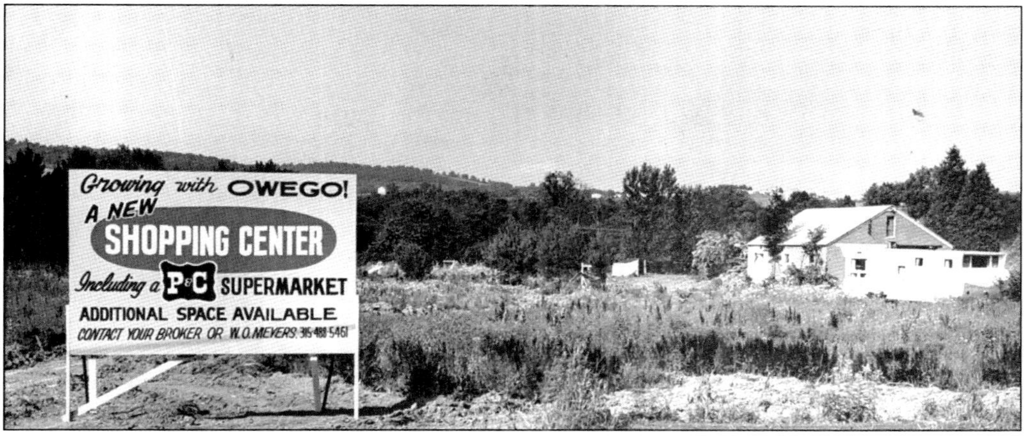

The sign in this August 1967 photograph was good news to a lot of people, but the local residents who lived close by had their doubts about the effect it would have on their properties. The plaza materialized, but a number of homes in the area disappeared to make way for new businesses and for the new Hiawatha Bridge that spanned the river just east of the village.

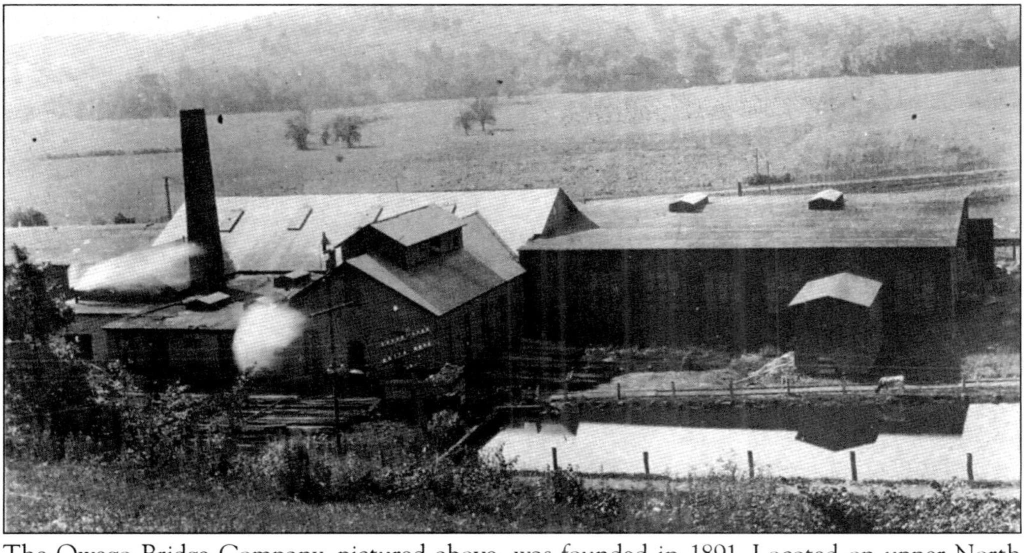

The Owego Bridge Company, pictured above, was founded in 1891. Located on upper North Avenue in the town of Owego, it turned out bridges and structural steel for buildings, and repaired boxcars. It closed in 1927, and today the buildings are used by the Open Door Mission, which operates a homeless shelter and thrift store.

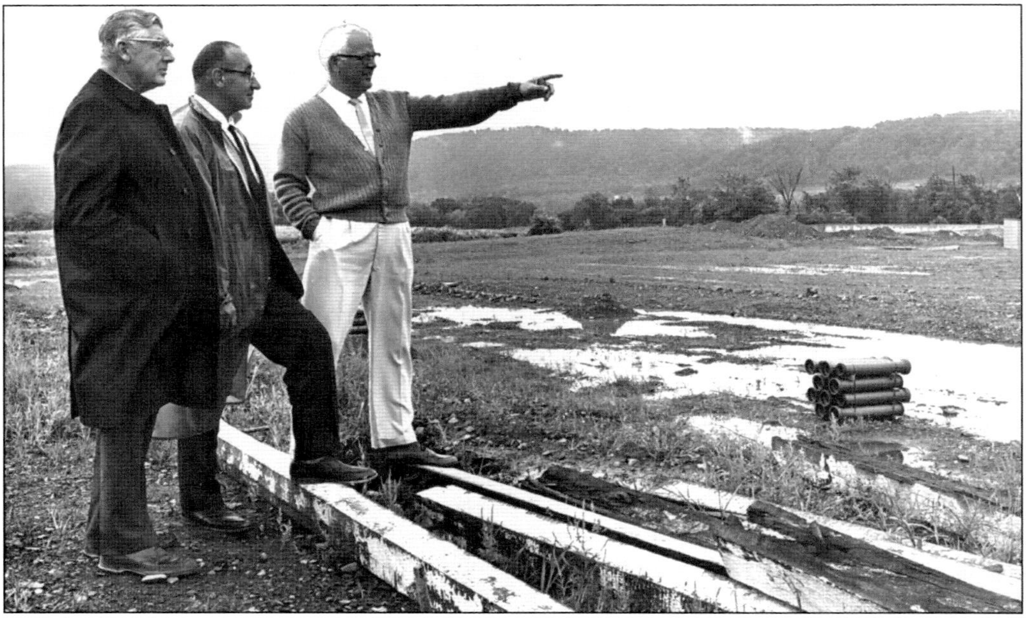

In September 1967, the general manager of Arrowhead Estates of Albany, Merton Litts, points to the spot where his firm has started building an $800,000 shopping center on Taylor Road in the town of Owego. Looking over the site are Town of Owego supervisor Charles Hills, left, and Charles Rich, town planning director.

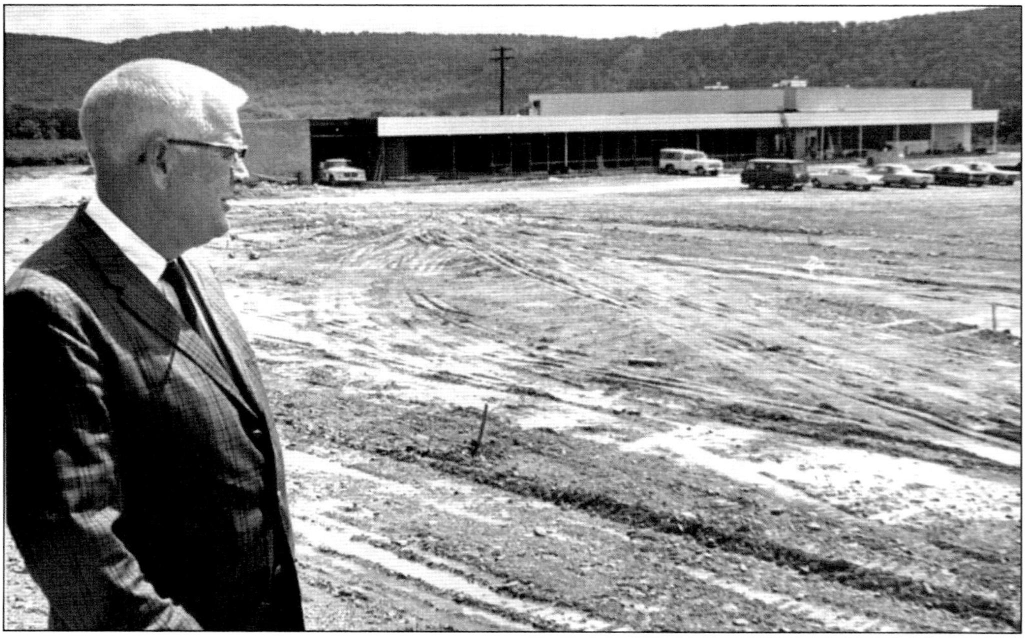

In June 1968, Merton Litts, the general manager for Arrowhead Estates, is observing the progress of a new shopping plaza that is being built on Taylor Road in the town of Owego. It was scheduled to open in July and would include a Victory Market and parking for 650 cars.

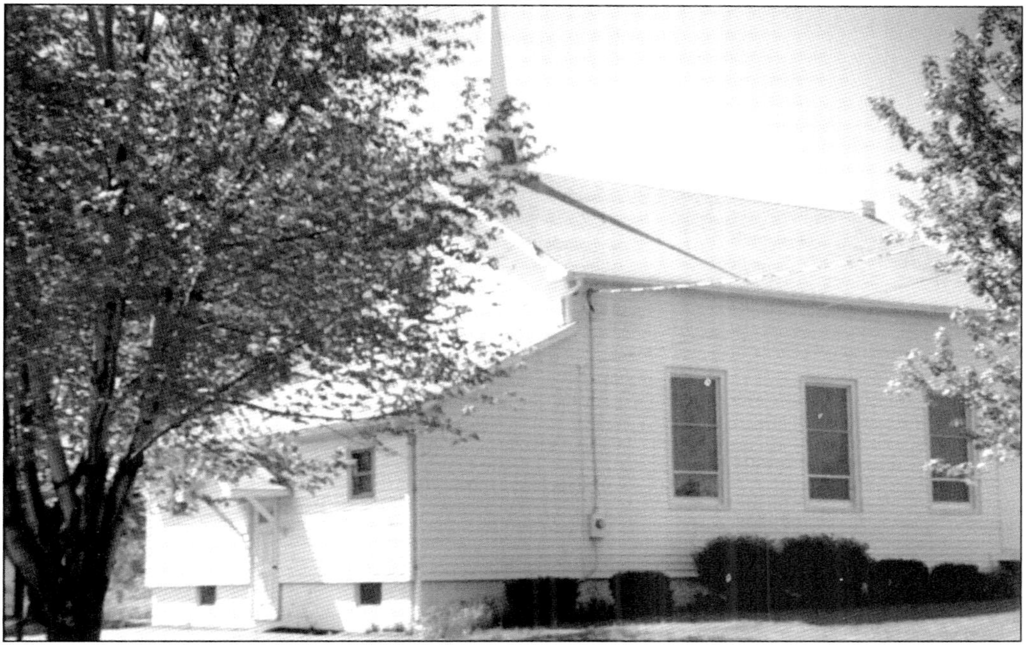

In 1830, Isaac Whittemore was the earliest settler in the area, located in the northeast part of Owego, on Whittemore Hill, near the county line. A Methodist church was built on land he leased to the society for the token sum of $1, so long as the building was used for church purposes. It was dedicated on August 19, 1852, and since that time, it has been used as such. In 1964, 112 years later, his great-great-great-grandson Rev. Norman G. Whittemore became pastor of the church that bears his name, the Whittemore Hill Methodist Church.

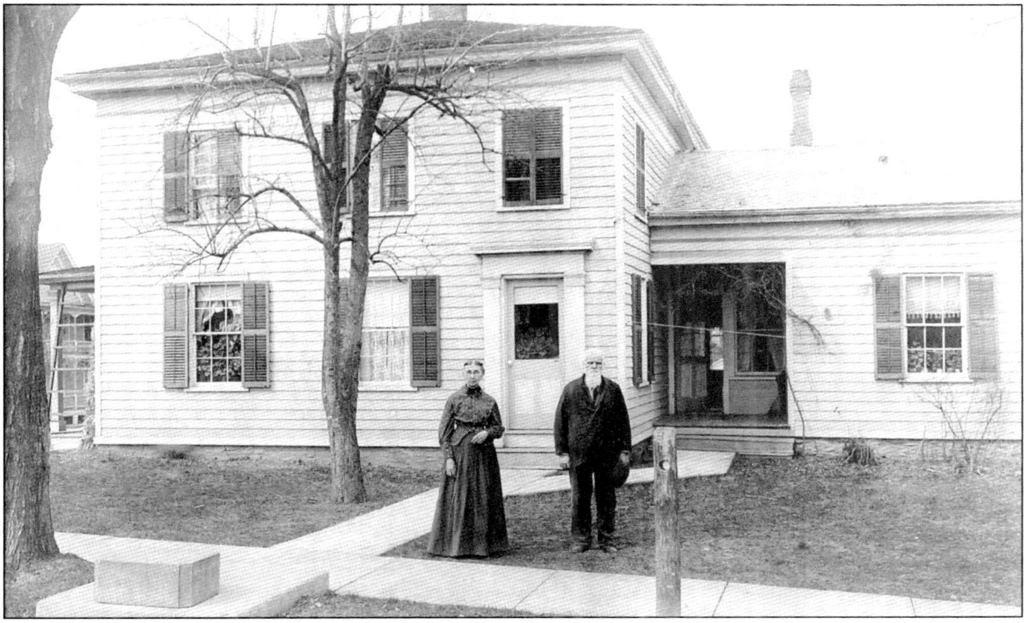

One of Isaac Whittemore's 12 children, Virgil, stands with his wife, Ruth, in front of their fine home on Whittemore Hill on part of his 200-acre farm.

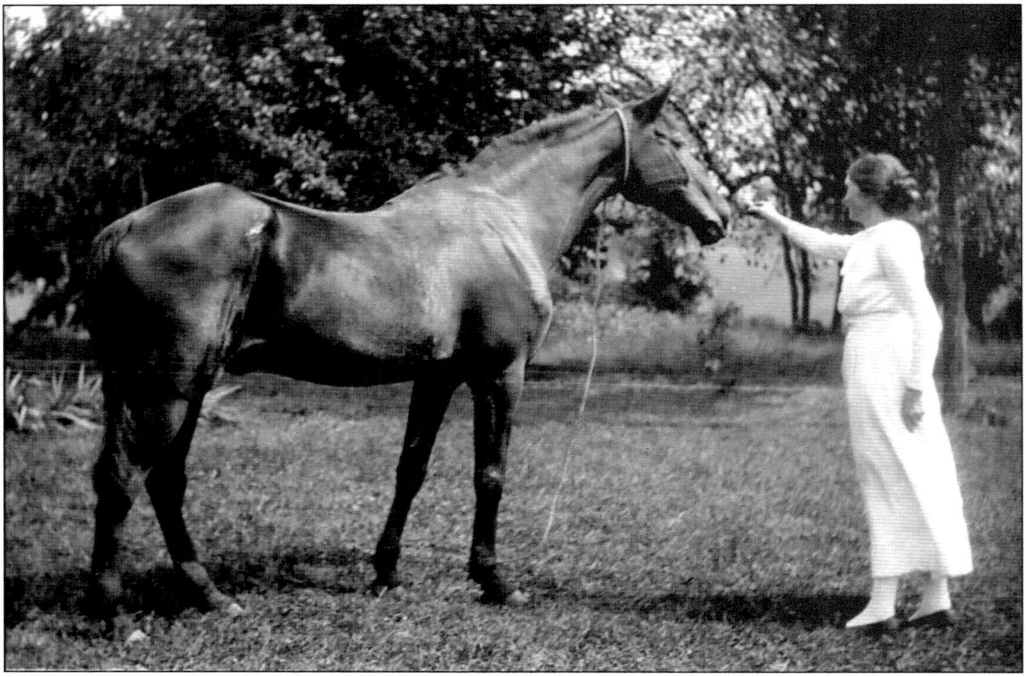

This beautiful horse belongs to Mary Ann Foster of Ivory Foster Road, around 1900. She was a schoolteacher who taught at the Beecher Hill School House in the town of Owego.

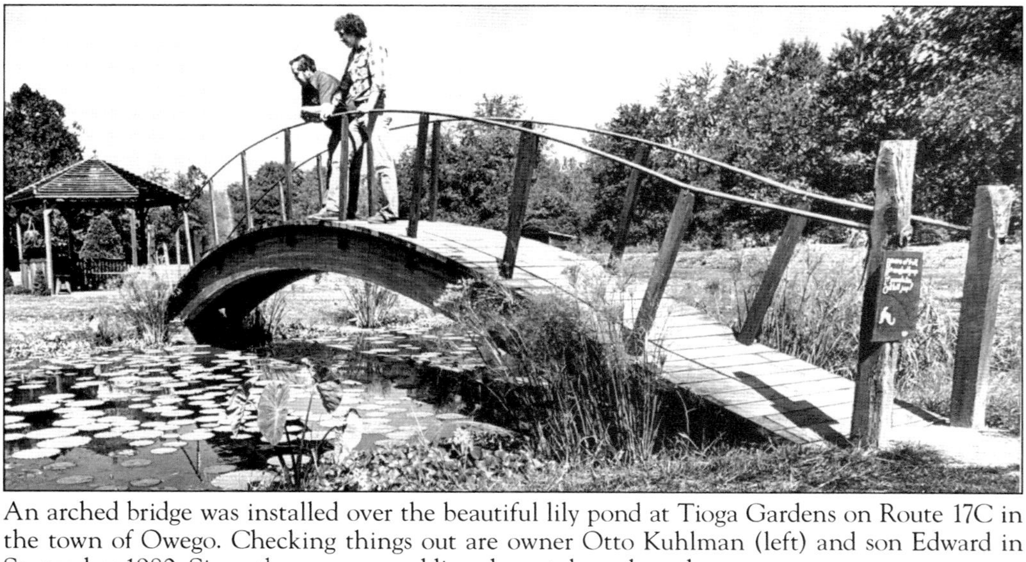

An arched bridge was installed over the beautiful lily pond at Tioga Gardens on Route 17C in the town of Owego. Checking things out are owner Otto Kuhlman (left) and son Edward in September 1980. Since then, many weddings have taken place there.

Seven

River Views

Writing about the town of Owego would not be complete without including the Susquehanna River. It divides the town in two, right across the middle, and its history is powerful, beginning when the Native Americans used it to their advantage, and when it was considered an official highway in 1813. It was the major route for the Sullivan-Clinton campaign during the Revolutionary War. The rafting of logs to Pennsylvania, with every salable object carried on them, even caused the dates for voting to be changed a couple of times, because the men would be gone at election time. The ice, the floods, and even the recreational activities caused major changes in laws to adjust to its presence. A New York State law was passed in 1876 to dredge the river between Owego and Binghamton to accommodate large steamboats carrying passengers to or from Hiawatha Island. Newspapers often reported on the progress of a handmade raft that carried the more adventurous fun-lovers down to Pennsylvania. When the ice broke up during the spring freshets, it was an annual event to gather on the riverbanks or the Court Street Bridge to watch the awesome sight of huge chunks crunching past. The winters today cannot be as cold as they were back then, because there are no more ice floes to watch.

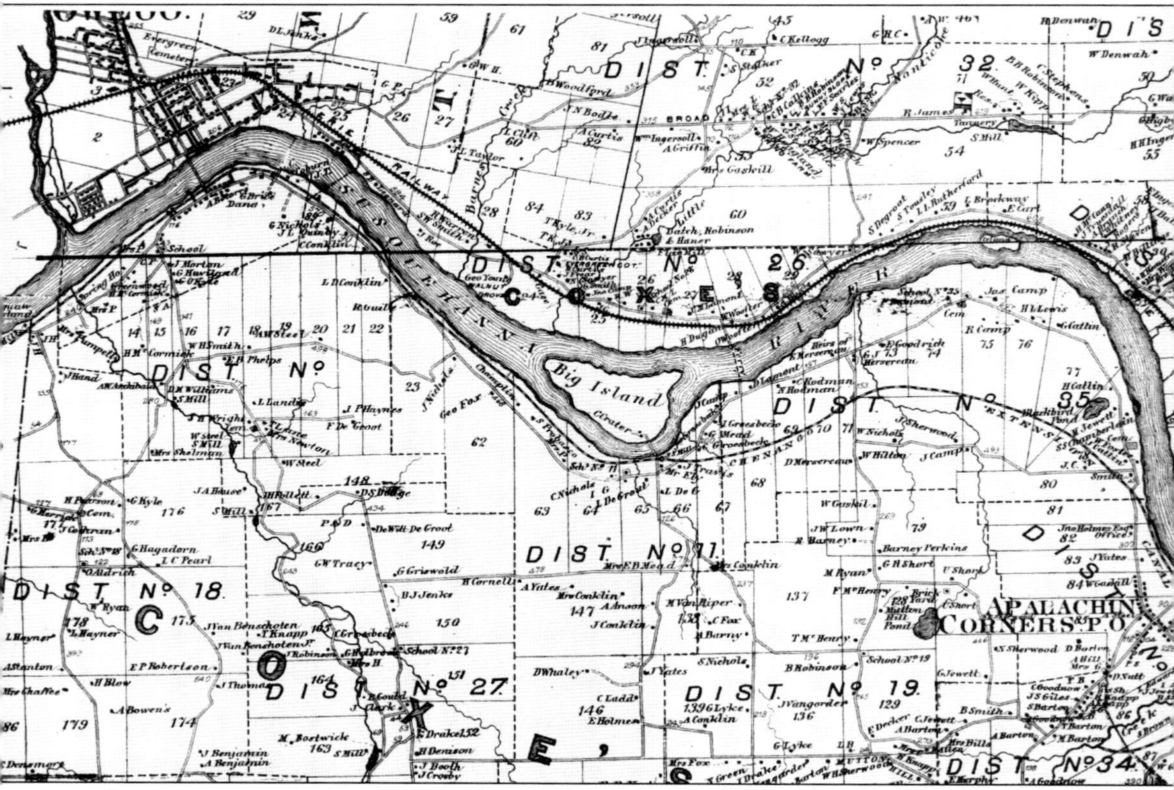

It is easy to see why so many people were drawn to the river, with its curves to challenge their boating and rafting skills or to simply sit on its banks and have a picnic. It had another side to its placid appearance too; many of the homes that were built on its shores often were flooded out.

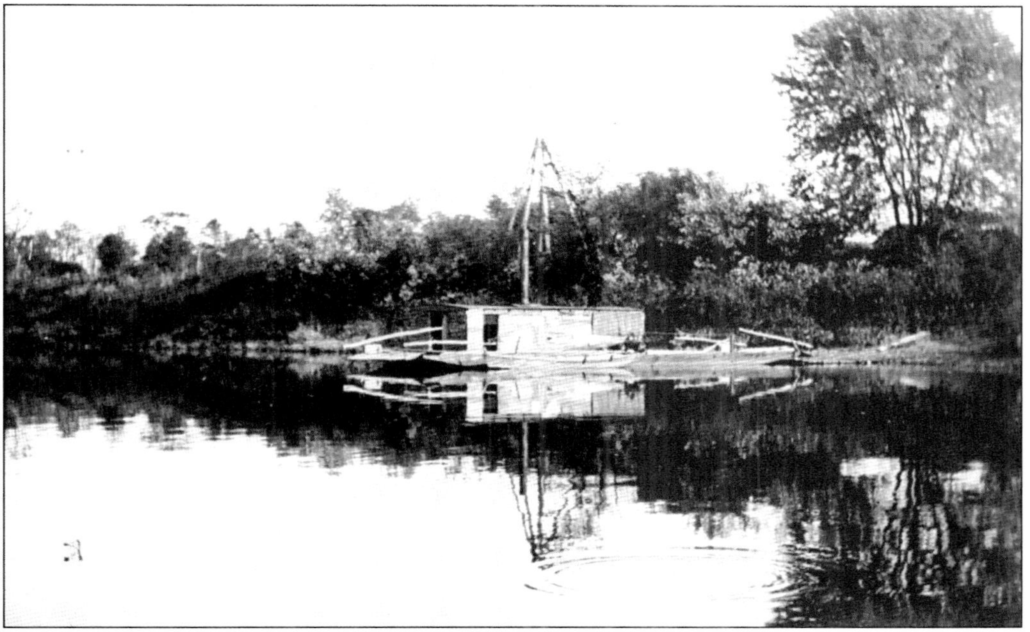

Rensselear Barton operated the Barton Ferry, located about three miles east of the village of Owego from 1873 until he died in 1898. His wife, Effie Ann Frear Barton, took over the running of the ferry until she died in 1911. She had the distinction of being the only woman in the United States to operate a steam ferryboat.

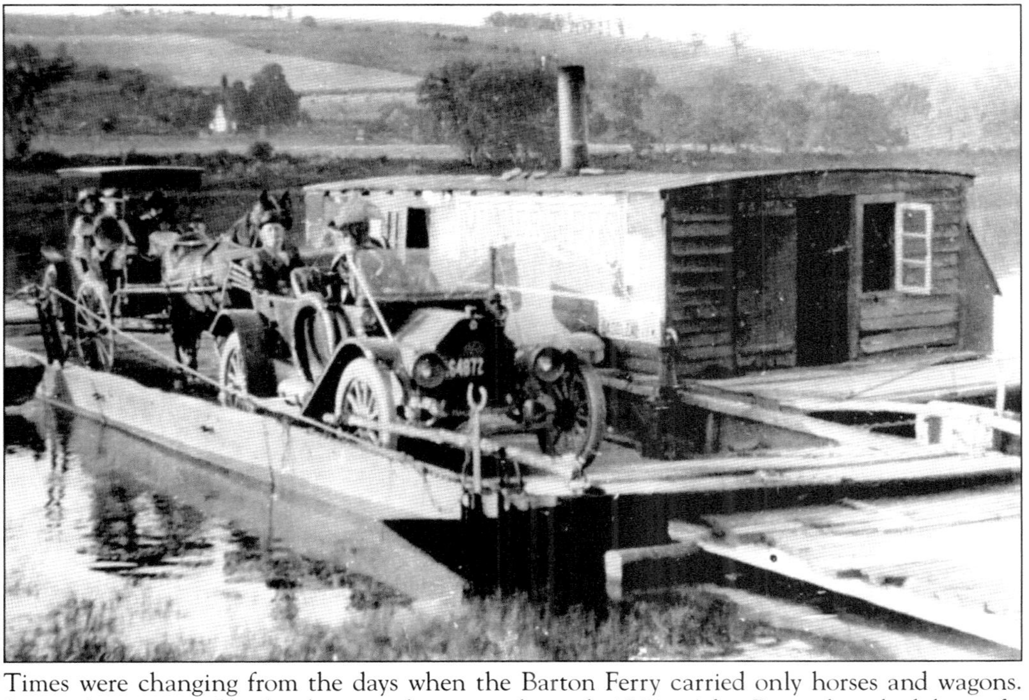

Times were changing from the days when the Barton Ferry carried only horses and wagons. Pictured is a view of both a horse and a car in the early 1900s. After Rensselear died, his wife, Effie Ann, took over the operation.

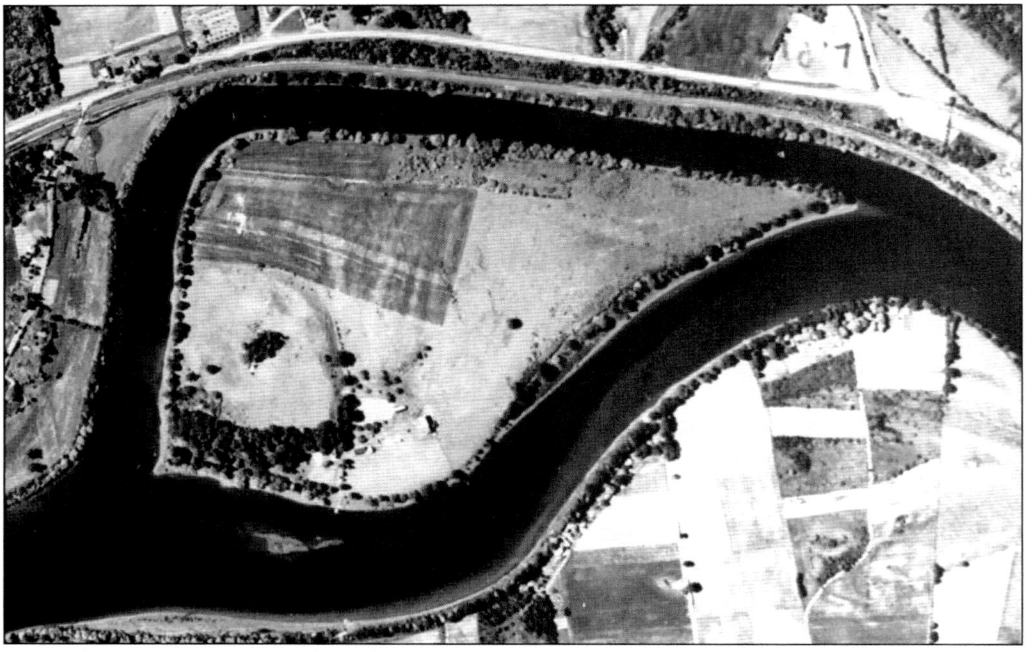

Hiawatha House, on Hiawatha Island, was built in 1876 and razed in 1932. The island was a popular summer resort from 1874 to 1888, and between the years 1876 and 1884, visitors came from 26 states and 9 foreign countries.

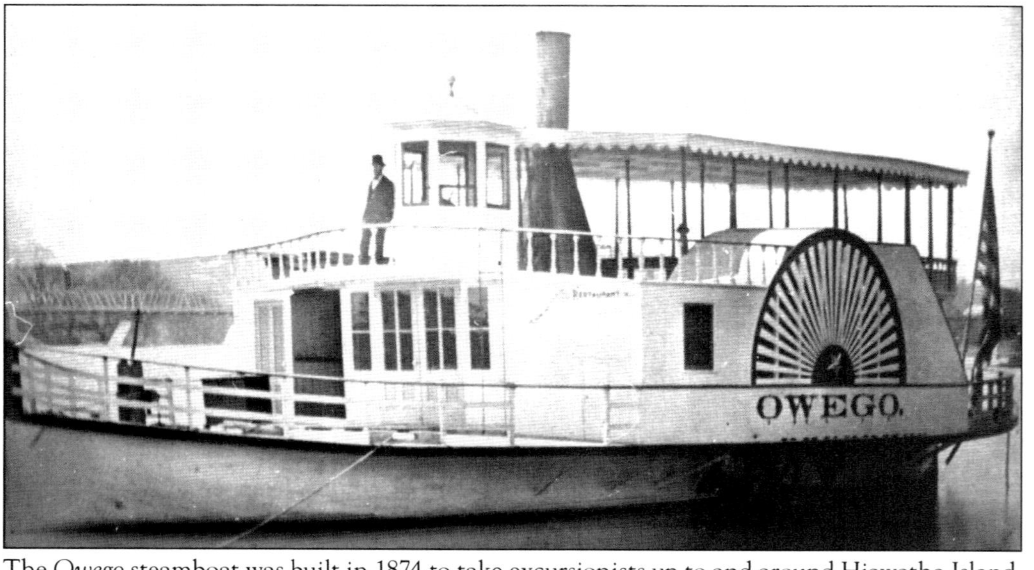

The *Owego* steamboat was built in 1874 to take excursionists up to and around Hiawatha Island. It proved to be so pleasurable that the steamboat company got permission to build a restaurant and dance hall there. It was like lighting a fuse on a firecracker, because it became the rage to sail up the Susquehanna River and join in the fun. The following year a barge was constructed and pulled behind the steamboat to accommodate the crowds.

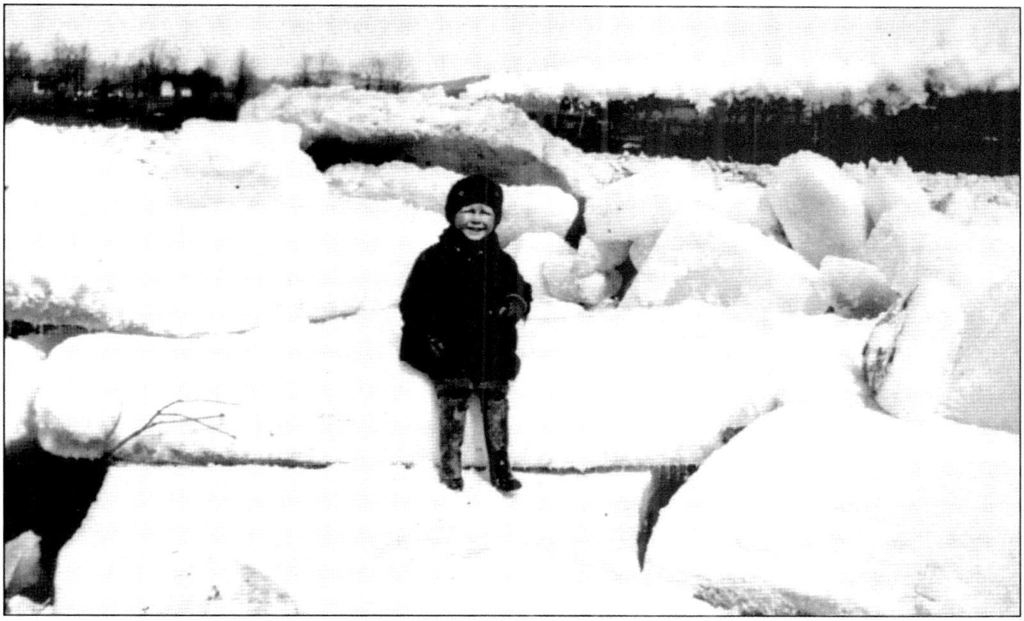

This small boy posing on a huge ice chunk in the Susquehanna River is Paul Longthorpe, whose mother, Vera Livingston Longthorpe Burnett, used to be the owner of Hiawatha Island in the 1920s. She sold most of it but kept two acres for herself until the early 1940s. The white streak of steam in the background is from the engine of an Erie Railroad train.

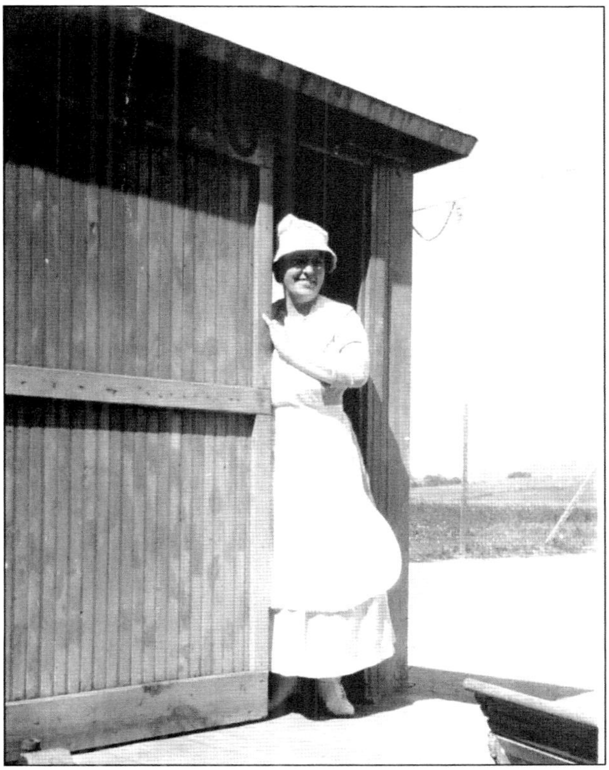

Peeking out from one of the buildings on the mainland across from Hiawatha Island, Florence Sleeper of Binghamton seems pretty content with the surroundings

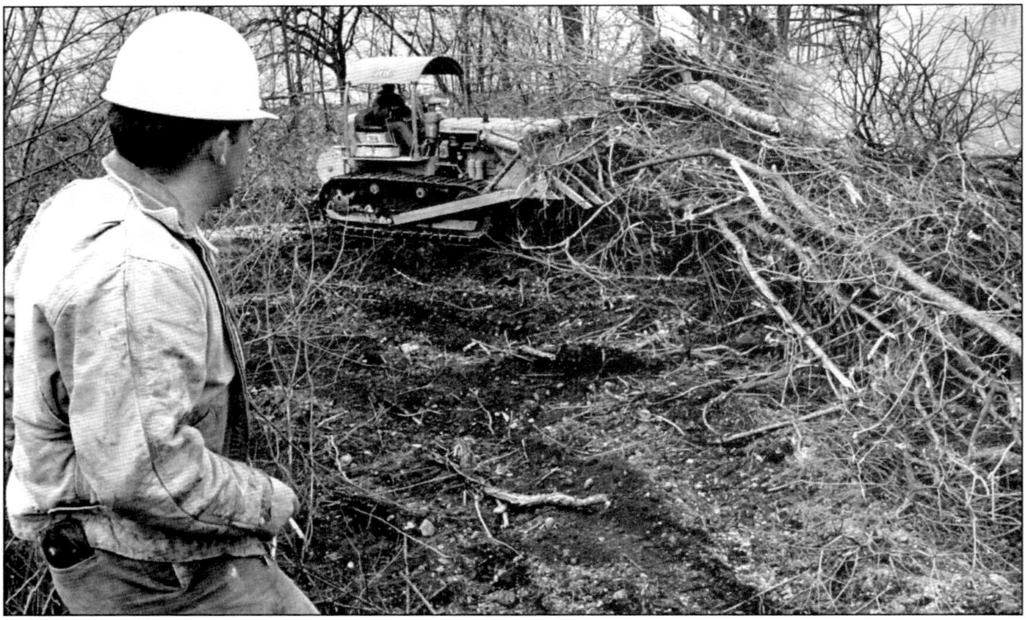

David Heaser (left), superintendent for Humphrey Construction Company, of Wichita, Kansas, supervises clearing of the right-of-way off Route 17 for the proposed bridge over the Susquehanna River, east of Owego. With the river in the background, Robert Manning of Binghamton operates the bulldozer.

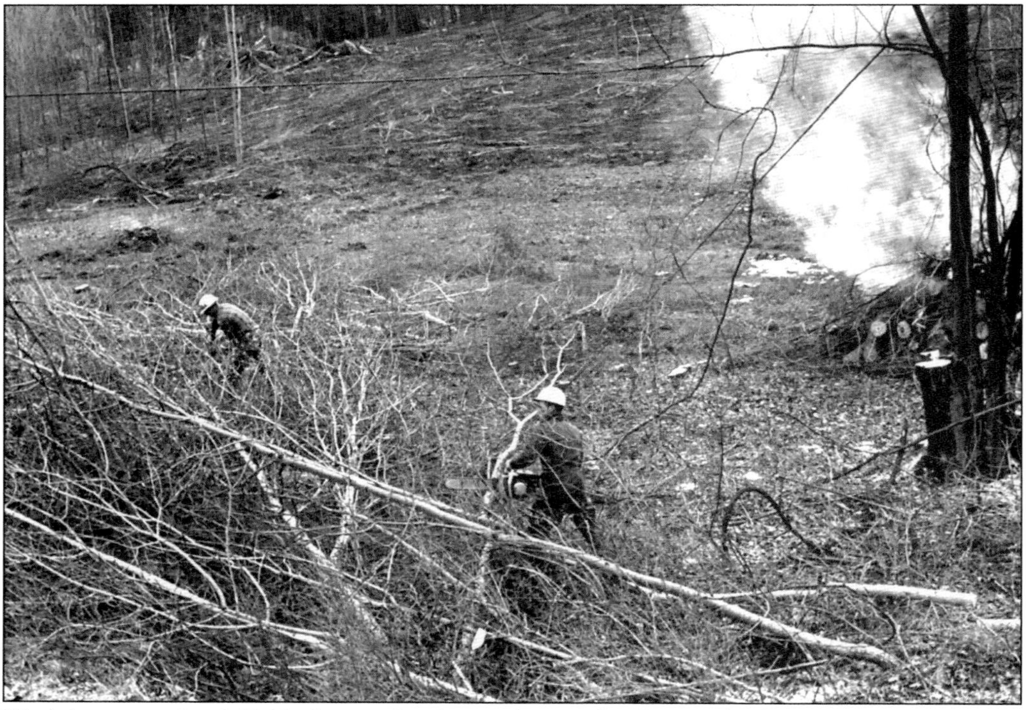

Work began in April 1966, clearing land to make way for the new bridge that would be put in near IBM, crossing from Route 17C to Routes 17 and 434 on the south side of the river.

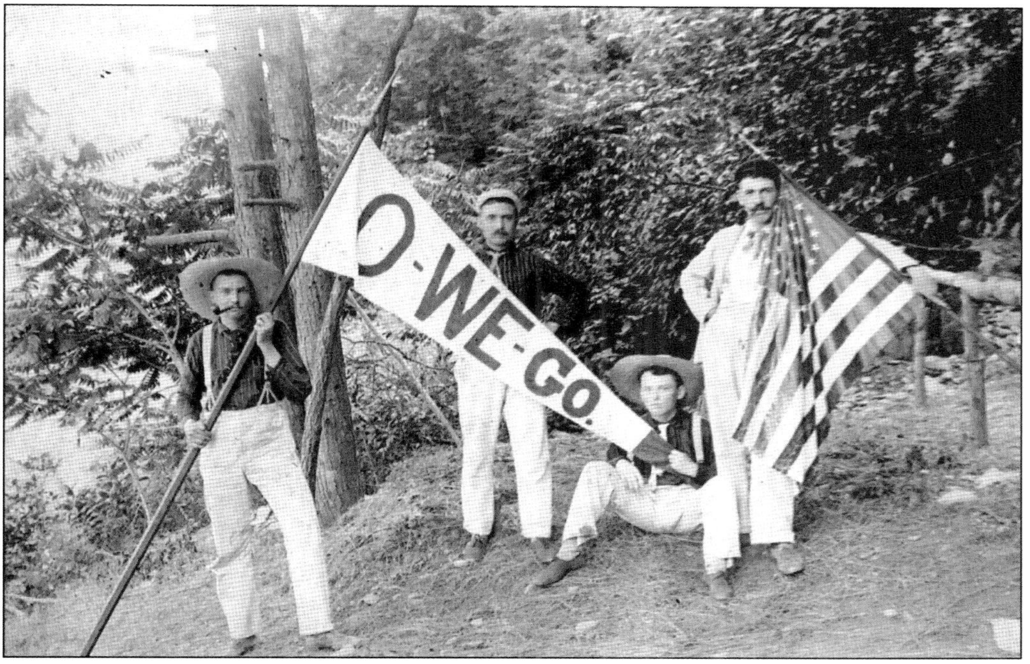

These unidentified rafters look as though they are enjoying themselves. They have probably stopped for a rest and posed for this photograph, displaying their flags.

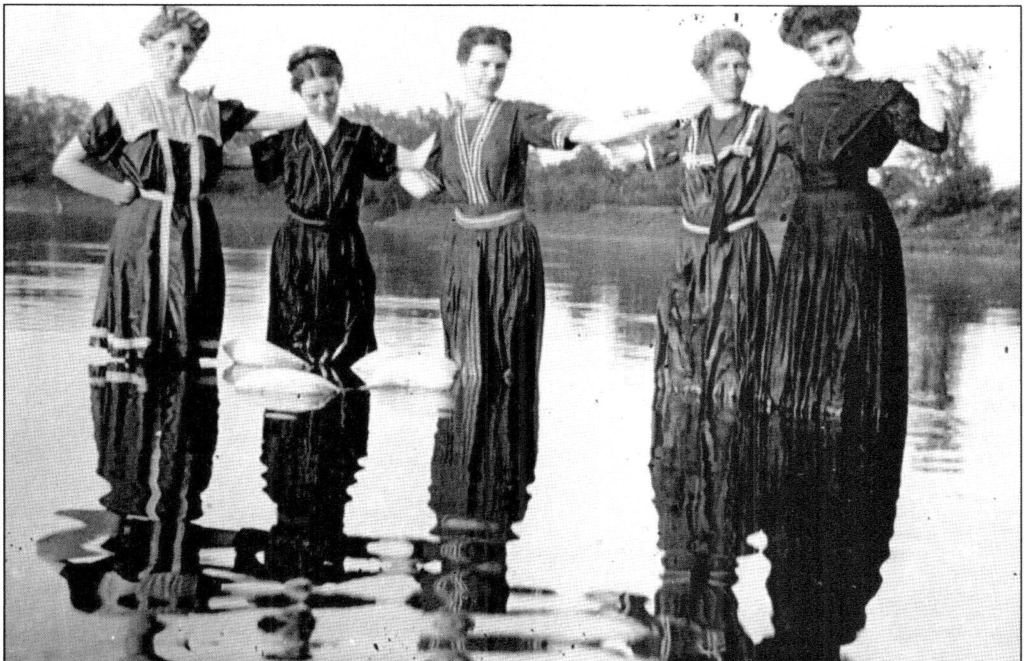

It is easy to understand why bathing suits today are so skimpy after looking at how cumbersome the suits were back in 1910. The group of girls shown in this photograph is from Binghamton and was staying at the cottages across from Hiawatha Island.

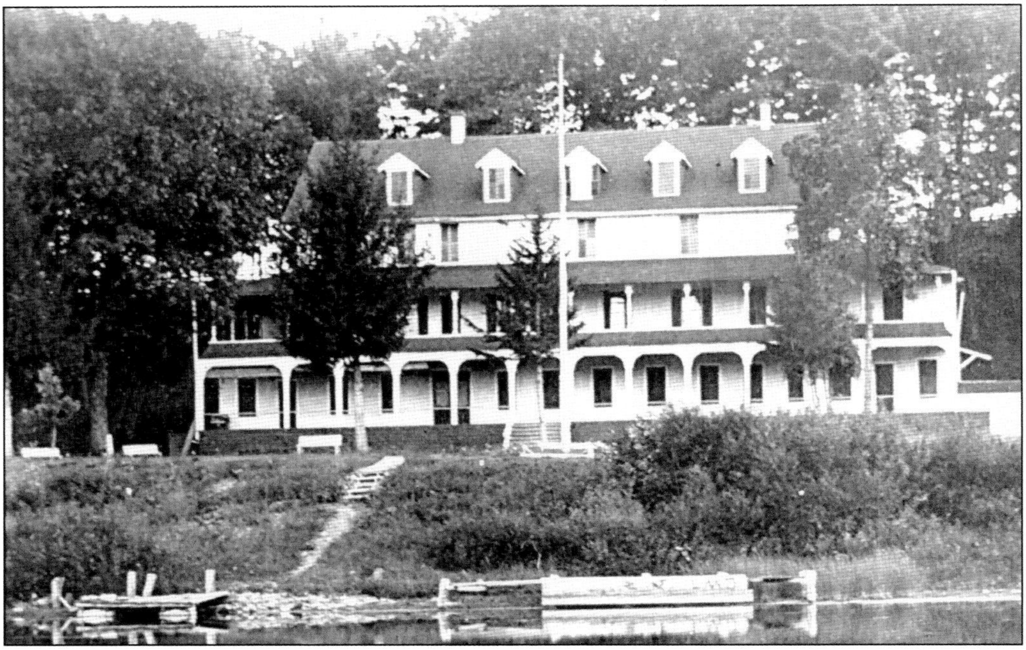

Visitors to Hiawatha Island today cannot believe that this beautiful hotel, the Hiawatha House, once stood there. It was built in 1876, when the island became a popular summer resort. After the island was sold in 1888, it was closed to the public and privately owned by Dr. Andrus S. and Jonas Kilmer of Binghamton. Since 1900, the island changed hands several times, and by 1932, the hotel was in such ruin that the owner had it razed.

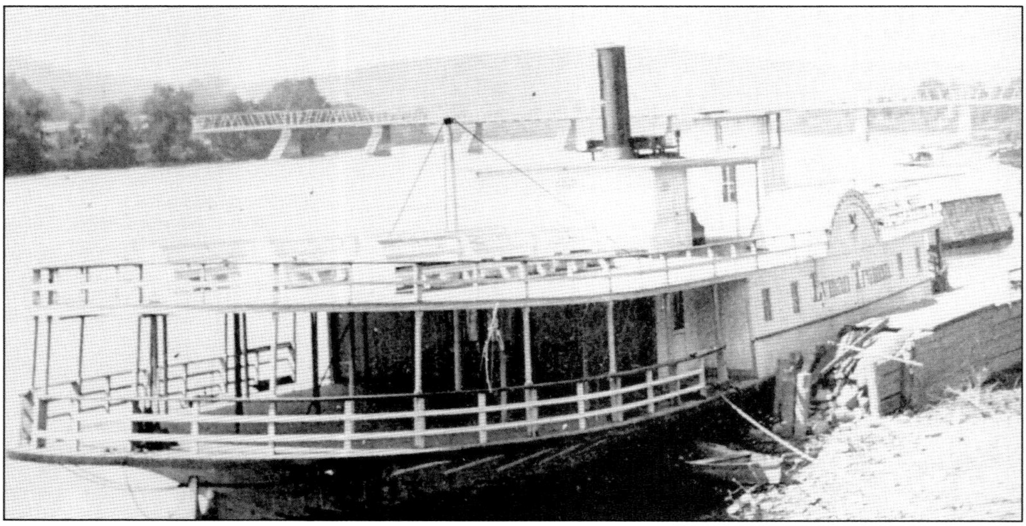

Because the *Owego* steamboat was too small to handle the crowds, it was sold, and the *Lyman Truman* was built to take its place in 1876, the same year a hotel was built on the island. This boat, too, was built on the riverbank, just below the Court Street Bridge. Crowds of curious onlookers came to see a huge 120-foot boat launched on March 9, 1876, into the muddy river.

This is one of the posters that lured thousands of visitors to Hiawatha Grove on Hiawatha Island in 1874. The steamboat *Owego* left on schedule from docks in the village, and the fun-seekers were not disappointed. Young couples especially loved to go there for dancing until the wee hours and to return on a moonlight trip back to the village of Owego.

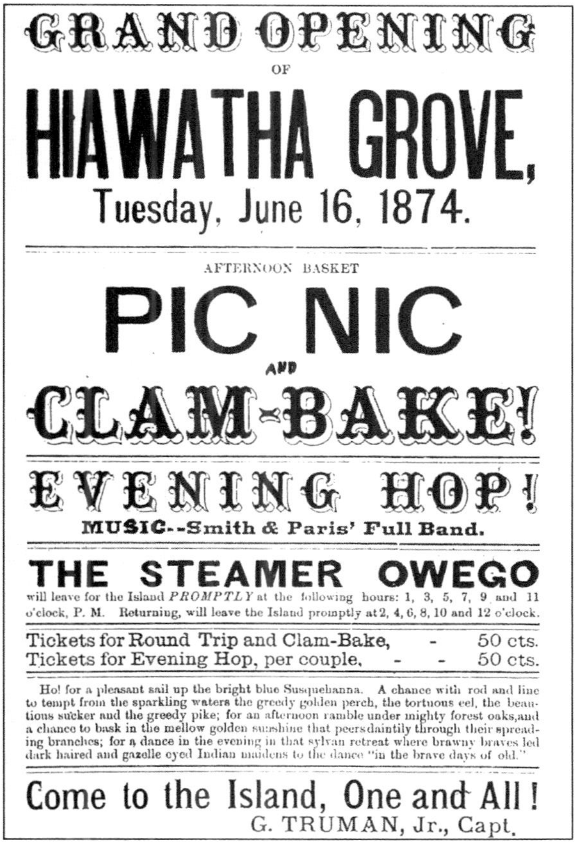

GRAND OPENING

OF

HIAWATHA GROVE,

Tuesday, June 16, 1874.

AFTERNOON BASKET

PIC NIC

AND

CLAM-BAKE!

EVENING HOP!

MUSIC--Smith & Paris' Full Band.

THE STEAMER OWEGO

will leave for the Island *PROMPTLY* at the following hours: 1, 3, 5, 7, 9 and 11 o'clock, P. M. Returning, will leave the Island promptly at 2, 4, 6, 8, 10 and 12 o'clock.

Tickets for Round Trip and Clam-Bake, - 50 cts.
Tickets for Evening Hop, per couple, - - 50 cts.

Ho! for a pleasant sail up the bright blue Susquehanna. A chance with rod and line to tempt from the sparkling waters the greedy golden perch, the tortuous eel, the beautious sucker and the greedy pike; for an afternoon ramble under mighty forest oaks, and a chance to bask in the mellow golden sunshine that peers daintily through their spreading branches; for a dance in the evening in that sylvan retreat where brawny braves led dark haired and gazelle eyed Indian maidens to the dance "in the brave days of old."

Come to the Island, One and All!

G. TRUMAN, Jr., Capt.

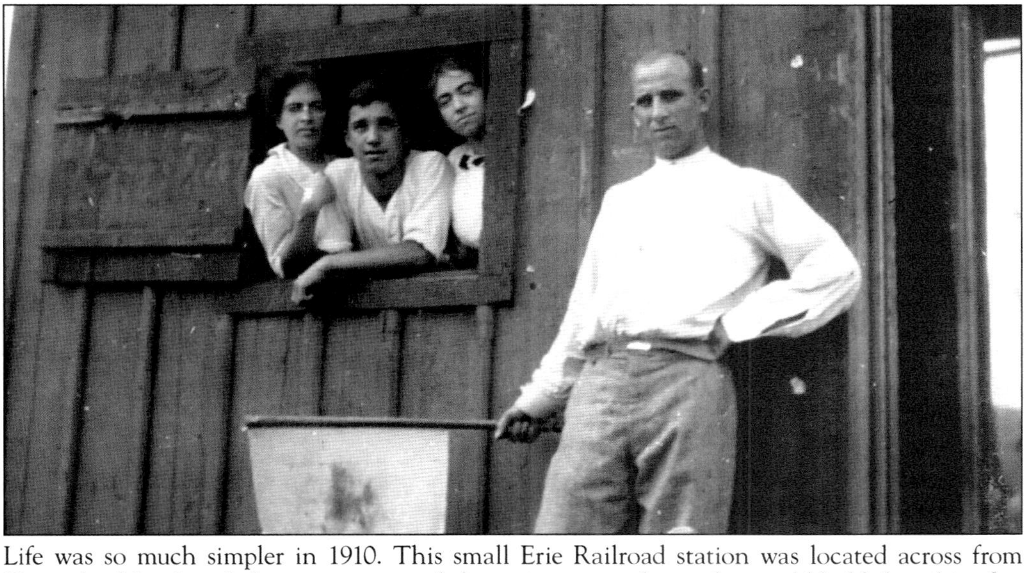

Life was so much simpler in 1910. This small Erie Railroad station was located across from Hiawatha Island, and if someone wanted the train to stop, he or she would hold the white flag out. The people shown here are visitors from Binghamton who vacationed at the cottages on the north side of Hiawatha Island.

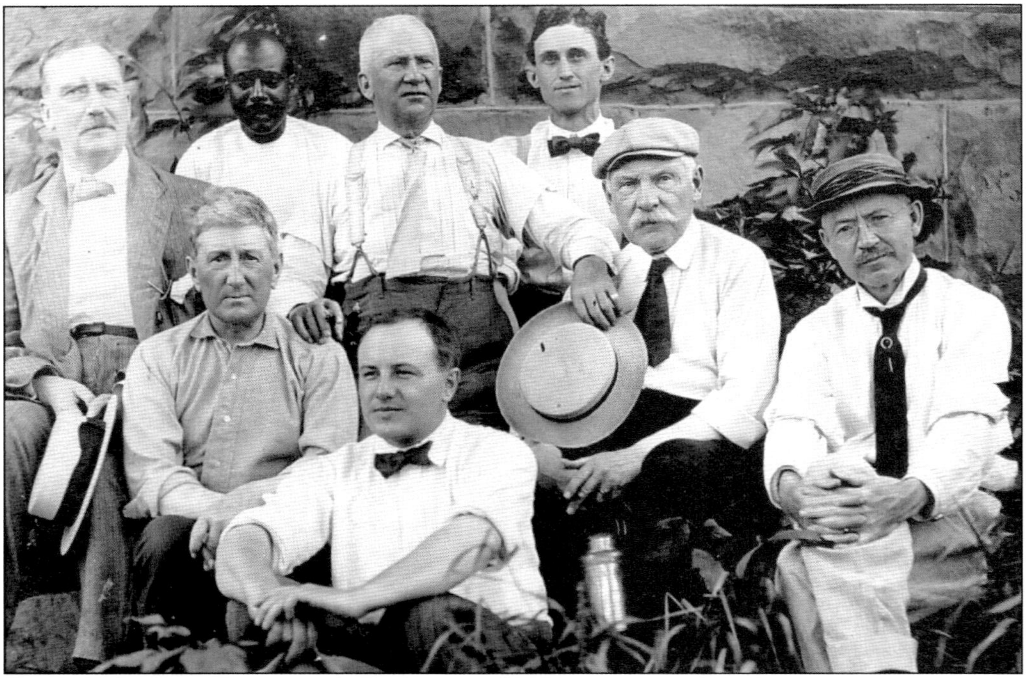

The *Tioga* houseboat crew is seen resting under the Ulster Bridge in Pennsylvania in August 1910.

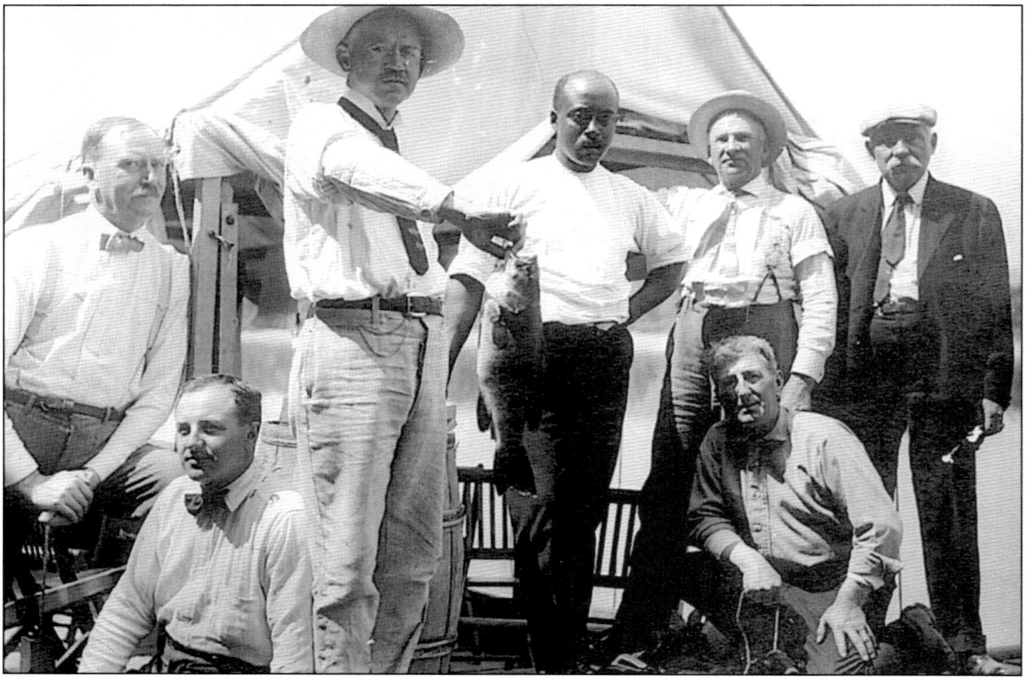

The Hortons of Owego were avid houseboat enthusiasts. In August 1910, they traveled down the river in their houseboat, the *Tioga*. Shown are Leslie S. Horton (seated left), George Henry Horton (kneeling), and H. J. Williams (standing with hand on hip). The others are unidentified.

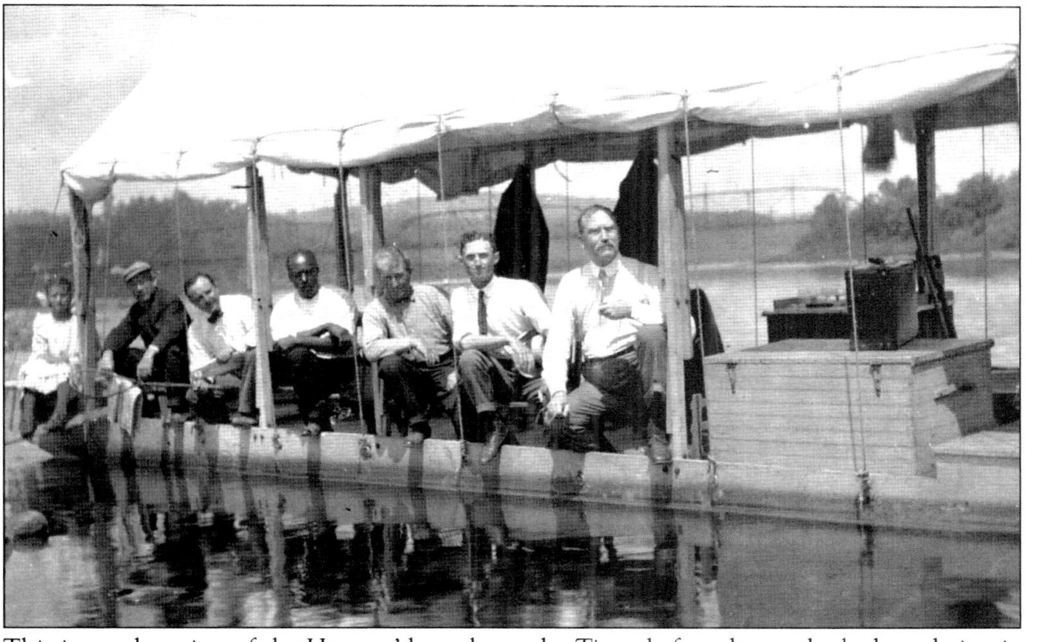

This is another view of the Hortons' houseboat, the *Tioga*, before they embarked on their trip in August 1910. Pictured are Leslie S. Horton (third from right), H. J. Williams (center), and George Henry Horton (third from left). The girl on extreme left and the man next to her, as well as the two men on the extreme right, are unidentified.

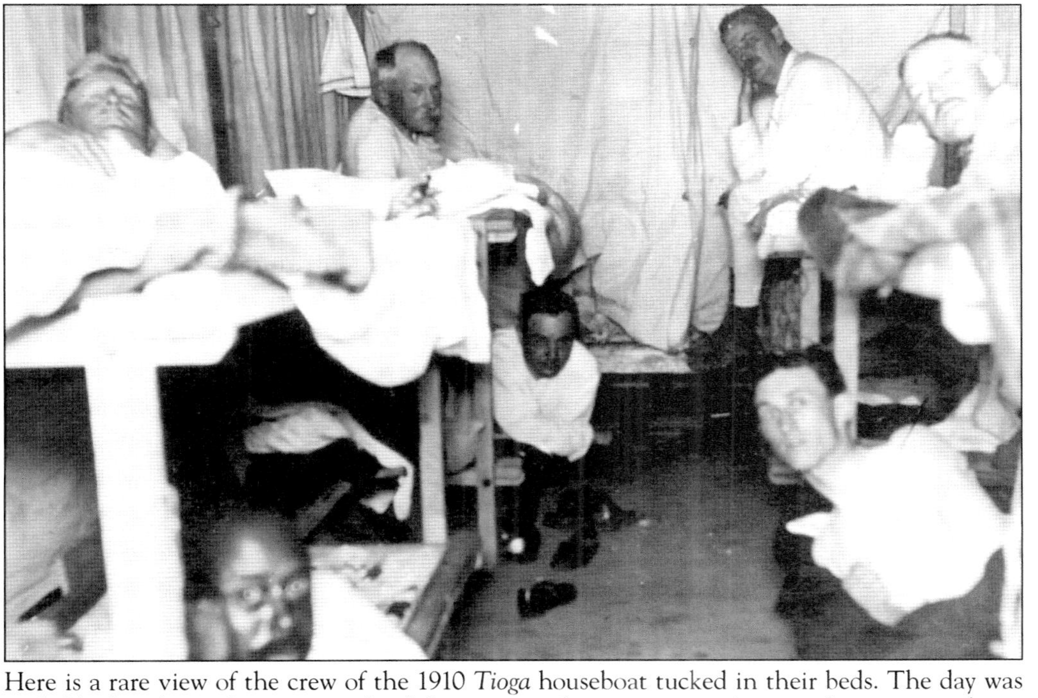

Here is a rare view of the crew of the 1910 *Tioga* houseboat tucked in their beds. The day was probably fun, but exhausting and exhilarating at the same time. Among those pictured are, Leslie S. Horton, George Henry Horton, and H. J. Williams.

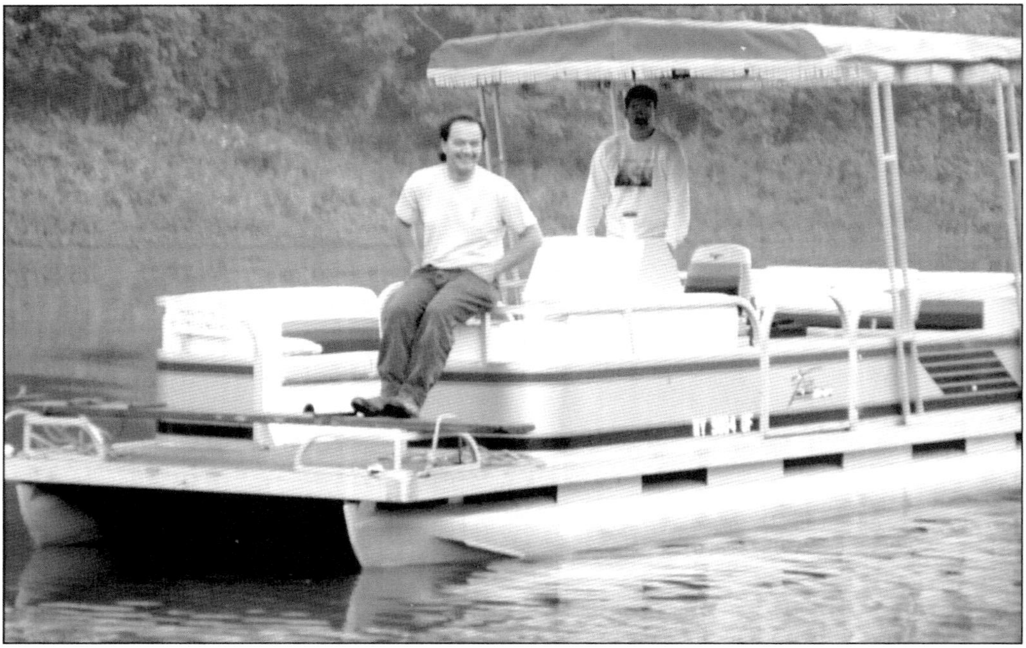

Fran Dunbar, sitting, and Dave Vogel, the driver, pilot a pontoon boat near Hiawatha Island in 1992. A concerned citizens' group, known as the Hiawatha Purchase Committee, carried visitors to and from the island for numerous fund-raising events in an effort to save the island from land developers.

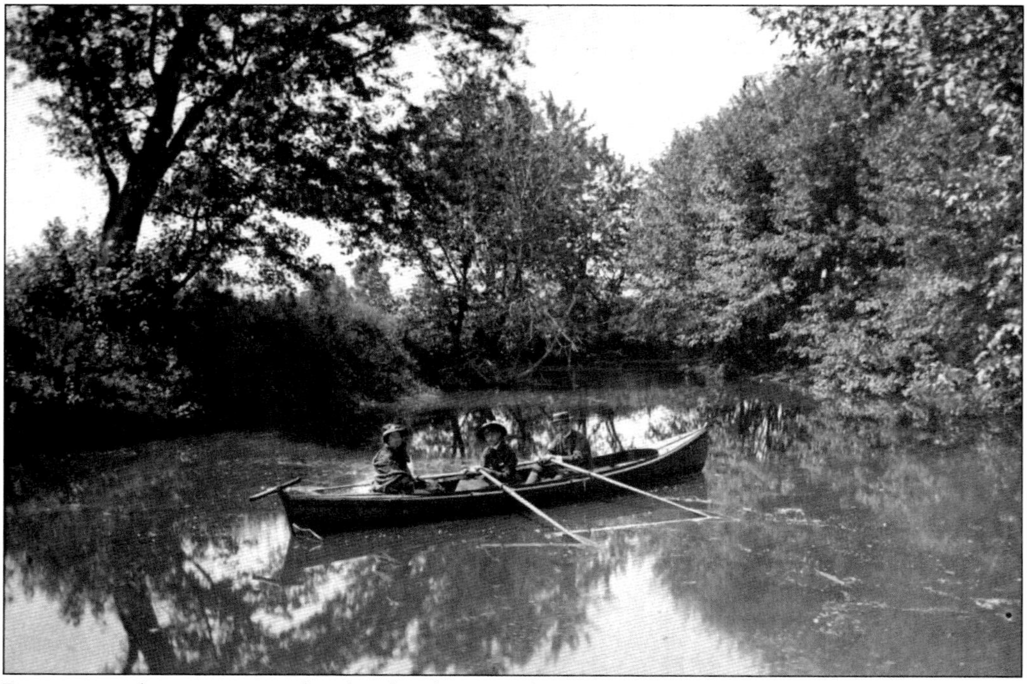

Rowing on the river seemed to be the thing to do on a warm, sunny afternoon. This group is enjoying the quiet surroundings of Little Nanticoke Creek.

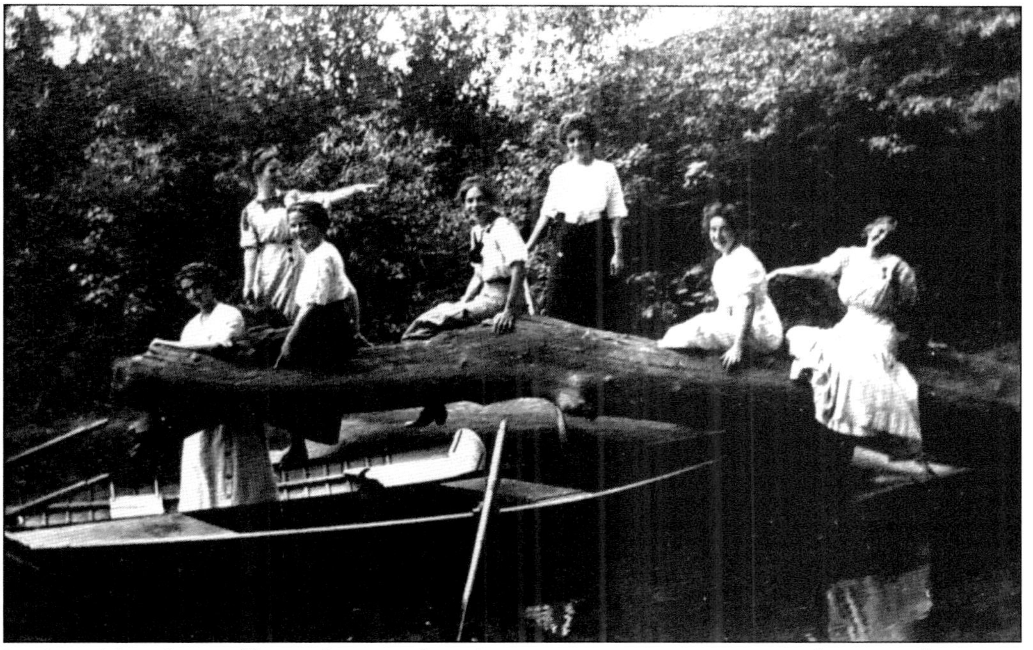

Looking like a bevy of butterflies on a log, these young women were part of a group that came from Binghamton and stayed in the cottages on the north side of Hiawatha Island in 1910. They are in the Nanticoke Creek, which runs through the Hickories Park and empties into the Susquehanna River.

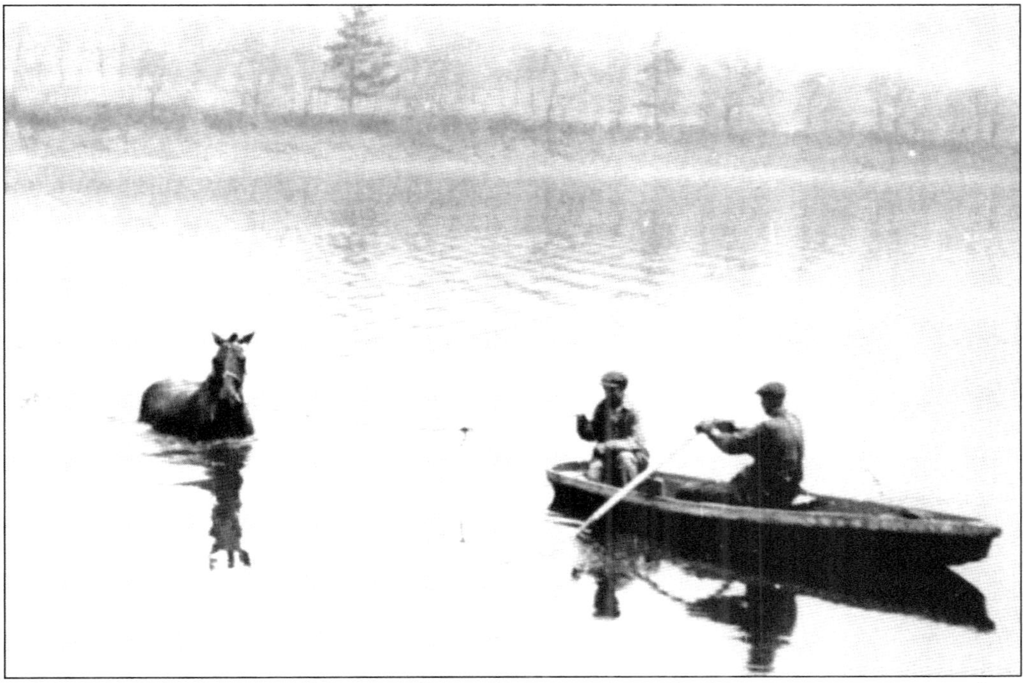

Walking your horse across the Susquehanna River at Hiawatha Island is one way to get him there when the water is low. Bill Burnett rows while stepson Paul Longthorpe holds the rope.

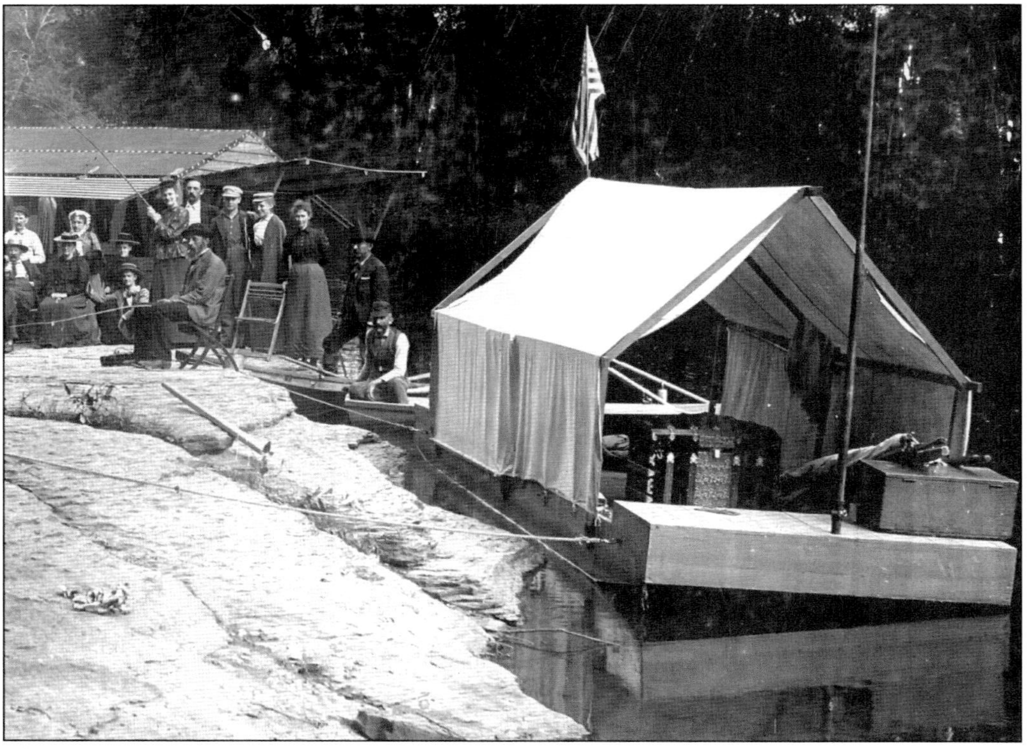

The houseboat *Tige* made more than one trip down the river. Here in 1893, the boaters tied up to shore at Keelers Eddy in Pennsylvania to picnic with their friends.

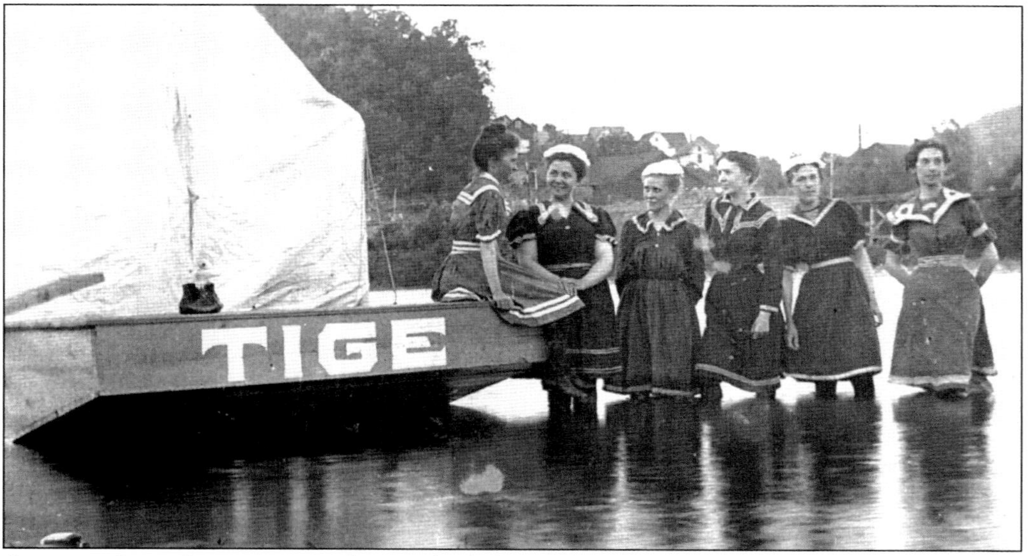

On a trip down the river, around 1893, the ladies of the houseboat *Tige* went for a dip. Wearing the latest fashions in swimwear, they are only up to their knees. Perhaps they do not want to get them wet.

Eight

Village Views

The village of Owego is the county seat and was incorporated in 1827. Native American artifacts have been uncovered over the years and explain why so many names used are derived from them, such as Ahwaga, Owego, Susquehanna, and Tioga. Beginning at the start of the 19th century, hundreds of wagons a day came from Ithaca with commodities such as salt, plaster, lathes, whiskey, and potatoes to load onto rafts from the village to ports in Pennsylvania and even as far as Havre de Grace, Maryland. After the Erie Railroad came through to Owego in 1849, roads were built, and transportation was improved, resulting in business expansion and an increase in population. Many who came were educated and refined, including doctors and lawyers—people who set a standard of living for the community and became leaders. Supreme Court justice of the United States John J. Taylor; Raphael Pumpelly, once the world's leading geologist; U. S. congressman Thomas Platt; New York State Supreme Court judges John M. and Charles E. Parker; and Helen Dean King, recognized for her scientific achievements, are just a few of them whose homes are still being occupied and beautifully maintained to this day. As a result, districts on Front and Main Streets have been placed on the National and New York State Registers of Historic Places.

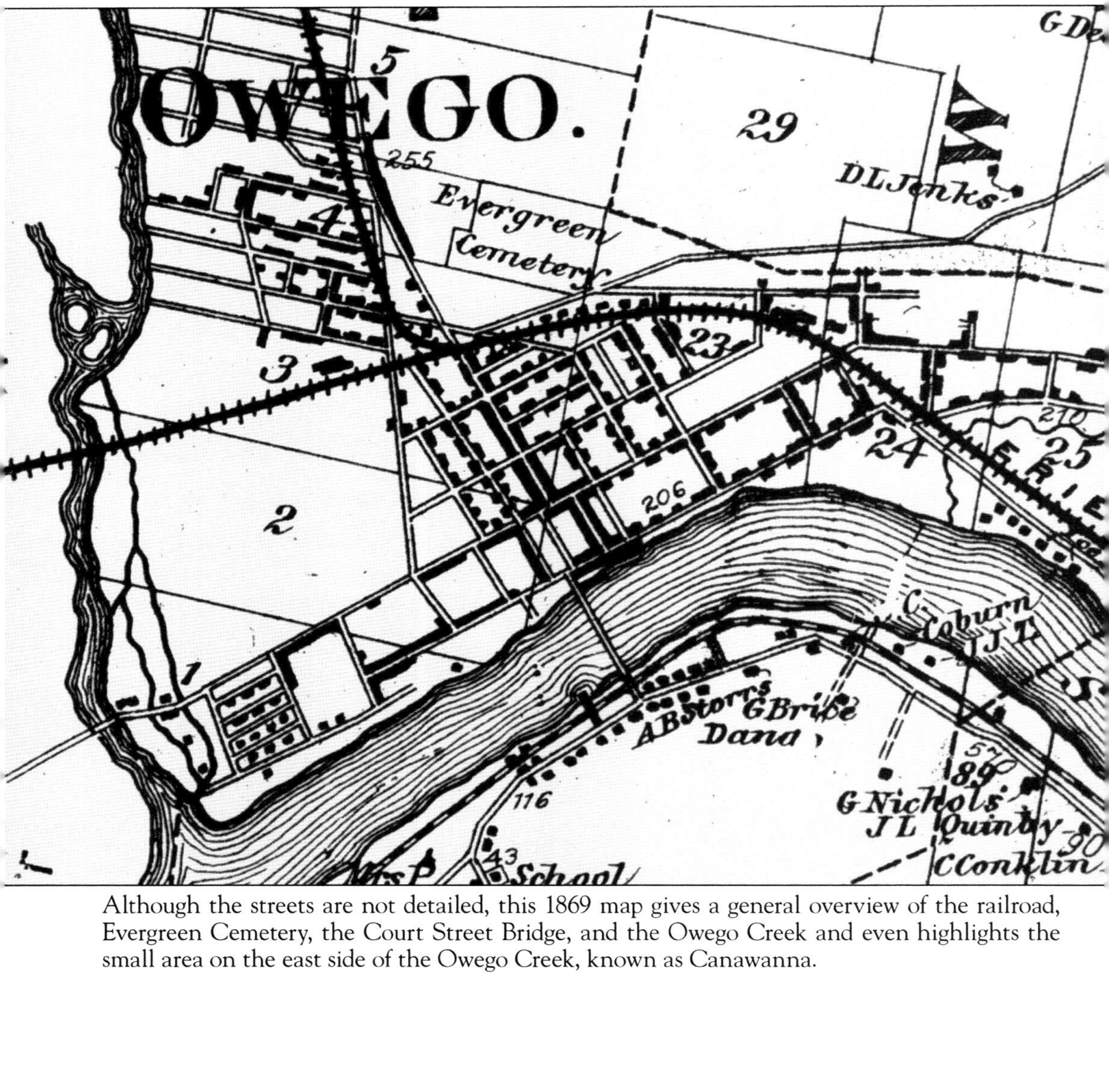

Although the streets are not detailed, this 1869 map gives a general overview of the railroad, Evergreen Cemetery, the Court Street Bridge, and the Owego Creek and even highlights the small area on the east side of the Owego Creek, known as Canawanna.

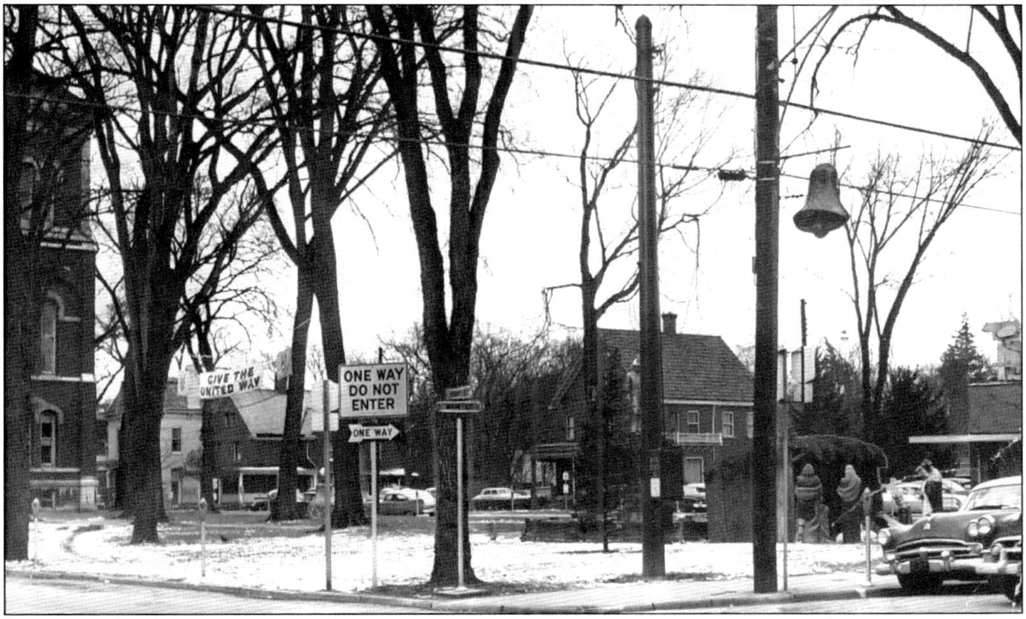

At the time this photograph was taken in January 1960, there was talk of converting the north side of Courthouse Square in the village into a parking lot. The debate had been going on for about three years, but after a public hearing, it was decided not to do it. The Christmas decorations are still in place, including the manger scene.

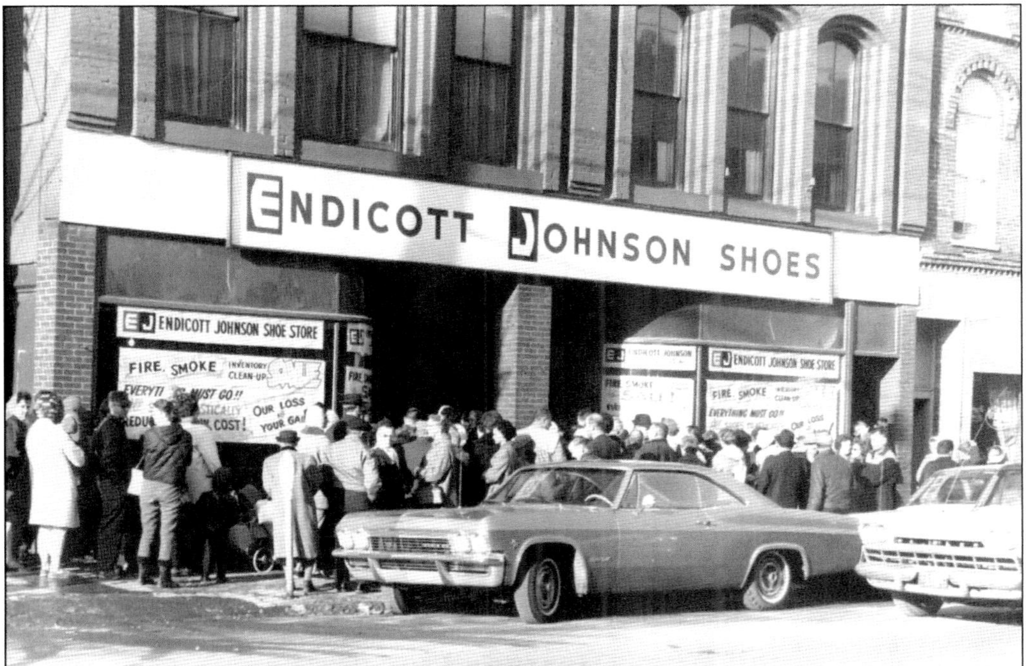

A huge fire raged through the Endicott-Johnson Shoe Store on Lake Street in February 1966. During inventory cleanup, a fire sale was held, and hundreds of people showed up to find a bargain. One of the store's signs reads, "Our Loss Is Your Gain!"

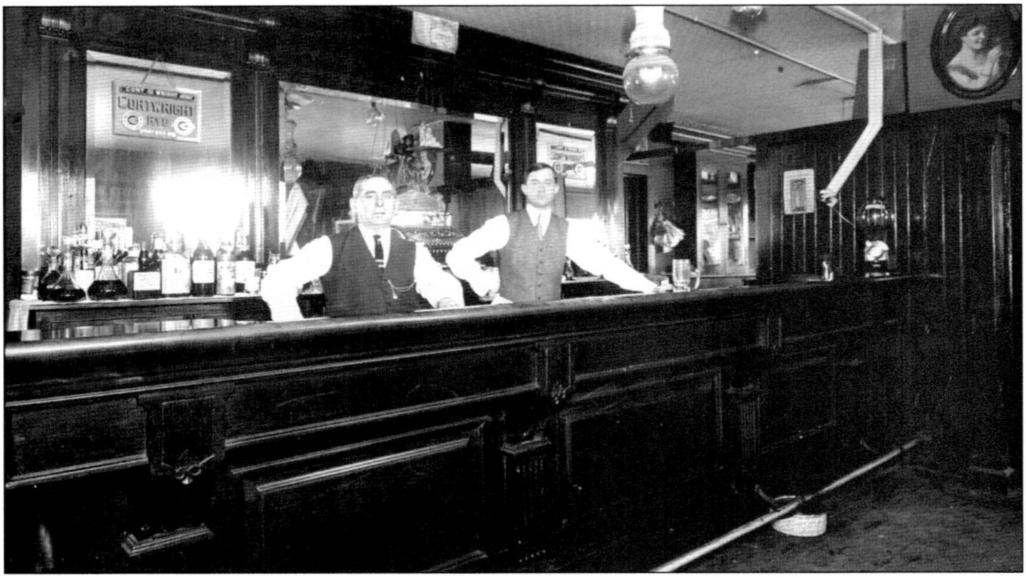

The spittoon is out, and John Potter, left, and owner John Driscoll are ready and waiting for some customers. The Cottage Bar was on the corner of South Depot Street and North Avenue in 1908, across from the Erie Railroad station.

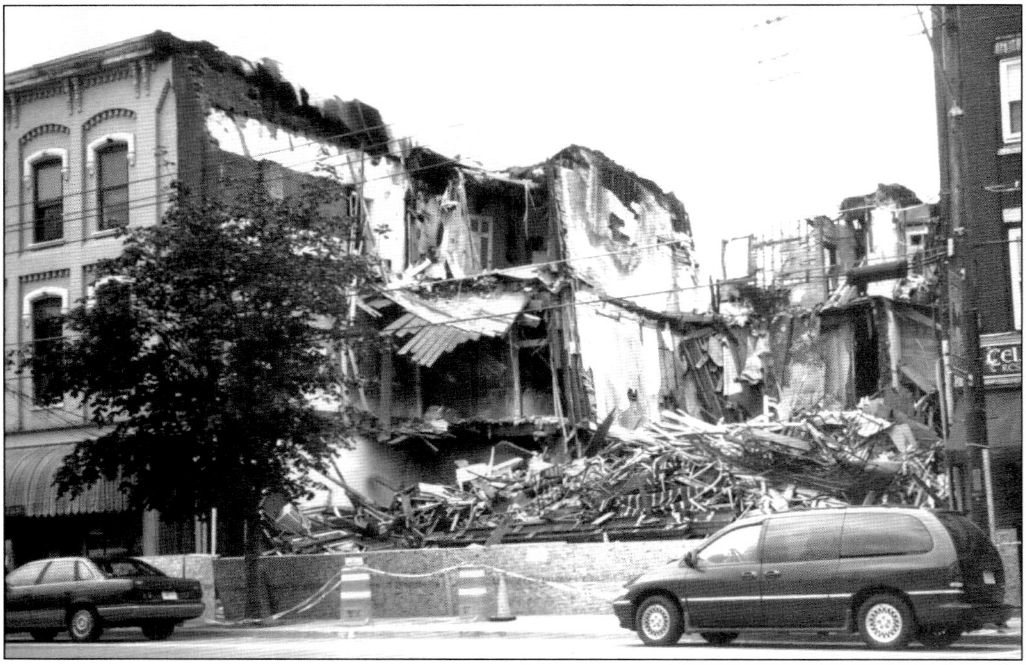

This was the result of a tragic fire on July 31, 2000, on Riverow, a section of Front Street in the village of Owego. It burned 202 Front Street to the ground, a building that once housed the Goat Boy and, at the time of the fire, the Cracker Barrel. The lot still stands empty, with much discussion about construction of a new building someday.

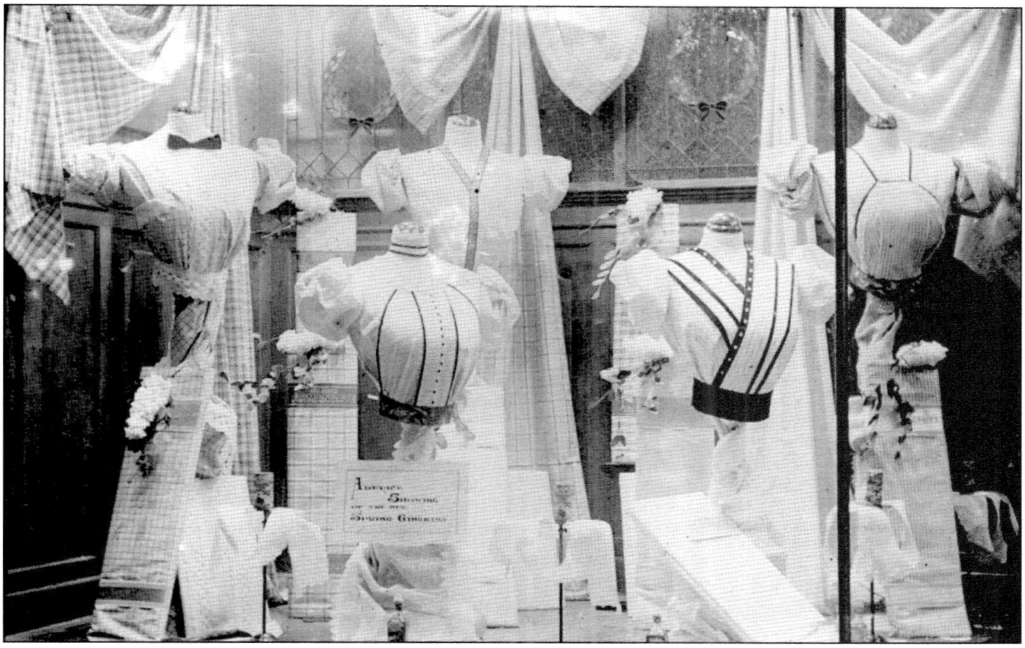

Women could not wait to see the latest fashions in the Goodrich store window at 196 Front Street. This photograph shows a few samples of what was coming. The sign reads, "Advance Showing of the New Spring Garments." This image is from around 1900.

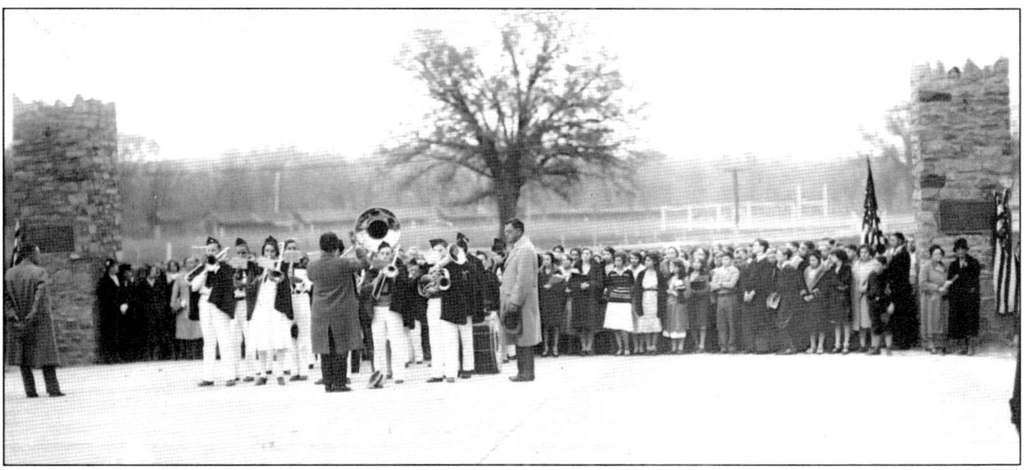

People gathered around, and the high school band played during the ceremonies for the dedication of the two stone pillars and tablets at Marvin Park in Owego on November 1, 1931. Village officials honored former mayor Charles D. Marvin, who purchased the park in 1924 and gave it to the village. In recognition of his generosity, the former Recreation Park was renamed Marvin Park.

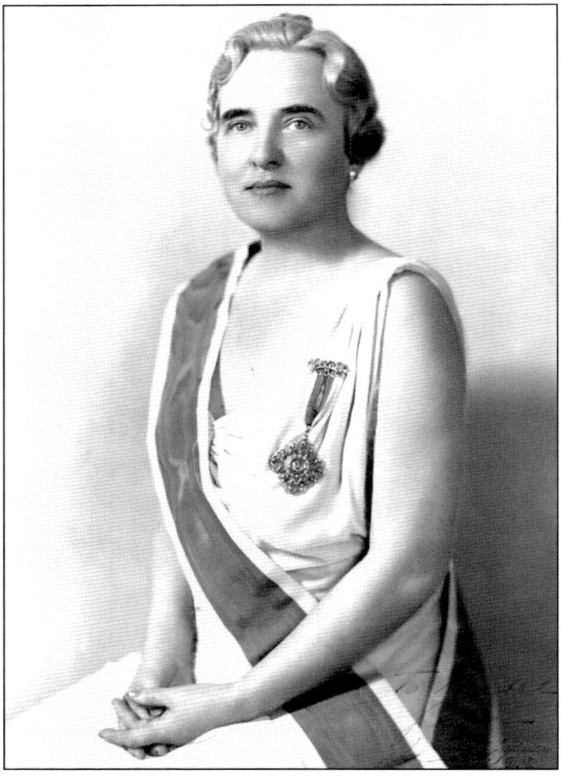

Not only did Gen. Henry Martyn Robert, author of *Robert's Rules of Order*, marry an Owego woman, but his son Henry Martyn Robert Jr. also found an Owego bride, Sarah Corbin. Shown in her formal attire, Corbin graduated from Owego Free Academy and Syracuse University. She taught history in the high schools of New York City and New Jersey and received recognition for her historical research. In 1938, she became president general of the National Society of the Daughters of the American Revolution.

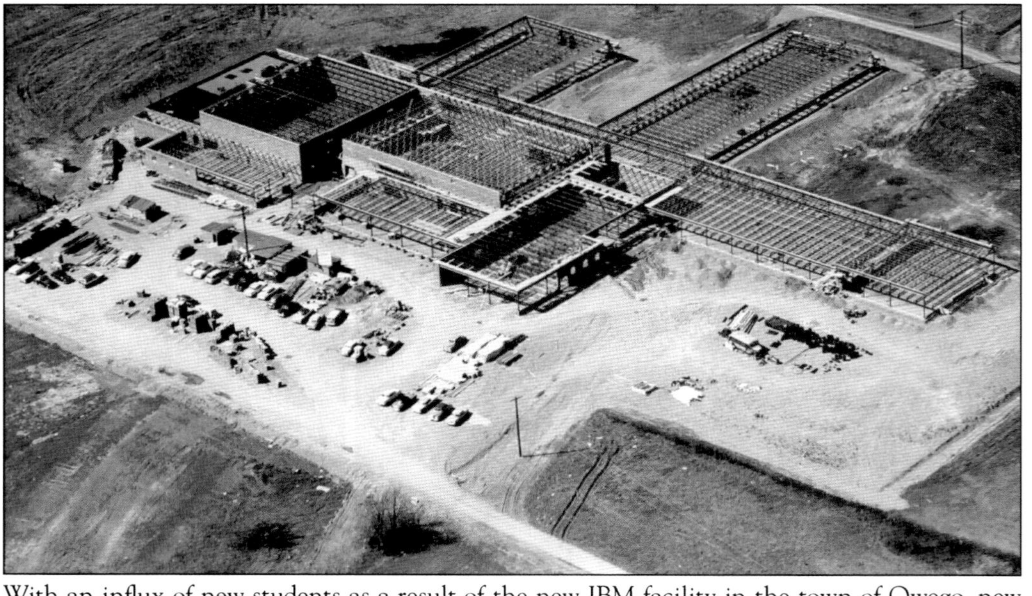

With an influx of new students as a result of the new IBM facility in the town of Owego, new and bigger schools were needed. Shown here in April 1958 is an aerial photograph of the new senior high school under construction on Elm Street in Owego. The $1,747,820 school opened in the fall. It later became the Owego Middle School and has now been closed and up for sale for several years since the new middle school opened in 2004.

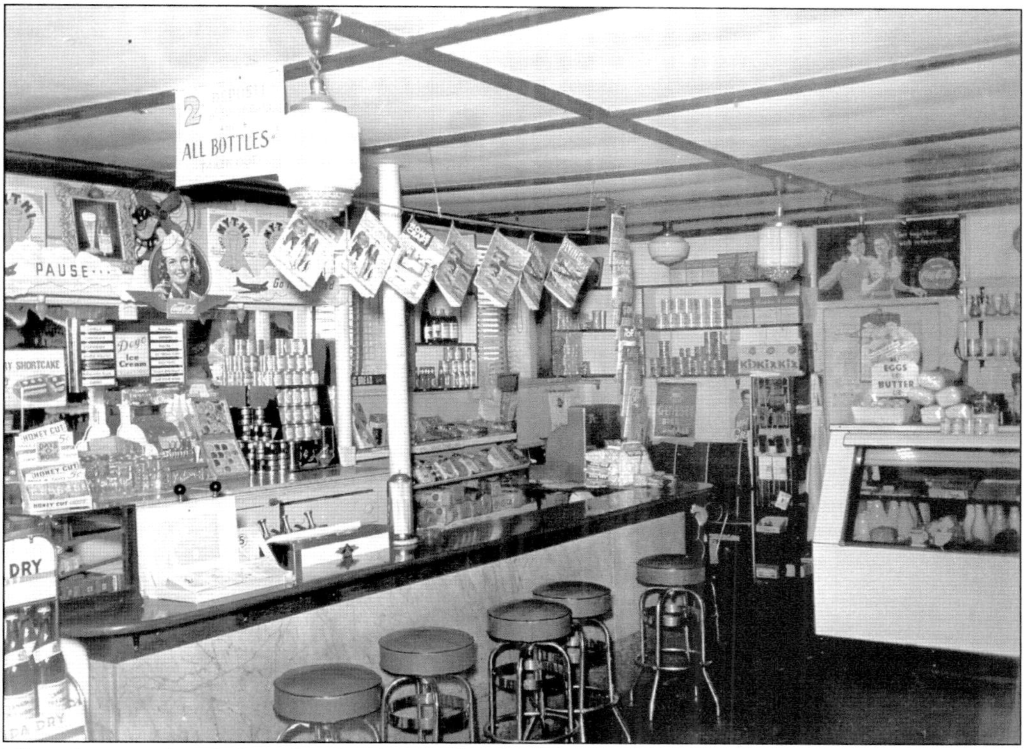

This photograph is believed to be the inside of Murray's Grocery Market at 106 North Avenue. For a small store, it looks as if it had something for everyone.

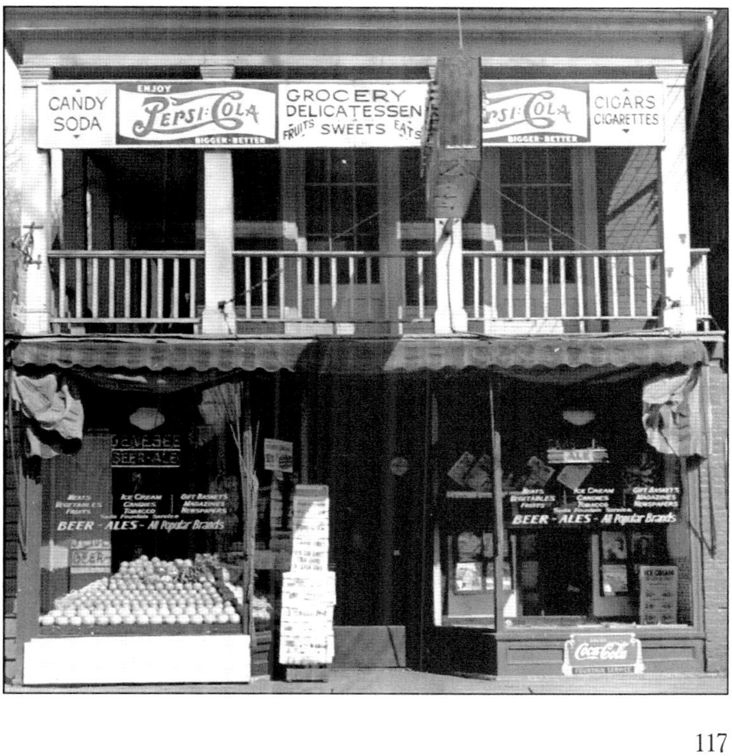

Murray's well-stocked grocery market used to be at 106 North Avenue in the village of Owego in the 1940s. Some people fondly remember the soda fountain inside and the great selection of movie magazines. The Community Shop occupies the site today.

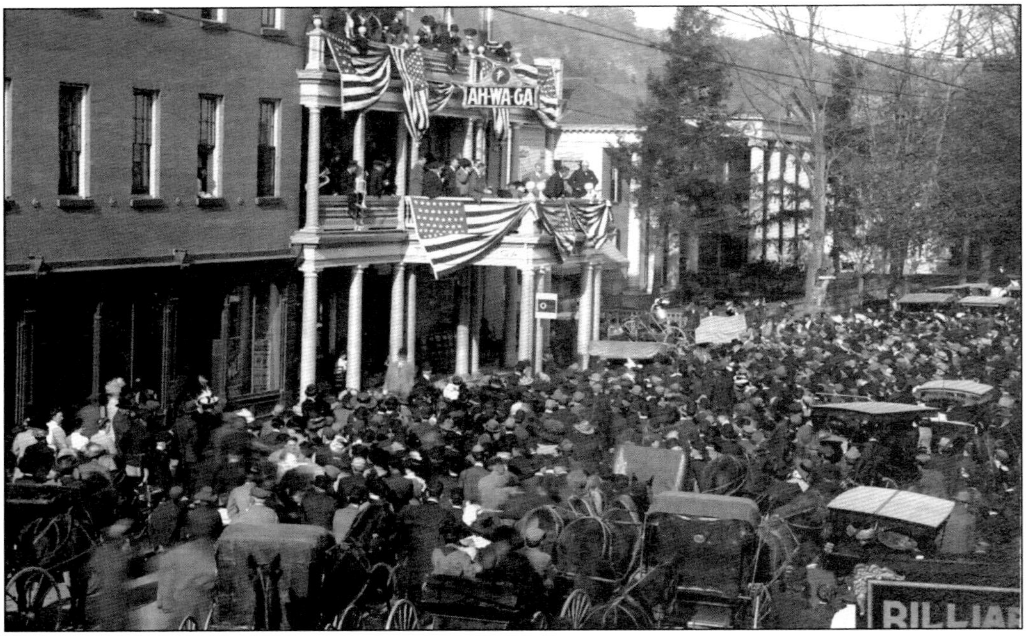

Theodore Roosevelt is shown here on October 24, 1910, speaking from the balcony of Owego's Ahwaga Hotel to a large crowd. He was making personal appeals to Tioga County voters to support the Republican ticket. A quote in the local newspaper read, "He made a corking good political speech."

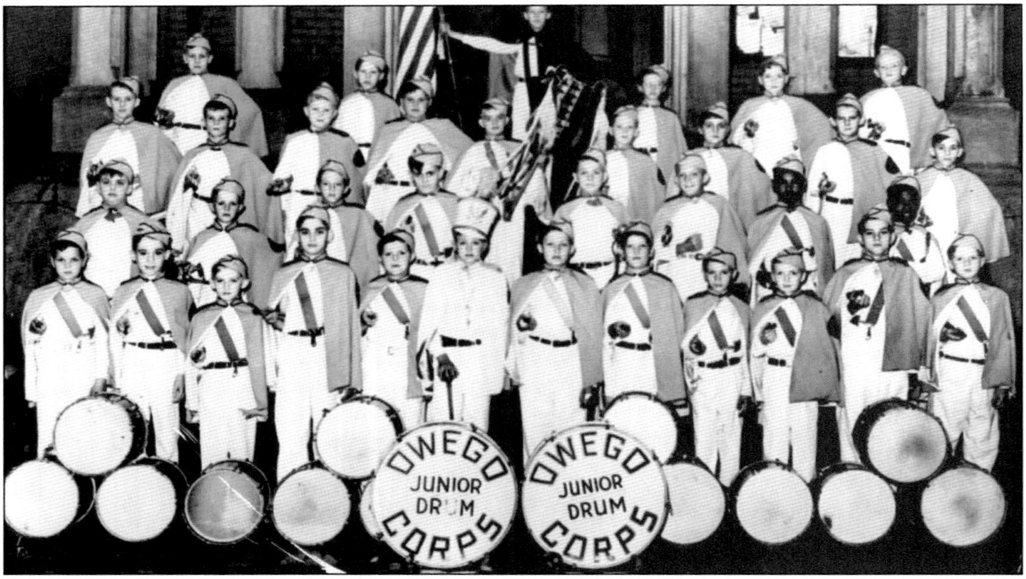

Owego Central School opened in 1907 at 231 Main Street and by 1942 had a junior drum corps made up of fourth- and fifth-grade students, sponsored by the American Legion. They are striking a pose on the courthouse steps, probably just before or after a local parade. The bugle bell player, fifth from left in the third row, is nine-year-old Fred Ford, who went on to contribute over 60 years of his time and talent to creating and directing drum and bugle corps in New York's Southern Tier.

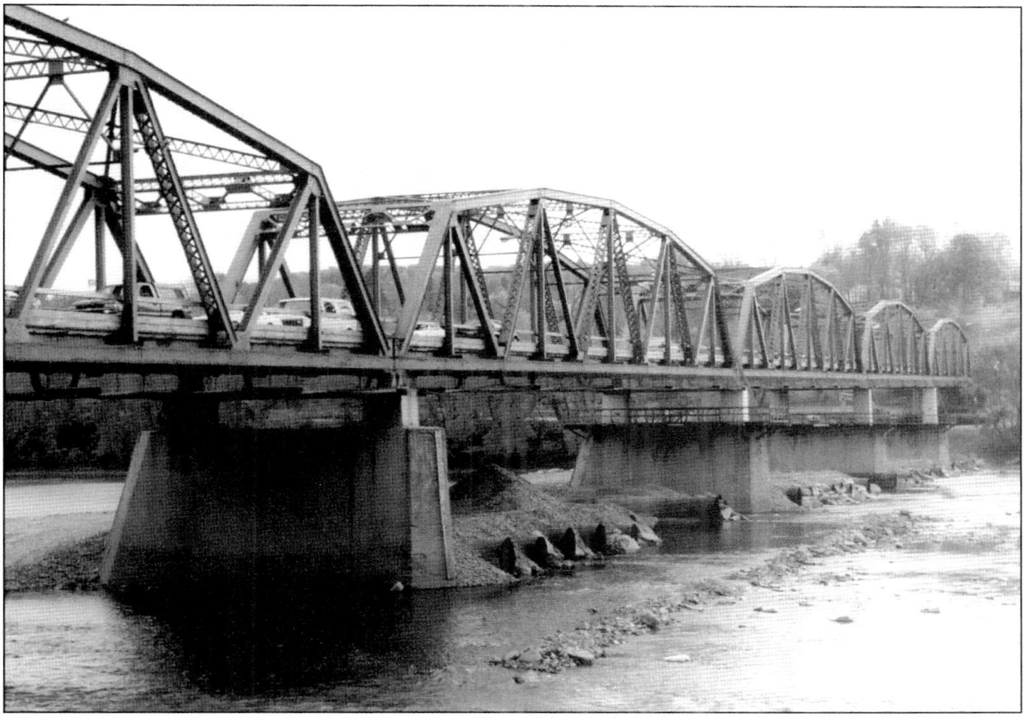

The old Court Street Bridge, built in 1933, is still being used in this 2001 photograph, but its days were numbered.

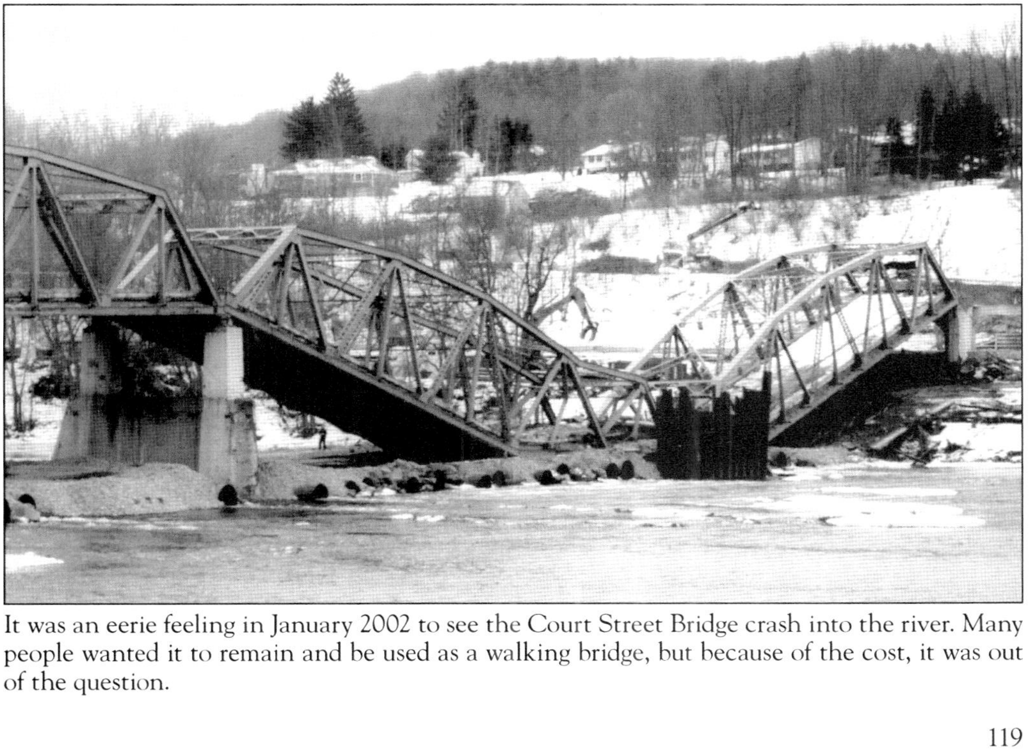

It was an eerie feeling in January 2002 to see the Court Street Bridge crash into the river. Many people wanted it to remain and be used as a walking bridge, but because of the cost, it was out of the question.

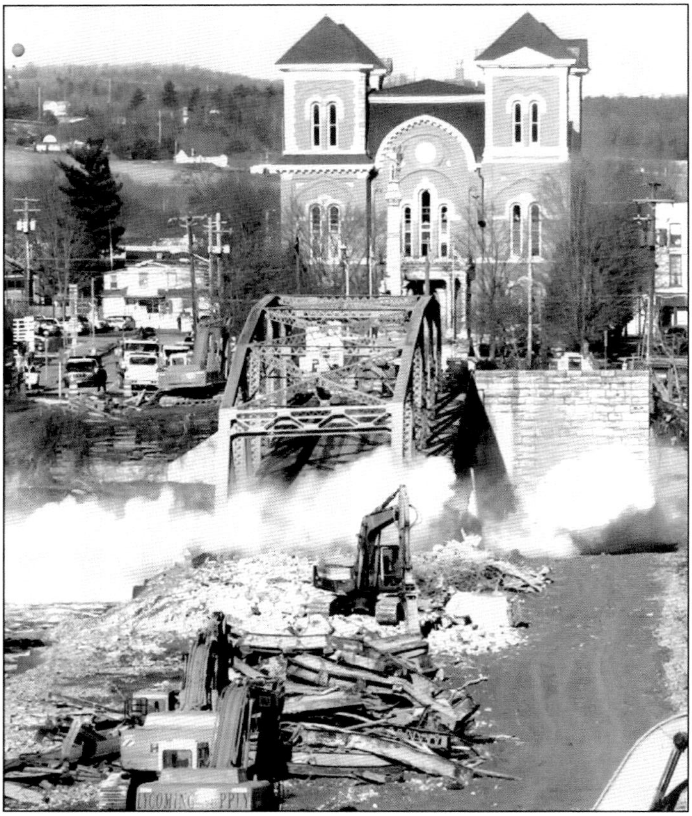

Imploding the north end of the Court Street Bridge was quite a sight, but scary. People wondered if the old mid-19th-century buildings would be able to stand the shock, and they did.

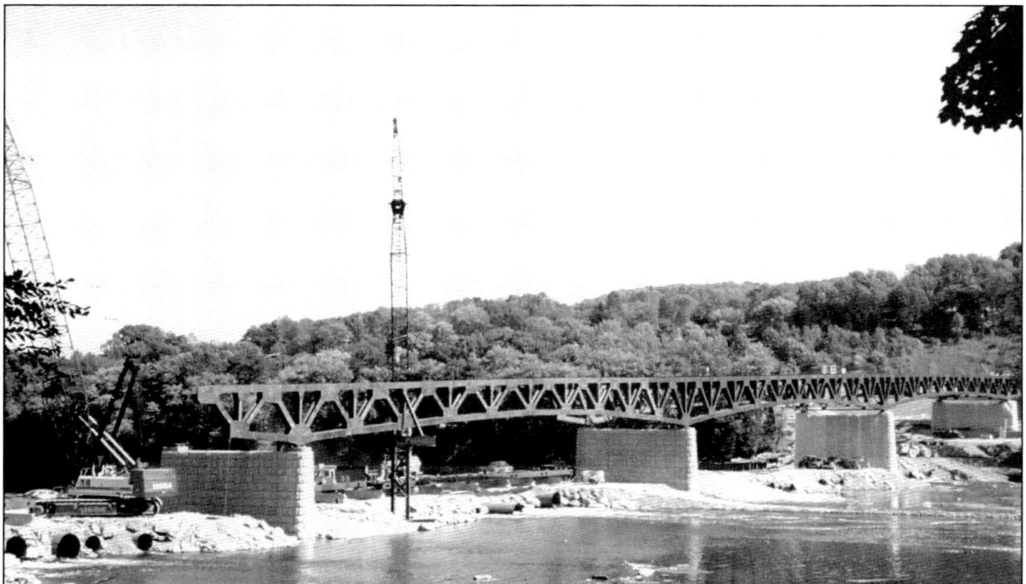

To watch the construction of a bridge is an event in itself. Here the Court Street Bridge is shown almost completed to the other side.

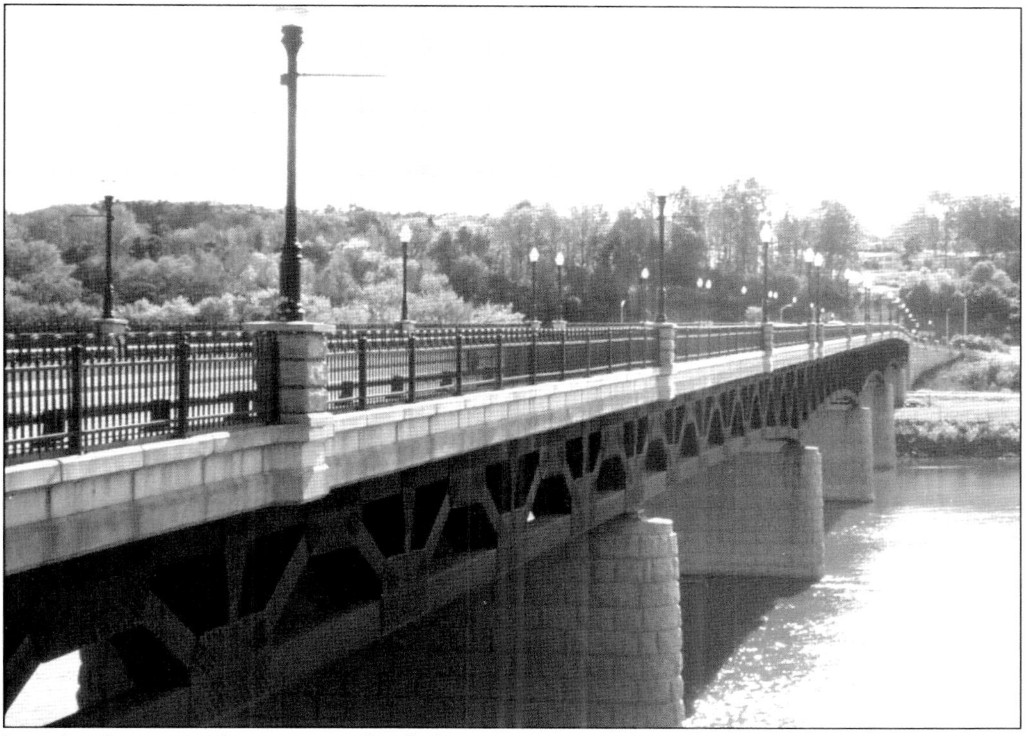

It took a long time from start to finish, but it was worth the wait for the beautiful new Court Street Bridge that opened to traffic on June 27, 2003.

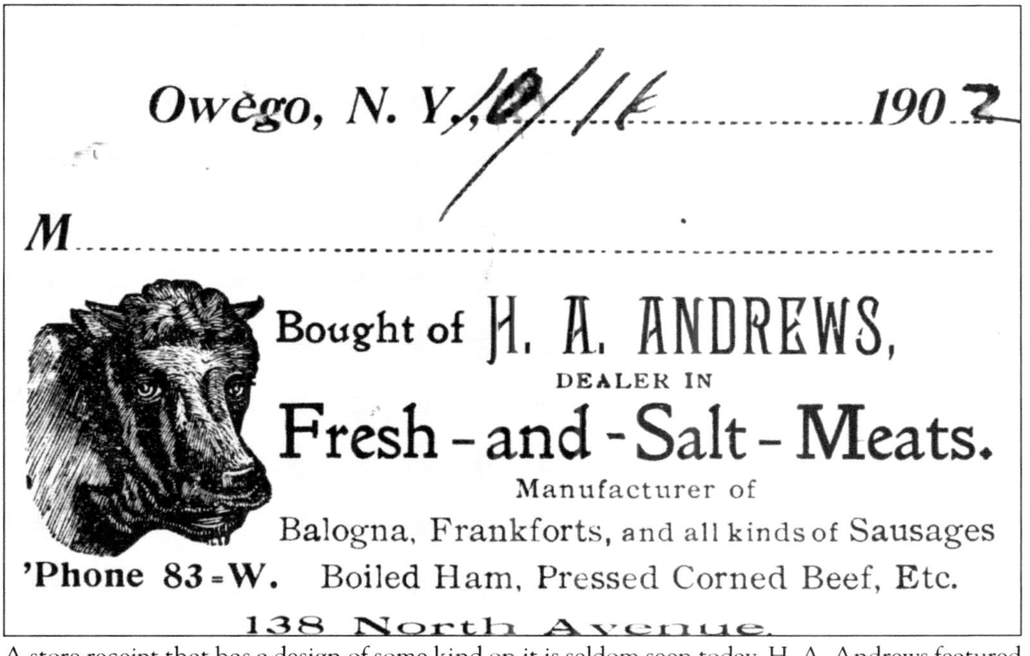

Owego, N. Y., 10/16 1907

M

Bought of H. A. ANDREWS,

DEALER IN

Fresh-and-Salt-Meats.

Manufacturer of

Balogna, Frankforts, and all kinds of Sausages

'Phone 83-W. Boiled Ham, Pressed Corned Beef, Etc.

138 North Avenue.

A store receipt that has a design of some kind on it is seldom seen today. H. A. Andrews featured a handsome-looking bull. Note the telephone number, 83-W; how easy is that to remember?

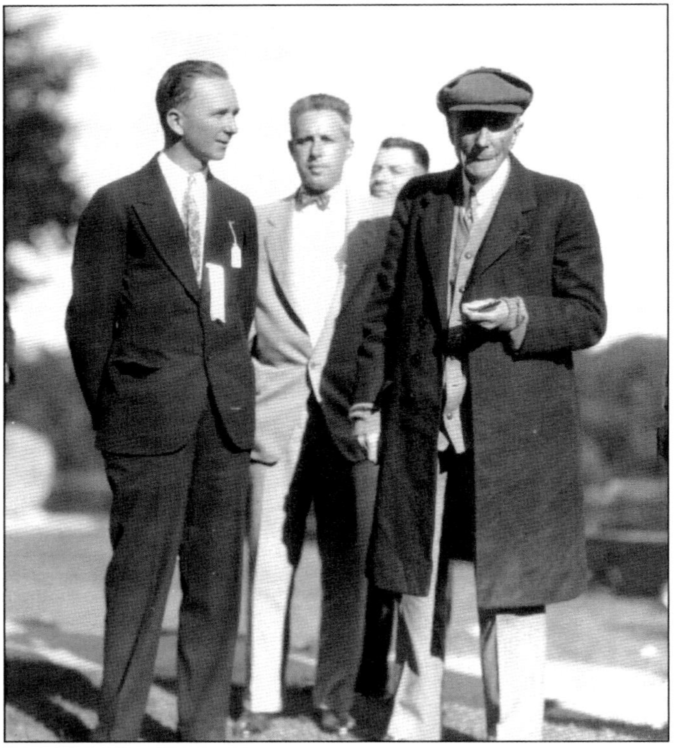

As a boy, John D. Rockefeller lived in the town of Owego for several years. After he made his fortune, he returned many times to visit old friends and reminisce about his boyhood days. In this August 9, 1927, photograph in Owego, he is shown being introduced to pilot Maj. Clarence D. Chamberlain, left, by Arthur Stiles, center. The man in the rear is an aide to Rockefeller. Major Chamberlain was the first man to fly nonstop to Europe (before Charles Lindbergh, but not alone in the plane). He flew to Owego soon after his return to the United States to attend the village centennial celebration.

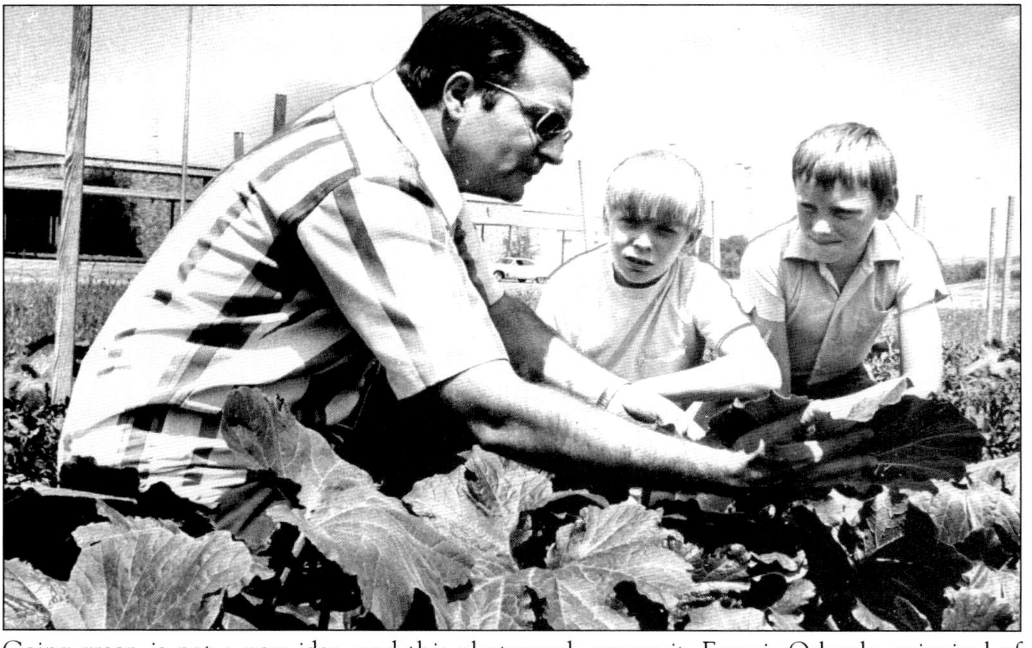

Going green is not a new idea, and this photograph proves it. Francis Orlando, principal of the Owego North Elementary School, demonstrates to the students how to appreciate nature. Shown working with him in the school garden in July 1971 are David Talcott (center) and Scott Andrews.

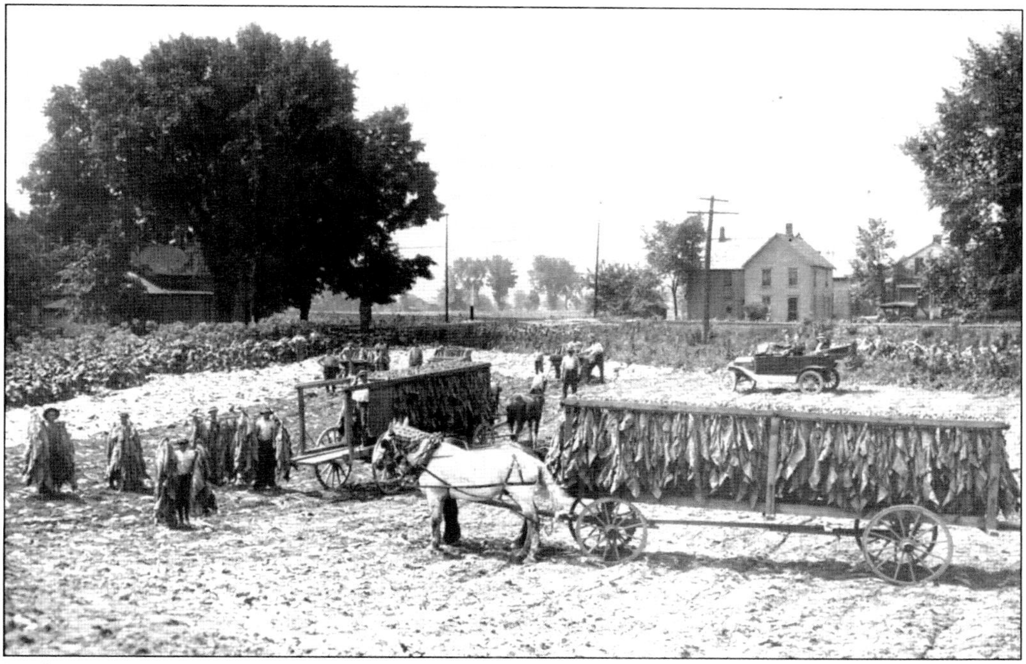

Back in 1919 there was a tobacco field where the old Owego Middle School now stands empty. The Pumpelly family grew the shoots in a hothouse on Front Street and planted them in the fields at Elm Street. Perhaps that is Spencer Pumpelly in the car in the background.

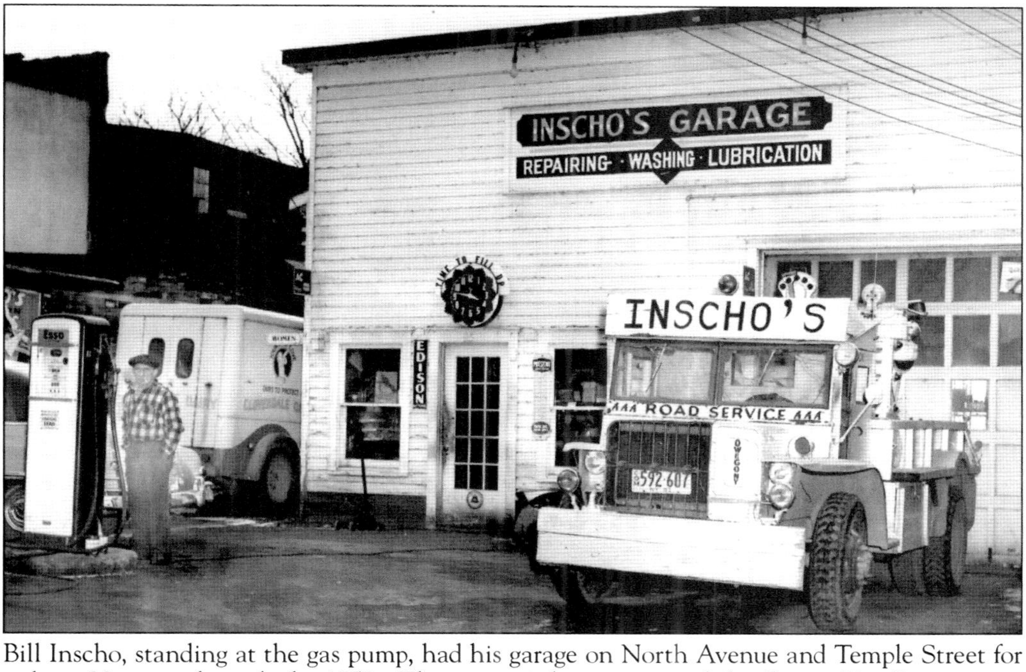

Bill Inscho, standing at the gas pump, had his garage on North Avenue and Temple Street for at least 20 years, through the 1950s. The garage is long gone, and the Owego Fire Department station has taken its place.

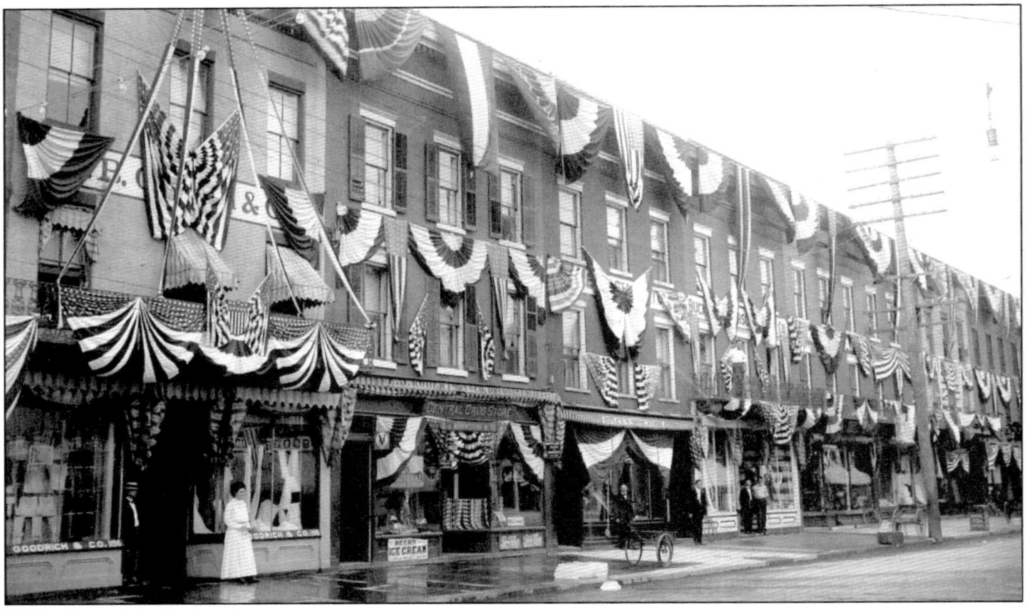

This is a great view of the stores on the south side of Front Street around 1900. The woman on the left is standing in front of the G. B. Goodrich and Company store, and judging by her pretty dress, it looks as if she just finished shopping there. Central Drug Store, to the right of Goodrich, was owned by E. J. Robertson, and next to the drugstore is the Ripley Shoe Company. Today this whole block of stores is known as Riverow.

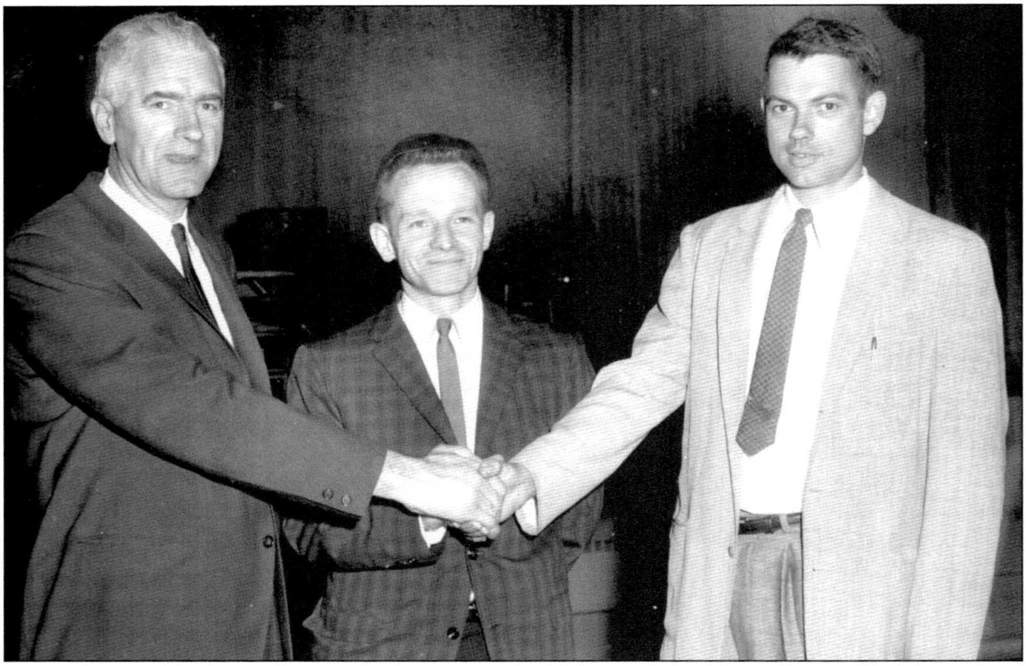

Harold Newcomb, president of the Owego-Apalachin Central School District Board of Education, welcomes Robert P. Jones and Edward Englehard, both of the town of Owego, to five-year terms on the board in June 1965. From left to right are Newcomb, Jones, and Englehard.

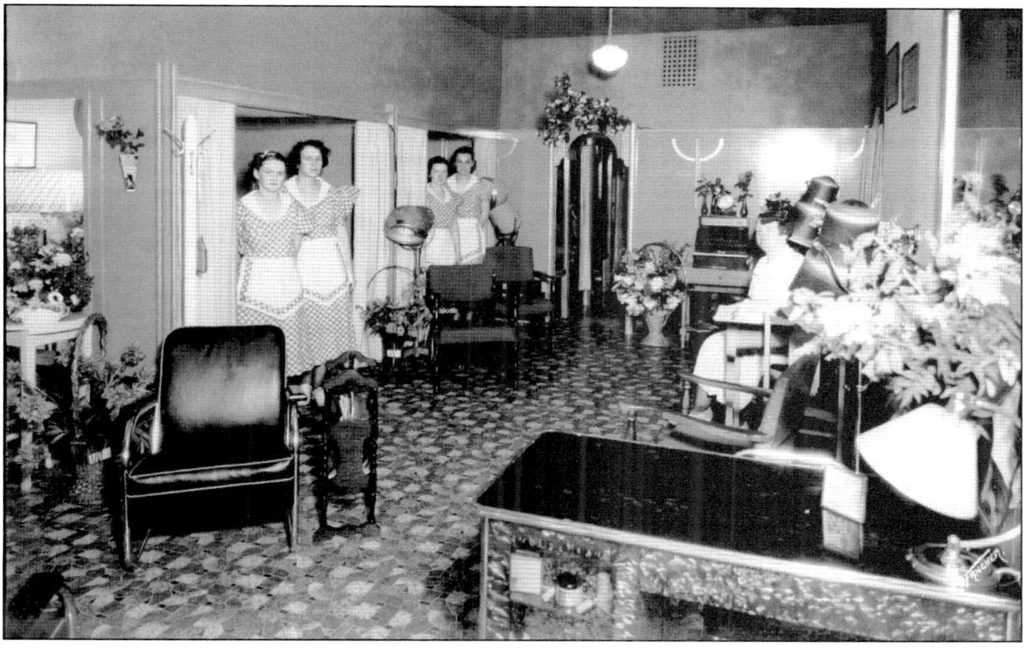

This beauty parlor, located at 80 North Avenue in the village of Owego in the 1940s, looks better than most of them do today. The four beauticians stand ready to serve the customers, while the owner, Rose Goodnough, sits, looking quite pleased with the surroundings.

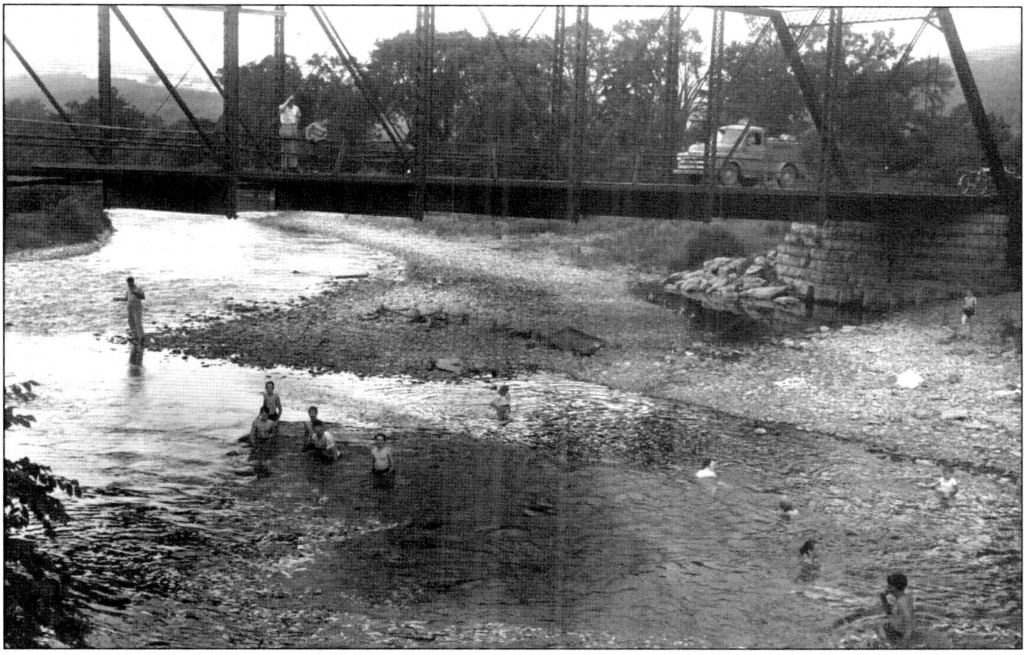

An ordinary sight before the municipal swimming pool was opened in 1957 was to peer down from the Talcott Street Bridge and see the kids swimming. The Owego Creek was dredged periodically to make it better for swimming; in fact, the schools would take the students there for swimming lessons.

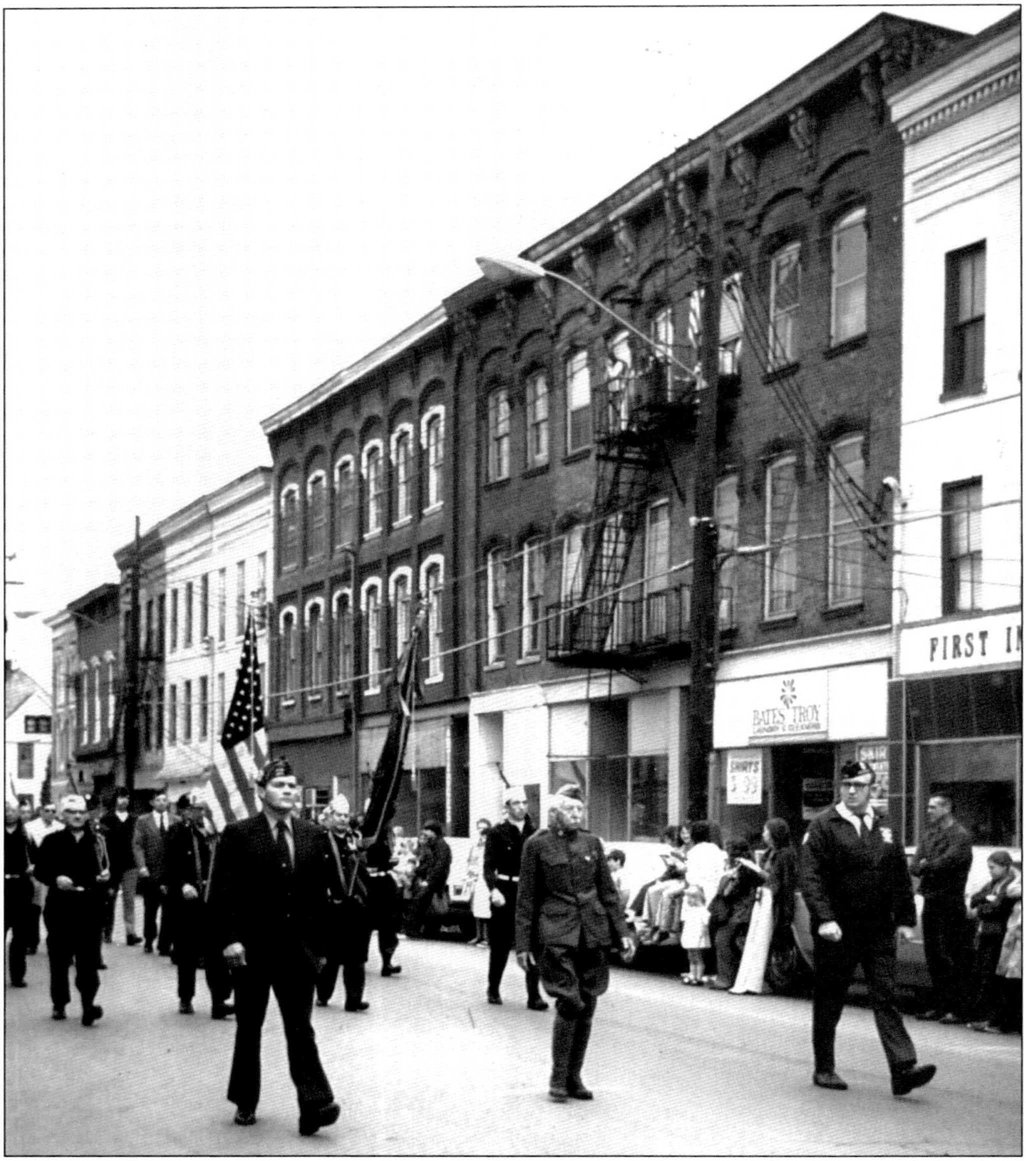

There were not many parades that World War I veteran Edwin T. Lay missed. In this photograph, taken on Front Street in Owego around the 1970s, he is shown marching with the American Legion Post No. 401 of Owego, of which he was a 65-year life member. He died on March 1, 1985, at the age of 89.

BIBLIOGRAPHY

Elliott, Dolores N., and William D. Lipe. *The Englebert Site*. Owego, NY: Tioga County Historical Society, 1970.

Gay, W. B. *Historical Gazetteer and Directory of Tioga County, New York, 1785–1888*. Syracuse, NY: W. B. Gay and Company, 1887. Reprint, Owego, NY: Tioga County Historical Society, 1978.

Kingman, LeRoy Wilson. *Early Owego*. Owego, NY: Owego Gazette Office, 1907. Reprint, Owego, NY: Tioga County Historical Society, 1987.

———. *Our County and Its People*. Elmira, NY: W. A. Fergusson and Company, 1898.

McEnteer, Thomas C. *Seasons of Change, An Updated History of Tioga County, NY by Tioga County Authors, 1990*. Owego, NY: Tioga County Legislature, 1990.

Morgan, Lewis H. *League of the Ho-De'-No-Sau-Nee, or Iroquois*. North Dighton, MA: J. G. Press, 1995.

Sedore, Emma M. *Hiawatha Island, Jewel of the Susquehanna*. Owego, NY: Tioga County Historical Society, 1994.